Australia's Paedophile Protection Racket

Shane Dowling

I0093238

Self-Published

A book written in the Public Interest

ISBN 978-0-6488909-0-4

Self-Published – Shane Dowling - Australia
Email: shanedowling@outlook.com.au

Website: www.kangaroocourtofaustralia.com

Send snail mail to:
Po Box 1280
Coolangatta
Qld 4225
Australia

NATIONAL
LIBRARY
OF AUSTRALIA

A catalogue record for this work is available from the National Library of Australia

Contents

Preface

I started publishing the judicial corruption website Kangaroo Court of Australia in January 2011 which I was motivated to do after a failed unlawful termination case that lasted 3 years against Fairfax Media where I had worked in sales. I documented the Fairfax case in a book published in 2009 titled "Love Letters from the Bar Table".

The aim of the website was, and still is, to focus on dodgy judicial appointments, judicial bribery and the fact that Australian judges are unaccountable when it comes to corruption. While other media write about these issues from time to time, I thought it needed to be collated in one place as only then would the gravity of the problem be obvious to the public. I believe I have achieved that goal to some degree but there is a lot more work to be done.

The elephant in the room that cannot be avoided is the paedophile protection racket being conducted by judges in the open where they give paedophiles suspended sentences or extremely lenient sentences that do not conform with the law or precedents.

My reporting of the paedophile protection racket has led to a vendetta by the NSW Supreme Court Chief Justice Tom Bathurst using the full resources of the Supreme Court and NSW Police Force to try to harass me, intimidate me and ultimately jail me twice. The allegation of Chief Justice Tom Bathurst's conduct is backed up by a police statement by Chris D'Aeth who is the NSW Supreme Court CEO and Principal Registrar.

The vendetta by Chief Justice Tom Bathurst started immediately after I sent an email to all the NSW Supreme Court judges on the 6th of September 2016 naming 15 judges, 2 registrars and 1 magistrate as being known paedophiles or suspected paedophiles which I published on my website a few days later. The email is still on my website and the allegations I made have never been disputed or complained about to me even though the court made a complaint to the police which led to a police charge that was later dropped.

What has given me some protection is the 1997 High Court of Australia precedent Lange v ABC which found that journalists and members of the public can make allegations of corruption against government officials and even if it isn't true, as long as the person believes it's true, then it is protected as political communication. And any laws that infringe on political communication are invalid. On my second jailing Justice Helen Wilson said she was "prepared to accept that the contemnor's beliefs in that regard are honestly held". But Justice Wilson went on the ignore the relevant precedents.

The basis of the book and what is covers is the "get Shane Dowling at any cost" strategy by Chief Justice Tom Bathurst as he tries to cover-up corruption in the courts by stopping the reporting and exposure of it by an independent journalist.

While some might not agree with some of the allegations, I make what can't be disputed is the paedophile protection racket being run the judges. This became obvious even at the highest levels of government and in September 2019 Prime Minister Scott Morrison announced the introduction of mandatory sentencing laws for paedophiles after he revealed that 28% of paedophiles convicted under federal laws did not receive jail sentences. By the time the new laws were legislated in July 2020, it had increased to from 28% to 39% of paedophiles convicted of federal child sexual abuse crimes did not receive jail sentences.

The hope is that by the time you get to the end of the book you will realise that the people who are meant to protecting our society and enforcing the laws are the ones who are breaking the laws the most and in this case, they are using it to cover-up and help facilitate the sexual abuse of children.

In the book, I have reprinted some articles that I have already published on the Kangaroo Court of Australia website. In those articles, there are numerous links which either show up underlined or say (Click here to read more) which I have left exactly as it is in the articles.

I have done that so you know if want more information or you want to watch the videos etc you can go to the Kangaroo Court of Australia website and find the article and click on the links and watch the video etc. To get the most out of the book you should use it in conjunction with the KCA website.

Because of a lack of financial resources, I have not had the book professionally edited. What I have done is put it through a grammar checker twice and proofread the book twice and some parts more than twice. Other parts where I have quoted have stayed as per the original article.

Introduction

The Book

Most Australians would be under the illusion that a lot has been done in recent years to protect children and the public from paedophiles, but the reality is that only the surface has been scratched, and now the paedophiles are fighting back. This book tries to shine a light on the situation as it currently stands.

As a journalist, I have been writing about the issue for several years on my judicial corruption website, Kangaroo Court of Australia, which resulted in me being stitched up for jail twice.

And that is a key theme of the book, showing the links and support between the government, the judiciary, the media and paedophiles via my own experience trying to shine a light on it by reporting it to the public.

Australia has been in the grip of a paedophile epidemic for decades. This was exposed by the Royal Commission into Institutional Responses to Child Sexual Abuse which ran from 2013 until 2017, handing its final report to the Governor-General in December 2017. This is similar to what has been experienced and uncovered in recent times in many other countries.

One thing that might set Australia apart from most other countries is the continual support and protection of paedophiles at the highest level of politics, the judiciary and the media since the Royal Commission finished in 2017.

Our current Prime Minister Scott Morrison has been doing what he can to protect Hillsong Pastor Brian Houston who is currently under investigation by the NSW police for failing to report his father's sexual abuse of children to the police. Paedophiles, especially paedophile priests, have continued to get looked after by the judiciary with lenient sentences. Scott Morrison announced on the 3rd of September 2019 that he would legislate so that paedophiles were given mandatory jail sentences and legislation was passed by the government in July 2020 but it is a Claytons law that will achieve very little as will become clearer as you read the book. It is the judges who are the problem, not the law.

Then there are Rupert Murdoch's paid puppets at News Corp and Sky News who, daily, have pleaded George Pell's innocence and attacked survivors while failing to reveal that Rupert Murdoch was awarded a papal knighthood in 1998 for his contributions to Church institutions and was made a Knight of St. Gregory while his wife at the time, Anna, was awarded the title of Dame of St. Gregory. This goes a long way to explaining why Murdoch has directed his paid puppets, the so-called journalists and commentators at News Corp and Sky News, to support Pell.

Rupert Murdoch Tweeted in 2014:

Rupert Murdoch ✔
@rupertmurdoch

Pope Francis appoints brilliant Cardinal Pell from Sydney to be no.3 power in Vatican. Australia will miss him but world will benefit.

11:50 AM · Feb 25, 2014 · Twitter for iPad

912 Retweets   **373** Likes

Rupert's paid puppets at News Corp and Sky News would have taken the Tweet as a direction from Rupert Murdoch to fully support George Pell, unless told otherwise.

Cardinal George Pell's Wikipedia page says he was a columnist, and a Tweet on Twitter says it was for Rupert Murdoch's tabloids for more than 10 years.

It is the judicial treatment of me when I wrote about, and named, paedophile judges that shines a light onto, not only judicial corruption but the paedophile protection racket that is operating in Australia. And if we have a paedophile protection racket, I would argue that it is mostly other paedophiles who are doing the protecting. This was the main basis for me naming the judges as paedophiles and that allegation has gone unchallenged by any of the judges.

Kangaroo Court of Australia website is born

The book starts with my background publishing the KCA website, and Kerry Stokes' attacks against me using a War of Law, as it sets the scene for the court's documented effort trying to silence me. This book also shows they have ultimately failed to silence me, at least at this point.

I set up the Kangaroo Court of Australia website at the end of 2010 and published my first article in January 2011. I set it up because I'd had a long-running unfair dismissal case against Fairfax Media which, with the help of corrupt judges, had abused the legal and court system with no media writing about it. So, I decided to become the media myself, something which anyone can do nowadays to fill the void by publishing a website focused on judicial corruption.

I also published my first book "Love Letters from the Bar Table" in 2009 about my battle with Fairfax Media.

In May 2011, Kerry Stokes, who controls mining and media company the Seven Group, tried to intimidate me with a lawyer's threatening letter when I wrote an article about him on KCA titled "Kerry Stokes, Seven Group Chairman and Australia's number one perjurer, has been charged with contempt of Court". I stood my ground and published the letter in another article titled "Kerry Stokes threatens legal action against blogger".

I didn't hear from Stokes and his lawyer again until 2014 which was the start of years of litigation designed to silence me which I outline in the first few chapters of this book. But that same litigation is a positive in that it has also allowed me to experience judicial corruption firsthand in the Supreme Court of NSW and it is rife as the judges have virtually no oversight and so are free to abuse the law like there's no tomorrow. I have found that there is nothing like having firsthand experiences to write about as one can do it with absolute confidence, and when outing corrupt judges, that is extremely important.

This book doesn't have all the answers, but its purpose is to wake people up to the fact that the paedophile epidemic that the Royal Commission into Institutional Responses to Child Sexual Abuse exposed is still there and needs to be dealt with because it leads to the highest levels in the government, the judiciary and the media.

Almost everything I write in this book has been raised in court either verbally or in written affidavits, so it is protected from defamation by the defence of "absolute privilege". This includes parts of the book being previously filed in legal documents in the High Court of Australia.

Kerry Stokes' SLAPP lawsuits

This book chronicles my recent experiences reporting on judicial corruption and the paedophile protection racket in the Supreme Court of NSW, and other courts, as Chief Justice Tom Bathurst and others try to silence me. This has led to me being jailed twice for the crime of journalism, possibly being jailed again in the near future, and also facing a malicious police charge involving the NSW police, Federal Police and the Commonwealth Director of Public Prosecutions (CDPP) that was dropped a few days before the hearing date.

To put everything into context, the first few chapters deal with various matters involving billionaire media and mining mogul Kerry Stokes and his associated companies that have sued me for defamation since 2014 using the SLAPP lawsuit model that is used by the wealthy and large companies to silence critics and stop journalists from exposing them. The SLAPP lawsuit model was made famous by McDonald's who used it in the UK in the matter McDonald's Corporation v Steel & Morris [1997], known as "the McLibel case" which lasted over 10 years.

The definition of a SLAPP Lawsuit as per Wikipedia is:

"A strategic lawsuit against public participation (SLAPP) is a lawsuit that is intended to censor, intimidate, and silence critics by burdening them with the cost of a legal defence until they abandon their criticism or opposition. Such lawsuits have been made illegal in many jurisdictions on the grounds that they impede freedom of speech."

"In the typical SLAPP, the plaintiff does not normally expect to win the lawsuit. The plaintiff's goals are accomplished if the defendant succumbs to fear, intimidation, mounting legal costs, or simple exhaustion and abandons the criticism. In some cases, repeated frivolous litigation against a defendant may raise the cost of directors and officers liability insurance for that party, interfering with an organization's ability to operate. A SLAPP may also intimidate others from participating in the debate. A SLAPP is often preceded by a legal threat."

For a SLAPP lawsuit to work, it requires corrupt judges to help felicitate it.

What lit the fuse that rattled Chief Justice Bathurst, and others, was an email that I sent to all the judges of the Supreme Court of NSW on the 6th of September 2016 naming 15 judges, 2 registrars and 1 magistrate as paedophiles or suspected paedophiles, and raising the $2.2 Australian mafia judicial bribery allegation that was reported by the ABC and Fairfax Media in 2015.

On the same day Chief Justice Tom Bathurst and the others received the email they went to the NSW police and made a complaint against me, even though they would have known that the email was protected as political communication. The NSW police took no action, so a couple of weeks later they went to the Commonwealth Director of Public Prosecutions who also took no action, instead referring the matter to the Federal Police for further investigation. The federal police also refused to charge me.

I was later charged by the NSW police, something which I believe only happened after political pressure by Chief Justice Tom Bathurst. The prosecution of the matter was taken out of the NSW police's hands and passed over to the CDPP after an honest magistrate, who heard the matter for directions, told the police prosecution that they didn't have jurisdiction because I had been charged with the federal crime and that there was a Supreme Court precedent that said the CDPP had to prosecute the matter. How exactly that worked I am not sure, but the police prosecutor didn't argue, and once the CDPP took over the prosecution it became obvious that they had no intention of following through with the matter because there was no case. The charge was withdrawn one week before the hearing date.

But the above police complaint was something that largely happened in the background without my knowledge while I was stitched up for two jail sentences.

The email and article naming judicial officers as paedophiles or suspected paedophiles

The email that I sent on the 6ᵗʰ of September 2016 is what escalated the battle with the courts, and it is reprinted below. I also published the email in an article a couple of days later, and that appears in full later in the book.

The email was nothing more than me doing my job as a journalist by putting allegations to people and then allowing them to respond before I publish. That has now been proven to be correct as the associated police charge for sending the email was dropped and the email is freely published on my website to this day.

The 6ᵗʰ of September 2016 email:

From: Shane Dowling [mailto:shanedowling@hotmail.com]
Sent: Tuesday, 6 September 2016 11:35 PM
To: victoria_bradshaw@courts.nsw.gov.au;
chambers.president@courts.nsw.gov.au;
dorothy_yon@courts.nsw.gov.au;
maree_harland@courts.nsw.gov.au;
chambers.macfarlanja@courts.nsw.gov.au;
trish_beazley@courts.nsw.gov.au;
morna_lynch@courts.nsw.gov.au;
giorgina_kotevski@courts.nsw.gov.au;
jasmine_geary@courts.nsw.gov.au;
chambers.gleesonja@courts.nsw.gov.au;
chambers.leemingja@courts.nsw.gov.au;
lynn_nielsen@courts.nsw.gov.au; adam_zwi@courts.nsw.gov.au;

kim_pitt@courts.nsw.gov.au;
cheryl.scholfield@courts.nsw.gov.au;
karen_adams@courts.nsw.gov.au;
linda.head@courts.nsw.gov.au;
renee_ingrey@courts.nsw.gov.au;
carla_wilson@courts.nsw.gov.au;
maria_heraghty@courts.nsw.gov.au;
chambers.johnsonj@courts.nsw.gov.au;
margaret_gaertner@courts.nsw.gov.au;
katherine_moroney@courts.nsw.gov.au;
jacqui.gray@justice.nsw.gov.au;
chambers.breretonj@courts.nsw.gov.au;
lisa_freeman@courts.nsw.gov.au;
colleen_sutton@courts.nsw.gov.au;
bernadette_heywood@courts.nsw.gov.au;
kate_moore@courts.nsw.gov.au;
chambers.mccallumj@courts.nsw.gov.au;
sally_mccrossin@courts.nsw.gov.au;
carol_lloyd@courts.nsw.gov.au;
chambers.slatteryj@courts.nsw.gov.au;
anita_singh@courts.nsw.gov.au;
chambers.schmidtj@courts.nsw.gov.au;
sue_page@courts.nsw.gov.au;
maria_kourtis@courts.nsw.gov.au;
chambers.garlingj@courts.nsw.gov.au;
catherine_young@courts.nsw.gov.au;
margaret.smith2@courts.nsw.gov.au;
anne_cochrane@courts.nsw.gov.au;
barbara_ruicens@courts.nsw.gov.au;
megan_grace@courts.nsw.gov.au;
lauren_channells@courts.nsw.gov.au; chambers.beech-
jonesJ@courts.nsw.gov.au; poppy_xenakis@courts.nsw.gov.au;
sara_bond@courts.nsw.gov.au;
shari_williams@courts.nsw.gov.au

Subject: Paedophile Judge list to be sent to the AFP, Australian Crime Commission, NSW Crime Commission and Royal Commission into Child Sexual Abuse for investigation

Dear Chief Justice Bathurst, Justice Hoeben, Justice Price, Justice Simpson other judges

I am writing to you all regarding the list of paedophile judges that I intended on making a formal complaint about to the AFP, Australian Crime Commission, NSW Crime Commission and Royal Commission into Child Sexual Abuse. The list is below.

Known paedophiles

Chief Justice Tom Bathurst – NSW Supreme Court

Justice Clifton Hoeben – NSW Supreme Court

Justice Derek Price – NSW Supreme Court (He is also Chief Judge of the NSW District Court)

Justice Carolyn Simpson – NSW Supreme Court

Judge Richard Cogswell – NSW District Court

Judge Garry Neilson – NSW District Court

Magistrate Doug Dick – NSW Magistrates Court

Suspected paedophiles

Justice Ian Harrison – NSW Supreme Court

Justice Lucy McCallum – NSW Supreme Court

Justice Peter Hall – NSW Supreme Court

Justice Michael Adams – NSW Supreme Court

Acting Justice Henric Nicholas – NSW Supreme Court (now retired)

Acting Justice Robert Hulme – NSW Supreme Court

Justice David Davies – NSW Supreme Court

Justice Peter Garling – NSW Supreme Court

Justice Stephen Campbell – NSW Supreme Court

Registrar Rebel Kenna – NSW Supreme Court

Registrar Christopher Bradford – NSW Supreme Court

If you are on the list and would like a right of reply to deny that you are a paedophile and argue that you should not be on the list, please email me by close of business Wednesday the 7th of September 2016. I will also likely publish the list on my website, if you would like me to publish a reply please send me one by 5pm Wednesday the 7th of September.

If you are not on the list but have evidence of paedophile judges, please contact me on the details below.

As we all know corruption in the NSW Courts is widespread and systemic. In July 2015 Fairfax Media and the ABC's Four Corners program reported that NSW judges had been bribed $2.2 million by the Mafia which was confirmed by Justice David Davies in December 2015. Maybe you have evidence that the above judges have also benefited from the Mafia bribes or other bribes. If you have evidence of judicial bribery, please contact me ASAP.

Regards

Shane Dowling

Email end

Not one judge has ever responded to the email, just the same as they all shut their mouths in 2015 when Fairfax Media and the ABC's Four Corners exposed NSW Judges for taking bribes of $2.2 million from the Mafia.

Doing jail time twice after Chief Justice Tom Bathurst let the dogs out

In 2014, Kerry Stokes started his War of Law against me with his first SLAPP lawsuit concerning an article I published about Seven paying Schapelle Corby, who was convicted of smuggling drugs into Indonesia, for an interview. The Australian Federal Police had raided Channel Seven a week or so before looking for evidence of Seven paying Corby, and my article focused on Kerry Stokes and his lawyers Justine Munsie, and they sued me.

The matter was given the name Munsie v Dowling. Stokes was given suppression orders, non-publication and a super-injunction by Justice Ian Harrison in the Supreme Court of NSW which meant that I couldn't even tell anyone there was a court case. I published an article telling people about it, and Stokes and Munsie hit me with a contempt charge as well for publishing an article saying they were suing me for defamation. The Super-Injunction was lifted a few days later after I argued in court that it should be lifted, but they followed through with the contempt charge and I was fined $2000 for breaching a Super-Injunction that should have never been issued in the first place.

Over the next couple of years I wrote numerous articles about the Munsie v Dowling court case and each time I did, Munsie and Stokes would run off to court, almost always at ex parte hearings (secret hearings), and get more suppression orders making me take down the new articles.

By 2016 I had decided to take a stand and not take down any more articles as there was no legal basis for all the suppression and non-publication orders and they were being issued by corrupt judges looking after their corporate mate with deep pockets. It turns out that Kerry Stokes' right-hand man, Bruce McWilliam, and his wife Nicky, are good friends with quite a few NSW Supreme Court judges such as Justice John Sackar, Justice Francois Kunc and others.

A key point to understanding my jailings and the conduct of the judges in the next few paragraphs is the timeline of the email I sent on the 6th of September, 2016 which is in the previous section of the book and adding that to the timeline of events after that.

In September 2016, I wrote an article about Capilano Honey suing beekeeper Simon Mulvany for accusing Capilano of selling poisonous and fake honey. Kerry Stokes was at the time the largest shareholder in Capilano when they were a listed company, and he still is a major shareholder after their privatisation in December 2018.

On Friday the 7th of October 2016, Capilano Honey's lawyers, who happened to be the same lawyers and barrister who represent Kerry Stokes, went to court ex parte and had wide-ranging suppression orders, non-publication orders and a Super-Injunction issued by Justice Peter Hall who is now the Commissioner for the NSW crime-fighting body, ICAC.

By this time, I knew the law well enough to know that the ex parte hearing could not be justified, and nor could the suppression orders, non-publication orders or Super-Injunction about which they emailed the paperwork to me that night. I would later be proven right after an application to review Justice Hall's orders found in my favour which was appealed by Capilano and I won again in a unanimous judgment in my favour. I had also had dealings with Justice Peter Hall in the Munsie v Dowling matter and knew he was rotten to the core, so I ignored his orders and published another article about it on the 9th of October 2016 titled "Capilano take out super-injunction to silence a 2nd journalist re: poisonous and toxic honey".

I did that because it was time to take a stand again against the dodgy suppression orders that the NSW Supreme Court was continually issuing to silence critics of rich individuals and large companies, or for their friends who I have no doubt were, and are, giving the judges kick-backs of one sort or another.

On Monday, the 10th of October 2016, Capilano's lawyers were back in court before Justice David Davies at 3pm, but I had only been notified late Friday night on the 7/10/2016 in their email and paperwork. I sent an email to Justice Davies asking for a later date for the hearing as I couldn't get time off work at such short notice, but Davies refused. Justice Davies heard their arguments in my absence and continued Justice Peter Hall's suppression orders, non-publication orders and Super-Injunction. Justice Davies also issued an order, at the request of Capilano's barrister Sandy Dawson, for the matter to be referred to the registry for the registrar to institute contempt preceding against me.

Once again, I ignored Justice Davies orders and published another article on the 13th of October 2016 titled "Capilano Honey want journalist jailed for exposing their toxic and poisonous honey". My mindset was that I had an obligation to warn people about a legitimate health and safety danger, and the court was aiding and abetting a company putting consumer's health at risk by issuing suppression orders that had no legal basis to be issued.

All the orders of Justice Peter Hall and Justice David Davies were overturned in 2018, firstly by a single judge, Justice Lucy McCallum, and then by 3 judges in the Court of Appeal. They had no choice because the whole situation with the Super-Injunction and suppression orders was scandalising the court.

I was notified on the 18th of February 2019 by the Crown Solicitor's office that the court would not be charging me contempt in the Capilano Honey matter, but I had that possibility hanging over my head for two and half years.

On the 21st of December 2016, Kerry Stokes instigated his third SLAPP lawsuit against me which related to me naming a well-known on-air host at Channel Seven and a well-known Channel Seven actress who were alleged to have had a sexual relationship with the then Seven CEO, Tim Worner. The matter became known as Jane Doe & Ors v Shane Dowling. Both women were named in a legal document that Amber Harrison filed with the Australian Human Rights Commission in her legal battle with Seven over her affair, and the hush money they paid, because of her affair with CEO Tim Worner.

The Tim Worner – Amber Harrison sex, drug and fraud scandal was all over the media, and as per usual, Seven's lawyers went to court ex parte and had Justice Stephen Campbell issue suppression orders and non-publication orders against me, even though there was no legal basis to do so. Justice Stephen Campbell set the matter down again for the 23/12/16. There were already things I had to deal with given it was 2 days before Christmas so I couldn't make it and there was no reason why he couldn't have set it down for a later date.

At that point, I had already decided to take a stand, in the Capilano Honey matter, against the scandalous abuse of suppression orders, non-publication orders and super-injunctions the Supreme Court of NSW was issuing for the rich and powerful when there was no legal basis to. It was, therefore, an easy decision to ignore the suppression orders and non-publication orders in the Jane Doe matter as well, not because I had issues with the Jane Doe's, but because it was part of my campaign against corruptly issued suppression orders that had no legal basis.

On the 23rd of December 2016, Justice Stephen Campbell continued the suppression orders and ordered the Registrar to consider charging me with contempt because I had ignored his suppression and non-publication orders, but they never did.

On the 2nd of February 2017, Seven's lawyers filed a Notice of Motion to charge me with contempt for breaching the suppression orders and non-publication orders. The following day, 3/2/17, I was in court for a directions hearing in the Jane Doe matter before Registrar Christopher Bradford.

Just winding the clock back for a minute, on the 9th of September 2016, a couple of days after I sent the infamous email mentioned above on the 6th of September 2016, I was in court for a directions hearing and I asked Registrar Bradford to stand down from hearing my matter because I had written on the internet that he was a suspected paedophile and known bribe-taker, but he refused, and luckily I recorded the hearing.

Back to when I was in court a few months later on the 3/2/17 before Bradford, I asked him to stand down from hearing the mater again on the same basis, and he refused again. So, I gave him a mouthful and later that day Bradford set in motion contempt charges for what I had said to him in court that day. I found this out when the Crown Solicitors office left me a voicemail and sent me an email. The contempt charge became known as The Prothonotary of the NSW Supreme Court v Shane Dowling.

At that point, the 3rd of February 2017, I was facing potential contempt charges in the Capilano Honey matter, the Jane Doe matter and The Prothonotary matter. I was also charged by the police in June 2017 for the infamous email I sent to the court. I did jail time for the Jane Doe matter in 2017 and Prothonotary matter in 2018, but they buckled on the other two matters.

They were all beat-up charges that can be traced back to the September 2016 email where I named the judges as paedophiles and suspected paedophiles and I dissect the charges in detail in later chapters. Evidence from the withdrawn police charge, a witness statement from the Supreme Court of NSW CEO Chris DÁeth, shows that Chief Justice Tom Bathurst wanted to stitch me up for jail time from the day he received the email I sent on the 6th of September 2016.

Becoming a fugitive on the run

I lived in Sydney from 2000 until November 2019 when I moved back to Queensland after the continual harassment by NSW judges who made it clear I will not receive justice in NSW courts and also after the Supreme Court sent NSW police to harass me again in May 2019. I figured between Kerry Stokes, Seven West Media, the NSW Supreme Court judges and the NSW police someone was going to stitch me up for jail again in the near future, so it was time to move. I go into further details in the book as they are still hunting me after the move.

A brief outline of events

January 2011 – I started publishing the website Kangaroo Court of Australia.

May 2011 – Kerry Stokes threatened legal action against me for an article I published titled "Kerry Stokes, Seven Group Chairman and Australia's number one perjurer, has been charged with contempt of court". I published an article about the threat and never heard from them again about it.

September 2013 – Kerry Stokes makes a complaint to the National Library of Australia about them archiving my website on their Pandora website. Kerry's son Ryan Stokes was chairman of the National Library of Australia at the time. More details are in Chapter 2 where Ryan wanted articles taken down from my website just before he was re-appointed as Chairman of the NLA.

April 2014 – Kerry Stokes and his lawyer Justine Munsie both sued me for defamation and started the proceeding at an ex parte hearing and were granted a Super-Injunction by Justice Ian Harrison. The matter was given the name Munsie v Dowling. Justine Munsie wrote the originating affidavit on behalf of Kerry Stokes which she admits in the affidavit. They have always refused to explain how one litigant can write an affidavit on behalf of another litigant. The only answer that I can come up with is that Munsie was not only being paid to represent Kerry Stokes but also being paid to be an applicant in the matter. Munsie and Stokes filed a Notice of Motion to charge me with Contempt of Court because I wrote an article letting people know they were suing me which was in breach of the Super-Injunction which meant I couldn't even tell people there was a court case. The Super-Injunction only lasted a couple of days because it was that dodgy but I was convicted of contempt and fined $2000 anyhow but never paid it because the Department of Justice refused to enforce it because they also knew it was dodgy. I deal with the Munsie matter in Chapter 1.

September 2016 – On the 6th of September 2016, I sent an email to all the judges of the Supreme Court of NSW naming 15 judges, 2 registrars and 1 magistrate as known paedophiles or suspected paedophiles and raising the ABC/Fairfax allegations of the $2.2 million Mafia bribe of NSW judges. I let them know that I would be writing an article about the issue and I gave them an opportunity to respond to the allegations in the email.

September 2016 – On the 6th of September 2016, without my knowledge, Chief Justice Tom Bathurst and court staff made a complaint to the NSW police and after they took no action they make a complaint to the Commonwealth Director of Public Prosecutions (CDPP) who sent it to the Federal Police for further investigation. I never found out until the following year.

September 2016 – On the 8th of September 2016, I published an article titled "Paedophile priest gets 3 months jail for raping 3 boys by NSW Supreme Court's Justice Hoeben" which has a copy of the email naming 15 judges, 2 registrars and 1 magistrate as known paedophiles or suspected paedophiles and raising the ABC/Fairfax allegations of the $2.2 million Mafia bribe of NSW judges. The article is still on my website and no one has ever complained to me about it.

September 2016 – On the 9th of September 2016, I was in the Supreme Court of NSW for a Directions Hearing before Registrar Christopher Bradford. I asked him to stand down as I had named him as a suspected paedophile in the email sent on the 6/9/16 and article which were both published on my website on the 8/9/16.

He refused. I recorded the hearing which I later published on my website.

October 2016 – The Kerry Stokes controlled Capilano Honey and CEO Ben McKee instituted defamation and injurious falsehood claims against me after I wrote about them suing beekeeper Simon Mulvany. The main article in question is titled "Australia's Capilano Honey admit selling toxic and poisonous honey to consumers". I discuss the matter in detail in Chapter 3.

December 2016 – The Kerry Stokes controlled Seven West Media pay for two female Channel Seven employees to institute defamation proceedings against me regarding allegations they had sexual relationships with the then Seven CEO Tim Worner. The allegations were made by former Seven employee Amber Harrison in a legal document filed at the Australian Human Rights Commission concerning her battle with Seven. One is a well-known actress and the other is a well-known on-air host. In February 2017 two more women were added to the claim but neither worked at Seven anymore which one must ask why Seven were paying for them to sue me. The matter was called Jane Doe and Ors v Shane Dowling. It is dealt with in detail in Chapter 4.

February 2017 – On the 2nd of February 2017 Seven West Media paid for the first 2 Jane Doe's to file a Notice of Motion to have me charged with contempt for failing to delete their names from the article were I had named them. I had decided a few months earlier before the Capilano Honey matter to take a stand against all the dodgy and corruptly issued suppression orders.

February 2017 – On the 3rd of February 2017 when I was in court, I had a run-in with Registrar Christopher Bradford after I asked him to stand down from hearing the matter and he refused. After an argument, he referred the matter to the duty judge but he also set in train the process to have me charged with contempt for what I said in court. I was accused of calling Justice Clifton Hoeben a paedophile and Registrar Christopher Bradford a suspected paedophile and known bribe-taker. I denied the allegations of what they claim I said.

I recorded the proceeding as I had previously asked Registrar Bradford to recuse himself from my matters on the 9th of September 2016 after I sent him the email naming his as a suspected paedophile, but he refused. I published an article on the 5th of February 2017 titled "Chief Justice Bathurst has journalist charged with contempt for accusing him of corruption" which has the recording embedded in it. More details are in Chapter 10.

February 2017 – On the 1st March 2017, the hearing for Contempt of Court in the Jane Doe matter was heard before Justice Ian Harrison and on the 15th March 2017, he handed down judgment and found me guilty of contempt. The sentencing hearing was on the 21st July 2017 and his judgment was on the 10th of August 2017 and I was sentenced to 4 months jail.

April 2017 – I was formally charged with contempt of court in April 2017 for what I said in court on the 3rd of February 2017 as well as 2 further charges of contempt for writing an article telling people I had been charged with contempt and the details of the charge. They had put illegal suppression orders on the matter because they didn't want the public to know they were stitching me up. The suppression orders were eventually lifted a few days before my appeal. More details are in Chapter 10.

May 2017 – The hearing for the Contempt of Court for what I said in court on the 3rd of February 2017 was held on the 4th of May 2017. Orders were issued for me to file and serve Notice of a Constitutional Matter to all Attorney-Generals which I detail in Chapter 11.

June 2017 – The NSW Police raided my unit and took my computers. I was at work but later that day I attended the Day St Police Station in the Sydney CBD and I was charged for the email I had sent 9 months earlier on the 6th of September 2016. I had tendered the email in court on the 4th of May 2017 as part of my defence for the Contempt of Court charge which is why I believe the Police raided my unit and charged me. The same people prosecuting me for the contempt charge were the same people, such as Rebel Kenna, who made the complaint to the police. The police charge was ultimately dropped as it was frivolous and vexatious but not before they gave Seven West Media a copy of my computer. I deal with the Police charge in Chapter 12.

August 2017 – On the 3rd of August 2017 I was found guilty by Justice Helen Wilson for contempt of court for what I said in court on the 3rd of February 2017.

August 2017 – On the 10th of August 2017 I was sentenced to 4 months jail by Justice Ian Harrison for contempt in the Jane Doe matter. Justice Harrison was named as a suspected paedophile in the email I sent on the 6th of September 2016, but he refused to recuse himself from hearing the contempt matter.

December 2017 – I was released from jail on the 9th of December 2017.

March 2018 – The CDPP sent me an email informing me that they would be formally dropping the police charge for the email that I sent on the 6th of September 2016. Details are in Chapter 12.

August 2018 – On the 22nd of August 2018 I was sentenced to 18 months jail with a non-parole period of 13 months by Justice Helen Wilson for what I said in court on the 3rd of February 2017.

November 2018 – My appeal against the conviction and sentence by Justice Wilson was heard on the 16th of November 2018. I was in jail and represented myself via video link. My appeal against conviction was dismissed but my appeal against the sentence was successful and it was reduced from 18 months jail with a non-parole period of 13 months to 4 months fixed which meant I was out of jail 5 weeks later on the 21st December.

December 2018 – I was released from jail on the 21st of December 2018.

May 2019 – On the 15th of May 2019 I received a visit from the NSW police who came to my place to harass me after a frivolous complaint by the NSW Supreme Court concerning emails I had sent to the court complaining about the fact that Justice Clifton Hoeben was hearing my matters as he was by then the defamation list judge. I had just spent 4 months in jail in part because I was found guilty of calling Justice Hoeben a paedophile and he refused to recuse himself from hearing my matters such as the Capilano, Jane Doe and Munsie matters. Justice Hoeben continued to have between 3 to 5 Court Sheriffs in court to try and intimidate me.

November 2019 – I moved to back to Queensland, after almost 20 years in Sydney, which is where I am originally from to try and get a far go and natural justice in court and get away from the harassing police who were working in collusion with Chief Justice Tom Bathurst and the courts. I deal with the harassment and move in Chapter 18.

February 2020 – On the 27th of February 2020 I received a hoax phone call from a "Damian Speers" who claimed he was from the Supreme Court of NSW and made threats against me if I do not take down certain articles etc. I deal with the call and associated attempted cover-up in Chapter 19.

The Players

Shane Dowling – Author of this book and publisher of the "Kangaroo Court of Australia" judicial corruption website since 2011. Self-represented litigant in numerous defamation and Contempt of Court cases. Author of the 2009 judicial corruption book "Love Letters from the Bar Table".

On the book cover - Front

Scott Morrison – Prime Minister of Australia – Good friends with Brian Houston who runs the fraud operation known as the Hillsong Church and he is currently under investigation for concealing his father's sexual abuse of children.

Chief Justice Tom Bathurst – Supreme Court of NSW – The driver behind the "get Shane Dowling" campaign as outlined in the book.

Bottom of front cover from left to right

NSW Police Commissioner Mick Fuller – Received a massive pay rise of $86,826 in March 2020 which took his annual package to $649,500. On Mick Fuller's watch, the police have refused to charge Prime Minister Scott Morrison's mate Brian Houston and have also harassed me based on frivolous complaints by the NSW Supreme Court as the book will show.

Premier Gladys Berejiklian – She has overseen widespread judicial corruption in NSW.

NSW Attorney-General Mark Speakman – Along with the NSW Premier he has overseen widespread judicial corruption in NSW and has failed dismally in his job.

On the book cover – back – From left to right

Justice Virginia Bell – High Court of Australia

Chief Justice Susan Kiefel – High Court of Australia

Justice Stephen John Gageler – High Court of Australia – It says on Wikipedia: "Gageler met his wife, Carla, while at the ANU. The family attends a Roman Catholic church, through the influence of Carla, although Gageler considers himself an Anglican." He was one of the judges who set Cardinal George Pell free and I believe he should have stepped down from hearing the matter as there is a clear case of perceived bias given he attends the Catholic church every week with his family.

Other key people in the book

Kerry Stokes – Mining and media billionaire. Legally he is best known for running the infamous C7 court case in 2007 where Seven sued 22 companies and people and they lost. It cost Seven $200 million in legal fees and Justice Sackville said Kerry Stokes "gave evidence that he knew was not true" and evidence that was "deliberately false" which is the definition of perjury.

Ryan Stokes – Kerry's son – Gifted the position as CEO of Seven Group which is the parent company of Seven West Media.

Justine Munsie – Partner at Addisons Lawyers – Seven West Media and Kerry Stokes are two of her key clients.

Richard Keegan – Special Counsel at Addisons Lawyers – Mr Keegan reports to Justine Munsie – He has been the day to day lawyer for all of the defamation matters against me.

Martin O'Connor – Partner at Addisons Lawyers – His name appeared on most of the paperwork for the defamation matters but I believe that was to conceal the fact that Justine Munsie, who also sued me personally in the Munsie v Dowling matter, was getting paid to represent Kerry Stokes and Seven West Media in all matters.

Bruce McWilliam – Commercial Director at Seven West Media. He is also Seven's head lawyer and the one behind the scenes running the legal cases against me on behalf of Kerry Stokes and Seven West Media. He is good friends with several judges such as Justice John Sackar. Both Justice Sackar and Bruce McWilliam are good friends with former Prime Minister Malcolm Turnbull.

Nicky McWilliam – Wife of Bruce McWilliam – She is also a lawyer and good friends with numerous judges such as Justice John Sackar and Justice Francois Kunc. Her name shows up in a couple of judgments because I asked at least two judges to recuse themselves given their known relationship with her but they refused.

For other people in the book go to the Kangaroo Court of Australia website and use the search box on the top left for more information about them.

Chapter 1

Kerry Stokes, Justine Munsie and the Schapelle Corby matter

The first few chapters deal with Kerry Stokes various lawsuits against me which is to show the corruption in the judiciary and give an understanding of my relationship with the court and the judges before they tried to silence me when I named numerous judges as paedophiles and suspected paedophiles in an email. I then published the email in an article which is still on my website to this day.

In May 2011 Kerry Stokes sent me a letter from his lawyers, Justine Munsie at Addison Lawyers, threatening defamation proceedings, because of an article I published titled "Kerry Stokes, Seven Group Chairman and Australia's number one perjurer, has been charged with contempt of court".

When I received the letter, I published another article titled "Kerry Stokes threatens legal action against blogger" and said in relation to the letter:

The letter raises two key issues. Issue one is that I said Kerry Stokes "has been charged" and the second issue is they claim I suggest that Kerry Stokes "has been charged and found guilty of perjury".

Issue one was clearly a smokescreen to conceal the real issue, which is issue two. A quick internet search will reveal that almost every media organisation in the country has said that Mr Stokes has been charged with contempt of court or to that effect.

So why did Kerry Stokes have his lawyers send me a letter complaining about it and not the other media organisations? (If his lawyers had sent a letter to the other media organisations, they have not taken it down from their sites). The only reason he raised it in his letter is to conceal the actual reason for his letter, which is he wanted me to take down the references to him being a perjurer.

Well, as I have previously stated on my website: "In a court of law any inference that can be reasonably drawn from the primary facts has to be taken at its highest. (See the decision of J Gyles in Choundary v Capital Airport [2006] FCA 1755 at 3 and 23)." See page 24 in my book "Love Letters from the Bar Table,".

And given that, as quoted in my previous articles, that Justice Ronald Sackville said in the C7 court case that Mr Stokes had given "deliberately false evidence" and "Mr Stokes evidence on this issue was not only implausible but, I must conclude, deliberately false," it is fair and reasonable to conclude that Mr Stokes is a perjurer until proven otherwise.

The letter from Mr Stokes lawyer, Justine Munsie, could and would be regarded as an attempt to conceal a serious indictable offence which is a crime. The lawyer is trying to hide Mr Stokes perjury.

End of quote

My reference to Kerry Stokes and Justice Sackville above is from the infamous C7 case where Mr Stokes, via his media interests

Channel 7 and C7, sued numerous parties which is outlined on Wikipedia which says:

"Seven launched what is considered to be the largest ever media lawsuit in Australia, naming 22 defendants including Nine, Ten, Optus, Austar, the AFL, the NRL, Fox Sports, PBL and Telstra. Primarily basing the claim on anti-competitive provisions in Part IV of the Trade Practices Act."

Stokes lost the legal battle and had to pay costs. Media reports estimated Seven paid out approximately $200 million in legal fees, which included their own and the other parties.

In February 2014 I published an article titled "Kerry Stokes, Channel Seven and Lawyer Justine Munsie Caught lying in the Schapelle Corby matter" which related to Channel Seven allegedly paying Schapelle Corby for an interview which was illegal because she had been convicted of a crime. The federal police raided Seven, trying to find evidence that Seven had paid Schapelle.

On Tuesday the 15th of April 2014 I received an email when I got home at about 7.30pm serving me with court documents that showed Kerry Stokes and his lawyer Justine Munsie were suing me for defamation and there was a super-injunction on the case which meant I could not even tell anyone that there was a court case. They had been to court the day before at an ex parte hearing (secret hearing) without my knowledge or consent. Ex parte hearings are meant to be very rare as they deny one party natural justice and their day in court. But in the Supreme Court of NSW ex parte hearings are quite common because the judges are so corrupt, they treat ex parte hearings as a right of the rich and powerful.

The disputed article had been on my website for over a month so there was no urgency for the legal action and their barrister, Sandy Dawson, told the court that if they didn't get a super-injunction, they wouldn't follow through with the case. Looking back in hindsight, the only reason they sued me is because Seven took action against the Australian Federal Police for raiding Seven and my article was holding up a settlement. The AFP paid Seven an undisclosed amount for the illegal raids on Seven. I was told the settlement was $1 million. In 2016/2017 Amber Harrison leaked text messages that showed Seven's head lawyer Bruce McWilliam discussing paying Schapelle Corby with Seven West Media board members, so they quickly sued Ms Harrison as well.

Given I publish a website focusing strongly on judicial corruption, I was very worried about the super-injunction as I knew there was no legal basis for one so I thought I was about to get stitched up and no one would know. So, I wrote an article telling people that I was being sued by Stokes and Munsie and I also emailed the Chief Justice and the Attorney-General etc complaining about the legality of the super-injunction as per the below email.

From: Shane Dowling <shanedowling@hotmail.com>
Sent: 16 April 2014 12:27
To: victoria_bradshaw@courts.nsw.gov.au
Cc: bernadette_heywood@courts.nsw.gov.au;
richard.keegan@addisonslawyers.com.au;
mail@addisonslawyers.com.au; tony.negus@afp.gov.au;
olsc@agd.nsw.gov.au; office@smith.minister.nsw.gov.au;
michael.phelan@afp.gov.au; jeffrey.kokles@afp.gov.au
Subject: Justice Harrison - Taking instructions from Kerry Stokes

Dear Justice Bathurst

Justice Harrison has issued suppression orders over defamation proceedings against me by billionaire media mogul Kerry Stokes. At no stage did anyone contact me or attempt to contact me which Mr Keegan from Addison Lawyers admitted to me.

This is a continuance of previous harassment by Kerry Stokes and his lawyer Justine Munsie from Addison Lawyers which was very clear in the affidavit filed by Ms Munsie. Justice Harrison should never have taken the action he did, and it leaves one greatly disturbed that he would aid and abet Mr Stokes and Ms Munsie. I have dissected their conduct further in the attachment *"Kerry Stokes has suppression order put on defamation proceedings against KCA publisher"* which I have also published on my website "Kangaroo Court of Australia"

It is very clear that there is not just perceived bias but actual bias by Justice Harrison and he should stand down from hearing the matter any further. Justice Harrison should also be investigated for his actions as we live in a democracy, not a dictatorship. It looks fairly clear that Kerry Stokes runs the Supreme Court of NSW which is consistent given Mr Stokes thinks he runs the federal police based on his recent actions and statements. Justine Munsie and the rest of the lawyers involved should be referred to the OLSC and at least be disciplined if not struck off as lawyers.

Regards

Shane Dowling

Kangaroo Court of Australia

I was in court on the 17th of April 2014 to argue against the super-injunction and wide-ranging suppression and non-publication orders that Justice Ian Harrison had put on the case.

While we were in court barrister Sandy Dawson handed up paperwork to have me charged with Contempt of Court for breaching the Super-Injunction by me publishing the article letting people know I was being sued and also for the email I sent Chief Justice Tom Bathurst and others as per above.

The following week Justice Ian Harrison handed down a judgment, Munsie v Dowling [2014] NSWSC 458 (24 April 2014), and I had won comprehensively. The super-injunction and suppression orders and non-publication orders were lifted but Stokes was not happy.

At 8.40pm on Friday the 2nd of May 2014 Justine Munsie sent me the below email:

From: Justine Munsie <justine.munsie@addisonslawyers.com.au>

Sent: 02 May 2014 20:40

To: shanedowling@hotmail.com

Cc: Richard Keegan <richard.keegan@addisonslawyers.com.au>

Subject: Supreme Court defamation claim

Mr Dowling

With apologies for the late hour, we are writing to advise that we intend to relist this defamation matter for further argument before the defamation list judge next week.

Could you please let us know what day or days are more convenient for you to attend so that we can arrange a mutually suitable time?

Regards

Justine Munsie | Partner

ADDISONS

I responded and said:

From: Shane Dowling <shanedowling@hotmail.com>

Sent: 02 May 2014 22:16

To: 'Justine Munsie' <justine.munsie@addisonslawyers.com.au>

Cc: 'Richard Keegan' <richard.keegan@addisonslawyers.com.au>

Subject: RE: Supreme Court defamation claim

Dear Ms Munsie

The day is not important but I am not in receipt of any notice of motion with a supporting affidavit which "must be served at least 3 days before the date fixed for the motion" as per UNIFORM CIVIL PROCEDURE RULES 2005 - REG 18.4

So, if you file and serve the notice of motion on Monday that means the "3 days before…" will take us to Friday as the earliest date for it to be heard.

Regards

Shane Dowling

Kangaroo Court of Australia

They went to court the following week without my knowledge before Justice Lucy McCallum with an application which was in effect a backdoor appeal against Justice Ian Harrison's judgment to lift the suppression orders. Justice Lucy McCallum should have been nowhere near the case and the transcript, which I later bought, showed that. McCallum also new Justine Munsie personally which is another reason McCallum should not have heard the matter.

Justice McCallum abridged the matter (expedited it) and set it down before the Duty Judge to have the matter heard urgently even though there was no urgency.

The matter went before Justice Peter Hall who in effect acted as the Court of Appeal and over-turned part of Justice Ian Harrison's judgment and made me take the article back down even though the article was published in Justice Ian Harrison's judgment. This to me was further evidence that somehow my article was holding up Seven's settlement with the AFP or was it just pure corruption to keep Kerry happy.

Peter Hall's judgment, Munsie v Dowling [2014] NSWSC 598 (16 May 2014), is just pure corruption and he knows it. Peter Hall will show up again in this book issuing a dodgy Super-Injunction in the Capilano Honey matter which the Court of Appeal ripped to pieces. This is worth noting because Peter Hall is now the Commissioner of the NSW Independent Commission Against Corruption (ICAC) and he is as crooked as they come.

Over the next few years, I would write about the court case and other associated matters involving Kerry Stokes and he would have his lawyers rush off to court, almost exclusively on an ex parte basis (secret hearings) and have orders issued for me to take down the articles.

Kerry Stokes won the Munsie v Dowling case even though they filed no evidence at the final hearing. Their barrister Sandy Dawson argued because I had my defences struck out on technicalities, they did not have to provide evidence and because they already filed evidence to support the interlocutory orders for suppression and non-publication orders.

But the only evidence they filed to get the interim interlocutory suppression and non-publication orders was hearsay evidence, predominantly for their lawyer Richard Keegan, and while hearsay evidence is allowed at interlocutory hearings it isn't allowed at final hearings which means they had no evidence to support their claim. Justine Munsie did file evidence to start the proceedings in 2014 but was on behalf of Kerry Stokes which makes it hearsay evidence and anyhow they refused to use it at the final hearing and the reason why will become obvious in a minute.

The way the whole case was managed and the fact that it lasted years helps explain why Justice Rothman heard the matter in April 2017 but didn't hand down judgment until May 2018. (See:

Munsie v Dowling (No 10) [2018] NSWSC 709 (21 May 2018)
He was trying to drag it out which is typical of a SLAPP lawsuit.

Stokes win was largely futile as the final judgment names almost all titles of the articles I had to take down which tells a large part of the stories and says at paragraphs 13 and 14:

Justine Munsie is the "first plaintiff" and Kerry Stokes is the "second plaintiff".

13. In or about February 2014, the defendant published an article titled "Kerry Stokes, Channel Seven and Lawyer Justine Munsie Caught Lying in the Schapelle Corby matter" ("the Corby Article"). The imputations in the publication are plain and obvious. The article imputes that the first plaintiff lied to the Australian Federal Police ("AFP") about Channel Seven's ability to comply with an AFP search warrant; the first plaintiff, a solicitor, attempted to assist her client, Channel Seven, to avoid revealing documents caught by an AFP search warrant, which she knew would prove that Channel Seven had concluded an illegal deal to pay Schapelle Corby for an interview and did so dishonestly; and the first plaintiff, a solicitor, has repeatedly committed perjury.

14. The same article also conveyed imputations concerning the second plaintiff that he: used threats and intimidation against the AFP to avoid having to reveal documents caught by an AFP search warrant, which he knew would prove that Channel Seven had concluded an illegal deal to pay Schapelle Corby for an interview; lied to the AFP about Channel Seven's ability to comply with an AFP search warrant; made dishonest threats against the AFP concerning their raid on Channel Seven; had repeatedly committed perjury; and is, or was, delusional.

Some of the article titles and descriptions in the judgment are:

31. "Known Adulterer and Womaniser, 7's Kerry Stokes Denies Sexual Relationship with Lawyer...". The article, as a whole and in its natural and ordinary meaning carries a number of

imputations which are defamatory of the first and second defendant. It imputes to the first defendant that: she was involved, or is involved, in an adulterous sexual relationship with the second plaintiff; by engaging in that adulterous sexual relationship

37. "Kerry Stokes and the NLA Lose Freedom of Information Legal Battle Against KCA Blogger"

39. "Channel Seven's Ryan Stokes Thrown under a Bus for Corruption as Chair of the National Library"

46. "ICAC Request Evidence re: Kerry Stokes & Ryan Stokes Getting Judicial Favours from NSW Judges".

Kerry Stokes and Justine Munsie both refused to give evidence or deny any of the allegations and so did Ryan Stokes who joined the matter as an applicant in 2015.

Stokes and Munsie were that corrupt they couldn't even enforce the costs they were awarded. They never went for damages as that would have meant they would have to provide evidence of the damage done. As Justice Ian Harrison said in his judgment there would have been very little damage.

The reason they could not get costs is that they could never explain why Justine Munsie wrote an affidavit on behalf of Kerry Stokes to start the proceedings in April 2014.

As you can see below Justine Munsie wrote an affidavit on the 14th of April 2014 and it says at paragraph 2:

"I am authorized by Mr Kerry Stokes, the second plaintiff, to swear this affidavit on his behalf and make this affidavit based on my personal knowledge or else on information provided to me by Mr Stokes or other employees and officers of the Seven West Media Group, of which Mr Stokes is Chair, and to whom I will refer in my affidavit, which information I believe to be true"

AFFIDAVIT

Name	Justine Melissa Munsie
Address	Level 12, 60 Carrington Street Sydney NSW 2000
Occupation	Solicitor
Date	14 April 2014

I say on oath:

1   I am a partner of Addisons and the first plaintiff.

2   I am authorised by Mr Kerry Stokes, the second plaintiff, to swear this affidavit on his behalf and make this affidavit based on my personal knowledge or else on information provided to me by Mr Stokes or other employees and officers of the Seven West Media Group, of which Mr Stokes is Chair, and to whom I will refer in my affidavit, which information I believe to be true.

3   Mr Stokes, the second plaintiff, is the Chairman of Seven West Media, whose media assets include the Seven Network which broadcasts news, current affairs and other programs throughout Australia.

Lawyers are allowed to write affidavits for their clients, but Kerry Stokes and Justine Munsie were both applicants in the case against me and one applicant can't write an affidavit for the other applicant. Why? Because it would show both applicants are working together to get their stories aligned which would be the crime of attempting to pervert the course of justice.

I have emailed them and their lawyers numerous times asking them about why and on what basis Justice Munsie wrote the affidavit for Kerry Stokes but they refuse to answer and every time I raised it in court the judges refused to take any action.

So how did it happen? I suspect it is like this: Justine Munsie was being paid to represent Kerry Stokes as she had done in 2011 when she sent me the first legal threat. But in 2014 Kerry decided he didn't want his name on the case so Justine said she would also sue me so it would become known as Munsie vs Dowling but she forget to change the affidavit to conceal the fact that not only was she being paid to represent Kerry Stokes but she was also being paid to be an applicant in the case.

This raises huge issues such as: If you pay someone to be an applicant in a case isn't that the same as bribing a witness etc? It is also a huge conflict of interest for a lawyer to be paid to be an applicant and also be paid to represent the other applicants in a matter.

This is what has brought them undone in enforcing the costs they have been awarded and claiming $100,000's if not $1,000,000's they, most likely Seven West Media, spent on the matter.

If you have costs awarded against you and you suspect the other party of fraudulently trying to claim money they aren't entitled to then you can make a complaint to the Office of Legal Services Commissioner - NSW who have a duty to investigate. And while Kerry Stokes, Ryan Stokes and Justine Munsie and their lawyers refuse to explain to me why Justine Munsie wrote the affidavit on behalf of Kerry Stokes they would have no option but to explain to the Office of Legal Services Commissioner and there is no credible explanation. They would also have to provide an itemised bill which they would have to commit another crime of fraudulently doctoring the bill to conceal that Justine Munsie was paid by the other applicants, Kerry Stokes, Ryan Stokes and/or Seven West Media. The Directors of Seven West Media would also have a lot of questions they would need to answer as well if the company paid for the legal fees.

Chapter 2

Ryan Stokes intervenes when he is not even a party to the proceedings / National Library of Australia

Sometimes when I write articles about judicial corruption people don't believe it because they think judges and the courts always act honestly. Well, this part of the book is classic corruption involving three Supreme Court judges, Justice David Davies, Justice Peter Garling and Justice Stephen Campbell. It involved the three judges issuing suppression and non-publication orders on articles to protect Ryan Stokes before he was even a party to the proceedings, although it could be argued that Justice Campbell waited until he was a party.

At the time Justice Davies and Justice Garling issued the orders, only Kerry Stokes and his lawyer Justine Munsie were suing me. So how did Ryan Stokes, who was not a party to the case, get orders in his favour? Talk about a scandal!

It involves Kerry Stokes making a complaint about my website to the National Library of Australia in 2013, where Ryan Stokes was chairman of the Library from 2012 to 2018, in relation to the two articles I wrote in 2011 titled "Kerry Stokes, Seven Group Chairman and Australia's number one perjurer, has been charged with contempt of court" and "Kerry Stokes threatens legal action against blogger".

Evidence I obtained under freedom of information laws pointed to the possibility that Ryan Stokes, in his position as Chairman of the NLA, intervened in the complaint and I wrote two articles about it in March and May 2015. In June 2015 Ryan Stokes position as Chairman of the NLA was up for renewal but they must have perceived the articles I had written were an obstacle to his reappointment, so they wanted them removed from my website.

Background

I started publishing on the Kangaroo Court of Australia (KCA) website in January 2011. In about September or October 2011, the Pandora website which is owned by the NLA approached me. Pandora requested permission to archive my website on their website. Pandora selected Australian websites, so they are there for future generations and I agreed for them to archive the KCA website. I even put a message at the top right-hand side of the KCA website advertising Pandora with a link to the archived site. I didn't think it was a massive issue but something worth promoting.

Pandora archived the KCA website in November 2011 and re-archived it in November 2012, and it was due for archiving again in November 2013. I did not check until February 2014 and noticed they had blocked access to the archived site.

The Complaint

I phoned the National Library of Australia (NLA) (27/2/14 at 4.25pm – call lasted 22 minutes) and found out that someone had made a complaint at the beginning of September 2013 and that the NLA stopped access after receiving a legal letter from the complainant. They said the complainant said there were defamatory articles on my site and demanded the NLA take certain action as the NLA was liable for the archived site. The library stopped public access to the archived site on their Pandora website and stopped re-archiving my site.

I was told by an NLA staff member it is very rare for the NLA to block access and stop updating archived websites.

The key person I suspected as being the complainant was former Prime Minister Kevin Rudd because the federal election was in September 2013 and I had written several critical articles about him and his wife. Although, when Stokes instituted defamation proceedings against me in April 2014 for a post I published in February 2014 he became a suspect as well and even more so given his son was Chairman of the NLA.

The NLA would not tell me much more and did everything they could to conceal the identity of the complainant. So, for 12 months I was in a freedom of information battle with the NLA and the mystery complainant whose identity I did not know.

As it turned out the complainant was Kerry Stokes, and the complaint was sent to the Library by Channel 7's lawyer Justine Munsie from Addisons Lawyers. Kerry Stokes is chairman of Seven West Media, and Ryan Stokes is a director.

What is disturbing is that Mr Stokes son, Ryan, was the Chairman of the Australian National Library and even worse is that there was no legal basis for the NLA to stop archiving my website.

The complaint to the NLA would have related to 3 articles I wrote about Kerry Stokes in 2011 and 2013. The second article in 2011 was about a legal letter sent to me from Stokes' lawyer Justine Munsie threatening defamation action because of the first article I wrote. All three articles are still on my website and have never been the subject of court action by Kerry Stokes. Given Kerry Stokes failed to take legal action against me for those articles it is a bit rich for him to tell other people the articles are defamatory and threaten them with legal action as he has did with the NLA.

I made a Freedom of Information request to the NLA in March 2014 and they gave me virtually nothing. They admitted they had 7 relevant documents but gave me only a heavily redacted email chain on the 2-5-14.

I appealed to the Australian Information Commissioner who started investigating my matter in August 2014 and I received the judgment on the 27th March 2015 in my favour with the NLA ordered to hand over further documents to me.

While the judgement by the Office of the Australian Information Commissioner did not name Kerry Stokes, there are several things in the judgment that made it very clear it was Kerry Stokes. For example, at paragraph 76 it says:

"I have performed a simple internet search of the names of the third party and Mr Dowling. I found a 2014 article in Australian Financial Review newspaper directly related to the issues raised by the third party in his complaint. This article also names the law firm and the partner representing the third party and discusses defamation action. I am satisfied that the substance of the information contained in documents 1 and 2 is already well known."

At the time there were only 2 articles in The Australian Financial Review that I knew of and they are both in 2014 and both relate to me, Kerry Stokes and Channel 7's lawyer Justine Munsie from Addisons Lawyers. It was always going to be almost impossible for the Commissioner to write his report and for me not to be able to guess who the complainant was given what was in the report.

The bottom line to the judgment is that the National Library of Australia acted illegally by withholding documents to try to protect Kerry Stokes from being outed as the complainant. And Kerry Stokes is the father of the NLA Chairman Ryan Stokes, which by itself raises many questions for many people to answer.

I wrote two articles on the issue. The first titled "Kerry Stokes and the NLA Lose Freedom of Information Legal Battle Against KCA Blogger" published on the 29th of March 2015 and the second "Channel Seven's Ryan Stokes Thrown under a Bus for Corruption as Chair of the National Library" published on the 10th of May 2015.

Were the articles defamatory? Kerry Stokes and his lawyers were monitoring my website daily and running off to court, making me take down articles within hours of me publishing them. So why did they wait two months for the first article and a month for the second article before they went to court to get suppression and non-publication orders on the 5th June 2015? It raises another question of why the judges ordered the articles be taken down after so long, but that's another story.

Well, Ryan Stokes 3-year tenure as Chairman of the National Library of Australia expired on the 30th of June 2015 and he was up for re-appointment but it would have been embarrassing for the government to appoint him given the articles I had written. So off to court they went, and he was re-appointed for another 3 years a few weeks later.

How it worked in court

Kerry Stokes lawyers had an ex parte hearing in the Munsie v Dowling matter on the 5th June 2015 (a secret hearing they never told me about until afterwards) before Justice David Davies and he issued various orders making me take down the 2 articles. I ignored the orders as they were corruptly issued as Ryan Stokes was not even an applicant at the time which Justice Davies blatantly had to have known and there was no legal justification for the ex parte hearing. Justice Davies also makes an appearance later in the book in Capilano Honey matter where again his conduct and the court orders he issued were scandalous.

On the 11th June 2015, Justice Peter Garling continued the orders and once again I ignored the orders as I pointed out to Garling that Ryan Stokes was not a party to the case so he could not legally get court orders in his favour which Garling ignored. But Garling also issued orders for the lawyers to file a Notice of Motion to add Ryan Stokes as a party to the case or for Ryan Stokes to start his own proceedings as per the below court orders 4,5,6 and 7. That was an admission by Justice Garling he knew Ryan Stokes was not a party to the matter, had no legal basis for court orders for his benefit and it again scandalised the court.

Form 43
UCPR 36.11

D0000LRG6R

Issued: 11 June 2015 5:05 PM

JUDGMENT/ORDER

COURT DETAILS

Court	Supreme Court of NSW
Division	Common Law
List	Defamation
Registry	Supreme Court Sydney
Case number	2014/00114469

TITLE OF PROCEEDINGS

First Applicant	Kerry Stokes AC
Second Applicant	Justine Munsie

DATE OF JUDGMENT/ORDER

Date made or given	11 June 2015
Date entered	11 June 2015

TERMS OF JUDGMENT/ORDER

This matter is listed for Duty (Common Law) on 17 June 2015 10:00 AM before the Supreme Court - Civil at Supreme Court Sydney.
GARLING J MAKES THE FOLLOWING ORDERS:
1. The defendant is hereby restrained until 11am 18/6/15 from publishing the
a) 29 March article,
b) 10 May article and the
c) Stokes tweets
and any matter of any concerning the plaintiffs to the same effect as the 29 March article, the 10 May article and the Stokes tweets (each as defined in the affidavit of Richard Keegan sworn 11/6/15).
2. Order that by no later than 10am 12/6/15, the defendant is to remove from his website (http://kangaroocourtofaustralia.com/) the following publications:
a) 29 March article
b) 10 May article
c) Stokes tweets
each as defined in the affidavit of Richard Keegan sworn 11/6/15)
3. Order that service of these orders is to be effected by email to the defendant's emails shanedowling@hotmail.com by 6pm on 11/6/15.
4. Direct that any application to join Ryan Kerry Stokes as a plaintiff in these proceedings is to be made by notice of motion filed and served by email no later than 4pm 12/6/15.
5. Order that all affidavit or other materials to be relied upon in support of that application be served by email by 4pm 12/6/15.
6. Alternatively to Order 4, if so advised, if Mr Ryan Stokes determines to commence new proceedings, then such new proceedings are to be commenced on or before 4pm 12/6/15 by filing and service of a statement of claim by that time.
7. Stand the proceedings for hearing of the current Motion for injunctive relief and any motion filed with respect to the joinder of Mr Stokes to the proceedings to Common Law Duty Judge on 17/6/15.
8. Reserve all question of costs.
To Shane Dowling: If you disobey Order 2(a,b,c) of this order you will be liable to sequestration of

On the 17th of June 2015, the matter was before Justice Stephen Campbell. He added Kerry Stokes' son, Ryan Stokes, as an applicant for which he handed down a judgment while we were in court. And then in a second judgment published on the 19th of

June 2015, Campbell made me take down 4 articles and 3 Tweets from twitter. There should have been one judgment but that would have told the full story, which is embarrassing for the court and Justice Campbell, so he split it up the two judgments which helps conceal what really happened.

That's how the court works. If you have deep pockets, you can get the judges to do whatever you want. Even issue orders for your benefit against a party when you are not a party to any proceeding. I have no doubt Ryan Stokes had no intention of becoming a party to the case and it was only because I pointed out, when the matter was before Justice Garling, how dodgy it was that Garling issued orders for Ryan Stokes to become a party or start his own case.

Like his father, Ryan Stokes refused to write and sign any affidavits or give evidence in the witness stand for the matter.

Chapter 3

The Kerry Stokes controlled Capilano Honey try to stop allegations of selling fake and poisonous honey

In February 2016 Capilano Honey started suing beekeeper Simon Mulvany because he used his Facebook page, Save the Bees Australia, to accuse Capilano Honey of selling fake and poisonous honey. The major shareholder at the time was Kerry Stokes, and it was his lawyers that were used to sue Mr Mulvany. Capilano Honey was privatised on the 10th of December 2018 and Kerry Stokes is still a major shareholder.

In about August 2016 the Capilano / Mulvany lawsuit came to my attention, and I published an article on the 17th of September titled "Australia's Capilano Honey admit selling toxic and poisonous honey to consumers". The article started going viral and was also picked up by other media overseas. There was nothing wrong with the article as it was predominantly about Capilano Honey suing Simon Mulvany and Capilano took no action as there was no legal basis to do so. But it was obviously worrying Capilano as they were receiving bad press in Asia and they had government departments in other countries contacting them with concerns.

On the 25th of September 2016, I published another article titled "Channel Seven, Capilano Honey and Addisons Lawyers involved in judicial favours scam". Again, Capilano Honey took no action as there was no legal basis to do so.

On the 6th of October 2016, I published an article titled "Sex tape featuring Capilano Honey CEO Ben McKee covered up by Directors" and Capilano Honey used that article to run off to court and to get interim orders for a super-injunction, wide-ranging suppression orders and non-publication orders making me take down the first and third articles until the final hearing. Once again there was no legal basis to do so, and ultimately the court of appeal agreed with me.

This is a classic example of a SLAPP lawsuit and it is worth repeating the definition I wrote earlier: The definition of a SLAPP Lawsuit as per Wikipedia is:

"A strategic lawsuit against public participation (SLAPP) is a lawsuit that is intended to censor, intimidate, and silence critics by burdening them with the cost of a legal defence until they abandon their criticism or opposition.[1] Such lawsuits have been made illegal in many jurisdictions on the grounds that they impede freedom of speech."

"In the typical SLAPP, the plaintiff does not normally expect to win the lawsuit. The plaintiff's goals are accomplished if the defendant succumbs to fear, intimidation, mounting legal costs, or simple exhaustion and abandons the criticism. In some cases, repeated frivolous litigation against a defendant may raise the cost of directors and officers liability insurance for that party, interfering with an organization's ability to operate. A SLAPP may also intimidate others from participating in the debate. A SLAPP is often preceded by a legal threat."

After Capilano Honey went to court, I published an article on the 9th of October 2016 titled "Capilano take out super-injunction to silence a 2nd journalist re: poisonous and toxic honey" which is reprinted in full below:

Capilano take out super-injunction to silence a 2nd journalist re: poisonous and toxic honey

Last Friday Capilano Honey and their CEO Ben McKee instituted injurious falsehood and defamation proceedings against myself and this website at a secret hearing in the NSW Supreme Court. They were also granted a super-injunction and I am not allowed to tell anyone about the court case.

The court has also ordered me (7/10/16) to take down 2 previous articles from this website in an attempt to cover-up them selling poisonous and toxic honey. I am going to stand and fight as this is clearly a national public interest matter regarding health and safety and undermines people's legal right to free speech.

I was denied natural justice as I was never told about the hearing and given I am not allowed to tell anyone about the case it also breaches the "open courts" principle.

All Australians should be alarmed that a food company like Capilano Honey can get a secret super-injunction so they can conceal their corrupt conduct.

I am now the second journalist that Capilano Honey and their CEO Ben McKee have sued in frivolous and vexatious defamation proceedings although I am the first where they have sought a super-injunction to cover it up from the public. The first article that they want me to take down is actually an opinion piece regarding them suing the first journalist Simon Mulvany, the health dangers and Capilano breaching court orders to file their full statement of claim. Court orders that Capilano and Ben McKee are still in breach of now.

If Capilano Honey and Ben McKee had truly been defamed, then they would want everyone to know they are suing me for defamation to send a message to others, not trying to conceal it like they are with a super-injunction.

They have sued me for 2 posts. One published on the 17th of September 2016 titled: "Australia's Capilano Honey admit selling toxic and poisonous honey to consumers" (Click here to read) and a second one published on the 6th of October 2016 titled "Sex tape featuring Capilano Honey CEO Ben McKee covered up by Directors" (Click here to read).

Capilano and Ben McKee's lawyer Richard Keegan emailed the court documents to me at 7.42pm on Friday and said:

"This email is not for publication and the Court Orders prevent you from providing it to anyone apart from a legal representative for the purpose of advising you." (Click here to read the rest of Mr Keegan's email)

Court orders: (Click here to read) Affidavit of Capilano Honey's lawyer Richard Keegan: (Click here to read) Summons: (Click here to read)

If you have a good look at Richard Keegan's affidavit it becomes very clear what their real concern is. The article I published on the 17th of September 2016 titled: "Australia's Capilano Honey admit selling toxic and poisonous honey to consumers" has gone viral, including in some parts of Asia. Keegan's affidavit has stories from Brunei and Malaysia where they have quoted this website and the article. The article has had over 528,000 page views as of today, so it has had a fair impact.

On page 6, 7 and 8 of Richard Keegan's affidavit, he seems to confirm the existence of a sex tape and refers to a transcript of the tape on page 87. But page 87 is missing as the judge has said they do not have it give me a copy. Once again, I am denied natural justice as how can I defend myself against evidence I am not allowed to see?

Interestingly, they have not sued me for a 3rd post published on the 24th September 2016 which is titled: "Channel Seven, Capilano Honey and Addisons Lawyers involved in judicial favours scam" (Click here to read) The fact that they have not sued me for this post I take as admission by Capilano Honey, Channel Seven, their lawyers and barrister Sandy Dawson whom I name in the post.

Capilano Honey has a lot of health and safety issues. For example, by their own admission Capilano Honey know their beekeepers are feeding their bees antibiotics and Chinese irradiated pollen yet refuse to do any testing to determine if it is safe for humans. And then there is the question of all the imports from China, Mexico, Argentina, Hungary and Brazil etc.

While Capilano fail time and again to address the issues and/or answer media questions, then it is more than fair to make allegations against them especially when it is backed up by evidence as my previous articles have. Each time I asked Capilano fair and reasonable questions before I published, and they refused to answer. They only want to answer easy questions or put out media releases by spin doctors that virtually say nothing.

I do not know the judge who issued the super-injunction, but I believe it would have been Justice Peter Hall given he was the Duty Judge for Common Law on Friday. I wrote an article about Peter Hall in 2014 titled "Money talks at the Supreme Court of NSW. Billionaire Kerry Stokes boy Justice Hall scandalises the court" so he is obviously not a fan of this website and vice versa.

Other media like Fairfax Media, who are sued for defamation on a regular basis, are not made to take down their articles until after the final hearing and then only if they lose. It is time corrupt judges stopped abusing their position for the rich and trying to silence whistleblowers.

Time to take a stand

Yes, I am in breach of the super-injunction telling you I am being sued by Capilano and Ben McKee but as far as I am concerned the super-injunction was illegally issued by a nameless judge who has failed to publish reasons for his corrupt secret hearing which breaches common law. So as far as I am concerned the injunction is null and void.

The matter is listed again at 3.00pm on Monday the 10th of October before the Duty Judge (Common Law) which is currently listed as Justice David Davies. I cannot make it and will email him an alternative time and update this post accordingly.

End of article

I sent Justice David Davies and others the below email on the 9th of October 2016:

From: SHANE DOWLING

Sent: Sunday, 9 October 2016 11:51 PM

To: victoria_bradshaw@courts.nsw.gov.au; supremecourt.enquiries@justice.nsw.gov.au; anita.singh@courts.nsw.gov.au

Subject: Scandalous denial of natural justice in NSW Supreme Court - hearing time change – Capilano & Anor v Dowling

Dear Chief Justice Bathurst, Justice Davies and Registrar Bradman

I am writing in regards to a defamation matter that was instituted against me on Friday the 7th of October 2016, was served on me by email late Friday night and has been set down for the duty judge (common law) at 3pm Monday the 10th of October 2016. This is scandalous and I cannot make it as I will be at work. All other litigants that have proceedings commenced against them get at least 30 days to prepare and what makes it worse is that I am a self-represented litigant so if anything I should get more time to prepare not a ridiculously short time to prepare.

Be that as it may, if a time is settled quickly I can make it to court at 11am on Tuesday the 25th of October or alternatively 11am Wednesday the 26th of October or Thursday the 27th of October. I will need to leave by no later than 11.30 as I will need to go to work but given it would only be a 5-minute directions hearing that should be fine. Otherwise, I am happy to consider dates after the 31st of October 2016.

It must be noted one of the articles the applicants complain about was published on my website on the 17th of September which they became aware of almost immediately yet took no action until the 7th of October then they expect me to jump when they say and the court obliges.

Why it has not been set down with at least 30 days notice for a directions hearing before the registrar which is the usual process, I find very disturbing. Why is Capilano Honey being treated special and getting favourable treatment? Is major shareholder Kerry Stokes bribing judges again?

For obvious reasons which I am sure you all will agree the Super-Injunction / Suppression Orders issued on Friday the 7th of October have been ignored because they were illegibly issued and are therefore null and void. I have written an article on my website, which explains why.

Some of the reasons which mean they were illegally issued are:

1. The hearing was an unjustified ex parte hearing (secret hearing) which I was not informed of, I did not attend and was therefore denied natural justice.

2. Given the ex parte hearing was unjustified then it becomes what it really was: Private communication between one party and the judge. As we know "private communication" is a very serious contempt of court.

3. There is no justification for the suppression orders given the articles complained of raise health and OH&S issues and are in the public interest which makes all orders null and void.

4. There are no published written reasons by the judge which is a breach of common law which makes the orders null and void.

5. The orders clearly state that the applicants do not have to give me all the evidence which again is a denial of natural justice which makes the orders null and void.

6. The applicants are also suing Simon Mulvany (since February 2016) for almost identical issues and there is no super-injunction on his matter. Why is that?

7. The applicants are in breach of court orders for failing to file their full statement of claim against Simon Mulvany so they think it is ok to breach courts orders. What action will the court take against Capilano Honey and Ben McKee given they are in contempt of the court orders and denying Simon Mulvany natural justice as justice delayed is justice denied?

Justice David Davies perceived bias and real bias

The orders say that the matter is listed before the duty judge (Common law) on Monday, which is currently David Davies. I have been before Justice David Davies before and he is a real grub. He is as corrupt as they get and admitted that the Mafia had bribed NSW Judges $2.2 million as reported last year by Fairfax Media on the ABC's Four Corners program. I have written 2 recent articles on him titled:

1. Justice David Davies – The sleazy, slimy corrupt go-to man at the NSW Supreme Court – published November 28th 2015

2. Justice David Davies confirms $2.2mill Mafia bribe & systemic corruption in NSW Supreme Court – published 31st January 2016

Justice David Davies is clearly not a fit and proper person to hear the matter, and there is clearly perceived bias and real bias against me.

Can you please supply me with:

1. The judge's name who heard the hearing on Friday the 7th of October.

2. The barrister's name who represented Capilano Honey. (Was it Sandy Dawson?)

3. A copy of the transcript from the hearing on the 7th of October.

4. A copy of the judges published written reasons for the hearing on the 7th of October.

I await your reply.

Regards

Shane Dowling

Kangaroo Court of Australia

Email end

Justice David Davies read the email but ignored it and went ahead with the hearing on Monday the 10th of October 2016 when there was no urgency to do so and even though I wasn't there. Justice Davies continued the super-injunction and other court orders.

Justice Davies also directed the registry to charge me with contempt for breaching the super-injunction when I wrote the article on the 9th of October 2016 titled "Capilano take out super-injunction to silence a 2nd journalist re: poisonous and toxic honey" telling people I had been sued by Capilano Honey and CEO Ben McKee. Justice Davies referred me to the registrar for contempt charges at the request of barrister Sandy Dawson who was representing Capilano Honey and Ben McKee.

What was so scandalous about it all is that there was no legal basis for the super-injunction, suppression orders and non-publication orders which explains why Justice Peter Hall never gave or published reasons for his court orders which was exposed in greater detail when I appealed his orders in 2018.

What made it even worse again is that Justice Davies published his decision, Capilano Honey Ltd v Dowling [2016] NSWSC 1441, which put him in breach of the super-injunction as a super-injunction means you cannot even tell people there is a court case. I wrote an article a couple of days after the hearing titled "Capilano Honey want journalist jailed for exposing their toxic and poisonous honey" on the 13th of October 2016.

Google, Facebook and Twitter

As with the other matters, the lawyers wrote many times to social media sites such as Google, Facebook and Twitter making sure they blocked links to the alleged defamatory articles on my website given I had refused to take them down. The suppression orders have been lifted but Google continues to block the articles even though I have complained to them and Capilano's lawyers.

Justice Lucy McCallum lifts the suppression orders after refusing to recuse herself

I applied to have the super-injunction, suppression orders and non-publication orders lifted and in July 2018 they finally were. The super-injunction had been lifted by consent a few months earlier as Justice Lucy McCallum pressured Capilano's barrister Sandy Dawson to do so as it did nothing more than embarrass the court as it was blatantly corrupt to issue the super-injunction in the first place.

What is interesting is that Capilano Honey and Ben McKee applied to have Justice McCallum recuse herself from the matter because I had sent in the infamous September 2016 email to the court naming Justice McCallum as a suspected paedophile and she refused to recuse herself. (See judgment: Capilano Honey Ltd v Dowling [2018] NSWSC 876 (4 April 2018).

Justice McCallum handed down her judgment lifting the suppression orders, Capilano Honey Ltd v Dowling (No 2) [2018] NSWSC 865 (8 June 2018), and it showed what a baseless and weak case Capilano Honey and Ben McKee had when the super-injunction, suppression orders and non-publication orders were issued on the 7th of October 2016. Once again, they had relied solely on hearsay evidence from their lawyer Richard Keegan which is inadmissible at the final hearing.

The judgment also showed that Justice Peter Hall who had issued the orders had given no reasons why he had done so. He ignored common law says he has to give written reasons. That by itself should send the corruption alarm bells ringing.

Capilano Honey and CEO Ben McKee appeal

Even though Capilano Honey and Ben McKee had comprehensively lost the battle before Justice McCallum to keep the suppression orders and non-publication orders they appealed which was at least in part a strategy to keep the suppression orders and non-publication going for a few more months.

Capilano and McKee filed the appeal within days and the matter was set down urgently in the Court of Appeal to hear an application to keep the suppression orders going until the appeal was heard. Justice John Basten continued the suppression orders but made some observations in his published judgment that supported me, especially in relation to the fact that Justice David Davies also breached Justice Peter Hall's super-injunction when he published his judgment. See: Capilano Honey Ltd v Dowling (No 1) [2018] NSWCA 128 (15 June 2018) at paragraph 13.

Court of Appeal – Justice Margaret Beazley, Justice John Baston and Justice Ruth McColl

The appeal was heard on the 19th of July 2018 and they handed judgment down on the 3rd of October 2018.

It was obvious at the Appeal that Capilano Honey was in major trouble and that their chance of winning was zero. The matter had already become a public issue with my article going viral and I also filed evidence of a Facebook post on the matter receiving almost 2 million views.

To make matters worse again for Capilano Honey and Ben McKee, a story broke in the media on the 2nd of September 2018 that testing had proven that Capilano's Allowrie brand honey was fake.

They were hoping for a corrupt judgment in the Court of Appeal which didn't happen this time and was never going to happen with all the public interest in the quality of Capilano's honey.

So, before the Court of Appeal handed down their decision one of Capilano Honey's and Ben McKee's lawyers, Alexander Latu from Addisons Lawyers, wrote to Google on the 7th of September 2018 asking them to again block numerous articles as per below:

Court Order Complaint to Google

SENDER	RECIPIENT	SUBMITTER
Alexander Latu	Google LLC	Google LLC
[Private]	[Private]	
_, AU	Mountain View, CA, 94043, US	

Sent on September 07, 2018

Re: Unknown

SENT VIA: UNKNOWN

NOTICE TYPE: Court Order

Explanation of Court Order

Dear Google, We are lawyers who act for the two plaintiffs in a civil proceeding against Mr Shane Dowling in the Supreme Court of New South Wales (see Orders Attachment at page 1 for more details), for defamation and injurious falsehood. Our client the second plaintiff is CEO of the first plaintiff. We have previously successfully written to Google seeking the removal of web search results based on orders made by the Supreme Court of New South Wales, as detailed below.   BACKGROUND Mr Dowling, the defendant, is the owner and author of the 'Kangaroo Court' website (www.kangaroocourtofaustralia.com). The 18 numbered links set out above in the earlier text box, which we will refer to as "Link 1" through "Link 18" respectively, are all links to Mr Dowling's Kangaroo Court website, or to Mr Dowling's Twitter account. Currently, those links are returned by Google's search results for certain terms including our clients' names. The link ...

Court order #1

SUBJECT

TARGETED URLS:
01. https://twitter.com/kangaroo_court/status/784126691064950784?lang=en
02. https://kangaroocourtofaustralia.files.wordpress.com/2018/01/affidavit-shane-dowling-12-1-18-compressed.pdf
03. https://kangaroocourtofaustralia.com/tag/capilano-honey/
04. https://kangaroocourtofaustralia.com/tag/ben-mckee/
05. https://kangaroocourtofaustralia.com/capilano-honey-poisonous-and-toxic-honey-investigation/
06. https://kangaroocourtofaustralia.com/2018/08/11/dying-cancer-patient-poisoned-by-the-same-weed-killer-found-in-capilano-honey-awarded-a395m/
07. https://kangaroocourtofaustralia.com/2018/07/07/coles-starts-australian-made-honey-war-against-woolworths-and-capilanos-imported-chinese-honey/
08. https://kangaroocourtofaustralia.com/2018/06/23/woolworths-organic-food-scam/
09. https://kangaroocourtofaustralia.com/2018/06/09/capilano-honey-lose-second-supreme-court-judgement-in-2-weeks-as-likely-class-action-grows-momentum/
10. https://kangaroocourtofaustralia.com/2018/06/04/kerry-stokes-capilano-honey-have-their-dirty-legal-tactics-against-simon-mulvany-exposed/
11. https://kangaroocourtofaustralia.com/2018/05/16/facebook-block-post-exposing-capilano-selling-imported-honey-while-the-accc-investigate-facebook-and-google-etc/
12. https://kangaroocourtofaustralia.com/2018/05/05/capilano-honey-want-whistleblower-simon-mulvany-jailed-for-exposing-their-polluted-and-poisonous-honey/
13. https://kangaroocourtofaustralia.com/2018/04/21/capilano-honey-sells-polluted-and-poisonous-honey-kerry-stokes-channel-7-claims/
14. https://kangaroocourtofaustralia.com/2018/04/15/capilano-honey-ceo-fails-to-sign-affidavit-declaring-their-honey-is-safe/
15. https://kangaroocourtofaustralia.com/2018/04/07/justice-lucy-mccallum-the-judge-helping-capilano-dump-their-cheap-chinese-honey-on-australian-consumers/
16. https://kangaroocourtofaustralia.com/2018/02/10/capilano-honey-ceo-ben-mckee-caught-on-video-talking-about-sex-with-a-staff-member-to-opposing-party/

It was a dirty trick by Capilano Honey and their lawyers as they knew they would lose the appeal. It also goes to show they have been running a SLAPP lawsuit since 2016 trying to conceal the truth from the public.

When the Court of Appeal handed down their judgment, Capilano Honey Ltd v Dowling (No 2) [2018] NSWCA 217 (3 October 2018), it was a unanimous decision in my favour and Capilano and McKee got smashed. The dodgy conduct of their barrister Sandy Dawson, lawyers Richard Keegan, Martin O'Connor and Alexander Latu was also exposed. At paragraph 122 of the judgment, one of the suppression orders was said to have an **"unjustifiable chilling effect on freedom of speech"**.

I was in jail at the time they handed down the appeal decision, which I discuss later, and it was a morale booster to have a win.

The Capilano Honey – Ben McKee matter has had everything, and it is something worthy of its own book because it is right up there with the infamous McLibel court case in the UK. See: McDonald's Corporation v Steel & Morris [1997] EWHC QB 366

During the proceedings, Capilano Honey tried to have evidence destroyed which they stupidly documented in a Deed of Release they wanted Simon Mulvany to sign. They settled with Simon Mulvany, but again that is a story in itself. They forced Mulvany to issue a statement apologising but it was only limited and to me was at least an admission that Capilano had been selling fake honey.

Capilano Honey and Ben McKee were ordered to file and serve witness statements by the end of 2019 and when they did I published them and pointed out that they support my case so they ran off to court and had orders issued, firstly by the duty judge Justice Button, and then by Justice Fagan a few days later making me take down the article based on a legal technicality.

Because they only signed off on witness statements and not affidavits I had to wait until the hearing and for them to swear the witness statements as being true and correct before I could publish them. I published an article on the 20th November 2019 titled "Capilano Honey does a Prince Andrew and shoot themselves in the foot" outlining the suppression orders.

The final hearing was set down for the 25th, 26th and 27th of May 2020 but ran over time to include the 28th of May and the afternoon of the 3rd of June. Justice Richard Button heard the matter, reserved his decision, and went on holidays. At the time of writing this book, he has not handed down a judgment. Justice Button did publish three interlocutory judgements which left a lot to be desired one of which was an application to have the matter transferred to Queensland given all parties are based here but Justice Button refused the request.

Chapter 4

Kerry Stokes controlled Seven West Media tries to protect Seven CEO Tim Worner during the fraud, sex and drug scandal – The Jane Does

In December 2016 former Seven West Media employee Amber Harrison started blowing the whistle on her 2-year affair with Seven CEO Tim Worner, their use of drugs and use of the company's money to help facilitate the affair and other affairs Tim Worner was having with female staff at Seven.

Amber Harrison left Seven in 2014 with Seven agreeing to pay Ms Harrison what was in effect hush money on a monthly basis for two years but Seven stopped the payments and Ms Harrison exhausted her legal avenues trying to rectify the situation.

On or about the 18th of December 2016 Amber Harrison emailed hundreds of journalists telling her story regarding Seven's treatment of her when she raised her sexual relationship with CEO Tim Worner with the HR Manager at Seven and also sent out copies of her complaint to the Australian Human Rights

Commission. Several of the major media companies published the story, and it was quickly all-over social media.

Amber Harrison named 4 other women, in a legal document filed with the Australian Human Rights Commission, as having had affairs with Tim Worner and raised the possibility that Mr Worner might have used his position as CEO to help their careers and/or salary at Seven.

One woman named by Amber Harrison is a well-known on-air host at Channel 7 and another is a well-known actress who worked Seven. The other two women named were administration staff who left Seven a long time ago.

I wrote an article on the 21st December 2016 naming the well-known on-air host at Seven West Media and the well-known actress at Seven. Seven's lawyers went to court the next day, ex parte (a secret hearing) when there was no legal basis to do so, and instituted defamation proceedings and had suppression and non-publication orders issued. The court gave the matter the name Jane Doe v Shane Dowling to conceal the name of the women from the public.

I wrote to Seven's lawyer, Richard Keegan from Addisons Lawyers, and asked who was paying the legal fees and Keegan wrote back saying it was the women who had retained him which implied the women were paying. This was proven to be a lie later when Richard Keegan was in the witness stand under oath and under sustained questioning, he ultimately admitted that Seven West Media were paying for the lawyers after initially giving evidence that the women were paying. Richard Keegan also admitted under oath that he was in regular contact directly with Seven's Chairman Kerry Stokes via email and phone calls regarding the matter.

This was a matter driven and paid for by Seven on the orders of Kerry Stokes for his and Seven's benefit.

On the 5th of January 2017, I wrote an email to the Directors of Seven asking many questions about the Tim Worner / Amber Harrison / Seven sex drug and fraud scandal that had been all over the media since it exploded at the end of December 2016. In the email, I also named and asked questions about the other two women who Amber Harrison named in her complaint to the Australian Human Rights Commission.

I published the email, with the two women's names, in an article on the 21/1/17. Kerry Stokes, Seven West Media and the women took no action even though Stokes and Seven had taken action immediately when I named the well-known on-air host and actress.

I published another article on the 19/2/17 titled "Kerry Stokes versus the world. Part 2. This time he wants to destroy free speech on social media". In that article, I pointed out the fact that they had taken against the first two women I named but taken no action when I named the second two women which I took as admission as it being true. As soon as I published the article, they were in court the next day, at another ex parte hearing (secret hearing), suing me for defamation on behalf of the other two women and seeking suppression orders and non-publication orders even though they had been named publicly on the internet for almost a month.

Kerry Stokes and Seven said "jump" and Justice Walton said, "How high Mr Stokes, how high" and he gave them exactly what they wanted and issued suppression orders and non-publication orders, so their names were also suppressed. So, then there was four Jane Doe's suing me for defamation being paid for by Seven.

It is scandalous that people get suppression orders and non-publication orders in defamation matters before they have made out their case at the final hearing. It is even worse when their names have been on the internet for almost a month and they are refused to sign affidavits refuting the allegations against them.

The second two women were no longer working for the Seven. One had left a long time ago and the other one left about the same time as I named her in the email I sent to Seven's directors.

So why would a company pay for two ex-employees to sue for defamation? Seven didn't care about the two women, they were trying to protect the CEO Tim Worner and the directors who were supporting him led by chairman Kerry Stokes.

When Amber Harrison blew the whistle, she started leaking evidence that raised questions about the conduct of the directors and they were worried.

Seven West Media spent $millions silencing Amber Harrison, firstly through hush money and secondly through a major court case, that was also played out in the media, in an attempt to protect CEO Tim Worner and the directors.

Seven has also spent hundreds of thousands if not millions in legal fees trying to silence me. Ultimately, it was a waste of money as they sacked Tim Worner in August 2019 after he drove Seven West Media headfirst into the ground where the company debt has ended up being greater than the value of the company. Kerry Stokes has to take full responsibility for the problems at the company and should have also resigned as chairman.

The final hearing for Jane Doe & Ors v Dowling was heard on the 26th and 27th of August 2019 with a final judgment on the 20th of September 2019. I published an article on the 31st of September 2019 that tells a large part of the story titled "Four mystery Channel Seven women awarded $600,000 plus costs in a defamation case against KCA journalist" which is published in full below.

Four mystery Channel Seven women awarded $600,000 plus costs in a defamation case against KCA journalist

Four Channel 7 female employees have won a defamation case and have been awarded a total of $600,000 plus indemnity costs which will likely bring the total to over $1 million against Kangaroo Court of Australia publisher Shane Dowling.

One of the women is a well-known on-air host at Seven, another is an actress on Seven and I understand one left Seven in 2017 and the fourth woman left sometime before 2017. The four women were named in a legal document that Amber Harrison lodged with the Australian Human Rights Commission in 2015 that claimed the women had sexual relationships with former Seven West Media CEO Tim Worner who was forced to resign (sacked) on the 16th of August 2019. The document also spoke of Tim Worner "grooming" women at Seven and in the industry for his "sexual gratification".

The reason I named the women was that they were named in a legal document and it told part of the overall story about the fraud and mismanagement at Seven. That mismanagement has ultimately led to Seven sacking their CEO Tim Worner and everyone knows Seven is for sale. Seven's debt is now greater than their market value and Chairman Kerry Stokes and the board don't have a clue what to do so they are looking to sell out.

While technically it was the women's court case against me it is Kerry Stokes' Seven West Media who paid the legal fees and Kerry Stokes who was in regular communication with the lawyers giving them instructions. Their lawyer Richard Keegan said 2 years ago when he was in the witness stand on the 1st of March 2017 when the matter was before Justice Ian Harrison:

Q. Mr Keegan, you have four clients in this matter?

A. I do, yes.

Q. They're all paying you individually?

A. I don't know whether they're paying individually or all together for the one proceedings.

Q. So you don't know?

A. That's correct.

Later in proceedings, Richard Keegan changed his tune. Did he commit perjury?

Q. You don't know who is paying?

A. No, I don't.

Q. So is it highly likely Seven West Media, is that right?

A. Yes.

Q. It is highly likely?

A. Yes.

Q. So Seven West Media are paying for their legal fees?

A. Yes.

It is important to confirm the fact that Seven West Media are paying for the matter for many reasons. Whoever pays for the court case controls it, and that means Kerry Stokes has ultimate control as chairman.

Richard Keegan again – Kerry Stokes heavily involved in the defamation and contempt case

Q. Have you spoken to Kerry Stokes in relation to this matter?

A. I have been in contact with him.

Q. So he's involved in this matter now?

A. Yes, he's concerned about the impact this is having upon his employees.

Q. And Kerry Stokes, how many times have you been in contact with Kerry Stokes?

A. Do you mean about these matters or ever?

Q. Yeah, about this specific matter?

A. They're all email.

Q. No, that's fine?

A. So I probably say five to ten emails.

Q. Five to ten, maybe up to fifteen?

A. No.

Q. So five to ten?

A. (Witness nodded.)

If Richard Keegan is saying 5 to 10 emails, I would expect the real number to be a lot higher and how many phone calls have there been? Kerry Stokes is not Executive Chairman so he shouldn't have had anything to do with the case and even an Executive Chairman should not have been giving instructions to a junior lawyer.

When I asked Richard Keegan again who was paying for the proceedings when he was in the witness stand on the 26th of August 2019 Justice Fagan wouldn't allow the question. What Justice Fagan didn't know was I already knew the answer and Justice Fagan just confirmed his bias.

All four women refused to show up to the final hearing on the 26th and 27th of August 2019, they all refused to sign affidavits, they all refused to give evidence in the witness stand under oath, they all refused to answer interrogatories or agree to the discovery of documents, there was no jury and the judge, Justice Desmond Fagan, lied throughout his dodgy judgment and relied on hearsay evidence from their lawyer Richard Keegan.

It should be no surprise that Justice Fagan stitched me up given that I publish a judicial corruption website, and I wrote about Fagan's criminal conduct on the bench a few weeks ago. (Click here to read more)

Richard Keegan admitted in the witness stand under oath and in front of Justice Desmond Fagan, that a junior lawyer at his law firm Addisons, who reported to partner Justine Munsie who has the Kerry Stokes / Seven West Media account, set up a fake GoFundMe page in the name of Amber Harrison. At the time Amber Harrison, who was in a well-publicised legal fight with Seven over her affair with CEO Tim Worner, had set up a GoFundMe to pay for her legal bills. The fake GoFundMe page was an exact copy of Amber Harrison's and would have confused people and put them off donating. Richard Keegan said in the witness stand that they had set up the fake website for market research which I judged as being blatant perjury by Keegan and admission of fraud and identity theft by lawyers at Addisons for impersonating Amber Harrison. On that basis, Justice Fagan should have ignored all of Keegan's evidence. (Click here to read an article about the fake GoFundMe page)

Details in legal documents before courts and tribunals are protected from defamation claims in what is known as "Absolute Privilege" which is section 27 of the Defamation Act 2005. Justice Desmond Fagan and the applicant's barrister Sandy Dawson admitted at the hearing on the 27th of August 2019 that documents lodged with the AHRC were protected by absolute privilege, but Justice Fagan has obviously done a backflip.

Dawson did argue that I had to wait until March 2017 before I could name them, but then he also did a backflip in his written submissions in reply to my submissions.

I'll briefly dissect a couple of the lies in the judgment: (Click here to read the judgment) Justice Fagan hasn't published the judgment on the internet which he has a habit of doing and it is very dodgy and corrupt so I scanned in the copy I was given.

Judgment lies:

In paragraph 2 Justice Desmond Fagan says that the 4 women work at Seven. As I already wrote I understand that is wrong and

2 left the company a long time ago and only the well-known on-air host and actress still work there.

In paragraph 7 I named the on-air host and the actress on my website in December 2016 and they went to court and got suppression and non-publication orders the next day even though the horse had bolted which is a good reason why they shouldn't have been allowed the suppression and non-publication orders.

I named the second two women in an article on the 21st of January 2017, but they took no action. A month later I wrote another article on the 19th of February again naming the second 2 women and pointing out they had not sued like the on-air host and actress which I said was telling. Only then did the second 2 women sue but only for the article I published on the 19th of February 2016 and they were also given suppression orders and non-publication orders to protect their names by Justice Walton. Their names had already been on the internet for a month, so they had no right to suppression orders and non-publication orders and Justice Fagan conveniently leaves that out of his judgment.

In paragraphs, 17 to 25 Justice Fagan does a big song and dance how I had failed to file the proper paperwork for a jury, and it didn't matter anyhow as a jury would have been a waste of time he said because of me wasting time in court. The reality is a jury would never have found me guilty of defamation when they saw none of the four applicants had filed sworn affidavits, none of the four applicants had shown up to court for the hearing, none of the four applicants would give evidence in the witness stand under oath and I wasn't allowed interrogatories or discovery. The jury would also have seen Richard Keegan's perjury in full flight.

In paragraph 51 Justice Desmond Fagan tells a huge lie in relation to Amber Harrison's legal document filed with the Australian Human Rights Commission which names the four women as having sexual relationships with Seven CEO Tim Worner. Justice Fagan says, "There has been no admissible evidence tendered to prove what the former employee may have communicated to the AHRC." That's a lie, and I tendered two pages of Amber Harrison's AHRC complaint as part of my defence which I filed in March 2017. Justice Fagan knows that as it was discussed numerous times in court as it was part of my defence and I also handed up another copy of the 2 pages on the day of the hearing. That's why Justice Fagan and the women didn't want a jury as they would have seen what was written in the AHRC complaint and the fact that women refused to refute it under oath or in any way other than having their lawyer deny via inadmissible hearsay evidence.

The 2 pages of the document I tendered to the court is the same document that a lot of other media referred to in reports but at the end of the day, it doesn't matter whether I had a defence or not because the applicant's had to prove their case. The four women failed to prove their case because they refused to give evidence in their own case. Perjury being a jailable offence stops a lot of people from giving evidence.

Justice Fagan also ordered me to take down whole articles instead of just the names of the women for no logical reason although he goes on a nutter's rant in the judgment trying to justify it. The real reason is that a lot of the articles I have to take down have little to do with the women except naming them but are about judicial corruption and one even talks about Seven's top lawyer Bruce McWilliam, who knows a lot of judges, stalking journalists via email and admitting he received judicial favours.

Justice Fagan has continued the non-publication orders when there is no legal basis to do so. It is only in exceptional circumstances that there should be non-publication orders, and this isn't one of them nor did the applicants identify any exceptional circumstance, otherwise it undermines the public's confidence in the judicial system.

We have all heard the names of Geoffrey Rush, Craig McLachlan and Rebel Wilson suing for defamation in recent times and that is the way it should be. It is what we call open justice, and it is what is meant to help keep the courts accountable.

Open justice is one of the fundamental attributes of a fair trial. That the administration of justice must take place in open court is a 'fundamental rule of the common law'. The High Court has said that "the rationale of the open court principle is that court proceedings should be subjected to public and professional scrutiny, and courts will not act contrary to the principle save in exceptional circumstances."

In Russell v Russell, Gibbs J said that it is the 'ordinary rule' of courts of Australia that their proceedings shall be conducted 'publicly and in open view'; without public scrutiny, 'abuses may flourish undetected'. (Click here to read more)

I said to Justice Fagan in my written submissions, which I had also said in court:

This is a SLAPP lawsuit and is part of a number of SLAPP lawsuits being run against me by Kerry Stokes and his companies Seven West Media and Capilano Honey. Kerry Stokes has a long history using a war of law strategy including the infamous C7 case where Seven had to pay $200 million in costs when they lost.

This particular SLAPP lawsuit has no legal basis and was designed to protect former Seven West Media CEO Tim Worner during the Amber Harrison sex, drug and fraud scandal. This is consistent with the same lawyers and Kerry Stokes' Seven West Media running the same scam in the Munsie v Dowling matter (No 10) [2018] NSWSC 709 (21 May 2018) which was Kerry Stokes, his lawyer Justine Munsie and Ryan Stokes suing me for defamation.

In the Munsie matter they also had no evidence at the final hearing, no witnesses except hearsay evidence from their lawyer Richard Keegan, the applicants never showed up to the hearing, no jury and I wasn't allowed interrogatories or discovery.

The decision is a judgment handed down by a corrupt judge who without a doubt in on the take and the judgment designed, at least partly, to try to intimidate all Australian citizens to protect an already corrupt judiciary who makes big dollars on the side. To prove the point, it was reported by Fairfax Media and the ABC in 2015 that NSW judges were bribed $2.2 million by the Australian Mafia to reduce one person's jail sentence. I made a formal complaint to ICAC, but it was swept under the carpet. (Click here to read more) If judges make $2.2 million just in a bribe in one matter how much are they making in total every year?

This website (KCA) is here to expose judicial corruption and I believe most fair-minded people who have a close look at the facts in this matter would be greatly disturbed at the state of open justice, natural justice and a fair go in Australia's courts. So, from that viewpoint, I think it is a good judgment as it makes it blatantly obvious to the public how corrupt the courts are.

There are a lot of twists and turns moving forward and there is still a current application in the High Court of Australia to have this matter removed to High Court, so we'll see what happens there. But as far I am concerned the High Court's Chief Justice Susan Kiefel needs to take ownership of the above judgment because Justice Desmond Fagan knew that there was an application before the High Court and he refused to adjourn the matter until the High Court had decided what to do. Justice Fagan was happy to hand down a dodgy judgment, so I can only assume that Justice Fagan knew he had the protection of the High Court and Chief Justice Susan Kiefel. And the High Court should have removed the matter to their court earlier as they are well aware of what is happening in this court case.

I'll have plenty more to say on this matter in the future as it is part of the huge press freedom issue being played out in Australia where more and more people with power are trying to silence the media.

End of article

Doing jail time for the Jane Does

In 2017 I did four months in jail after Jane Doe 1 and Jane Doe 2 instituted contempt proceedings against me. I deal with that in detail in a later chapter to keep the book in order as much as possible.

Chapter 5

Seven West Media and Seven Network v Shane Dowling

In April 2017 Seven West Media and its subsidiary the Seven Network instituted proceedings against the unknown owner of the website sevenversusamber.com claiming the owner breached suppression and/or non-publication orders issued in Seven's proceedings against Amber Harrison. The matter was known as Seven versus Publisher X.

A few months later Seven changed the name of the respondent from Publisher X to me claiming I was the owner of the website. The matter is now known as Seven Network (Operations) Limited & Ors v Shane Dowling.

At about the same time Seven started suing me the ownership of the website sevenversusamber.com was transferred to Kerry Stokes and/or Seven West Media as they claimed they owned the copyright to the word "seven". The international body who oversees domain name disputes ordered the transfer of the name to them.

The matter is still afoot at the time of writing this book (September 2020). I applied to have the matter transferred to Queensland as I moved here in November 2019 but Justice Kunc refused to make a decision, but he kept the contempt proceeding that Seven instituted against me in 2017, via a Notice of Motion, before himself in Sydney. I said to Justice Kunc he had obviously done that on the instructions of Chief Justice Tom Bathurst to stitch me up for more jail time.

I have already caught Justice Kunc lying and deceiving many times during the court case and I'll deal with that in more detail later in chapter 16. I applied to have all my matters transferred to the High Court of Australia as there is documented evidence that shows Chief Justice Tom Bathurst ordered senior staff to have me jailed because of the September 2016 email so I was never going to get a fair trial in NSW courts.

Below is the application filed in May 2019 to have the Seven matter moved to the High Court of Australia. I won't publish the other applications as they are similar but it's worth having a look at one application so you can see the corruption that the High Court regularly sweep under the carpet which they also did in this case.

IN THE HIGH COURT OF AUSTRALIA
SYDNEY REGISTRY

No. S145 of 2019

BETWEEN:

Shane Dowling
Applicant

and

Seven Network (Operations) L
First Respondent
Seven West Media Limited
Second Respondent

APPLICATION FOR REMOVAL

To: The Respondent
        Attn: Martin O'Connor – Addisons Lawyers – Level 12 / 60 Carrington
        St Sydney 2000

The applicant applies for an order under section 40 of the *Judiciary Act* 1903
removing the whole of the cause now pending in the Supreme Court of NSW
which is proceeding number 2017/116771 between Seven Network (Operations)
Limited and Seven West Media Limited v Shane Dowling.

Part I:

The matter be removed to the High Court of Australia.

Such further or other order as the court thinks fit.

Part II:

[A concise statement of the constitutional or other question.]

2.1 Does the NSW Supreme Court have the constitutional power and/or legal
authority to hear a matter that has evidence before the court the 18 NSW Judicial
Officers are paedophiles or suspected paedophiles and judicial bribery allegations.

2.2 Does the NSW Supreme Court have the constitutional power and/or legal
authority to hear a matter that has evidence before the court that is only before the

Shane Dowling   Ph: 0411238704
1/78b Ocean St, Bondi
Sydney, NSW 2026   Email: shanedowling@outlook.com.au

court because of a malicious complaint that Chief Justice Tom Bathurst ordered senior court staff to make to the NSW Police and Commonwealth Director of Public Prosecutions (CDPP).

2.3 Are SLAPP lawsuits (Strategic Lawsuit Against Public Participation) legal in Australia as this is a blatant SLAPP Lawsuit and is part of numerous other SLAPP lawsuits by Kerry Stokes and his associated companies.

Part III:

[A brief statement of the factual background to the application.]

3.1 On the 6th of September 2016 I sent an email to all the judges of the Supreme Court of NSW accusing 15 judges, 2 registrars and 1 magistrate of being paedophiles or suspected paedophiles and raising allegations of judicial bribery.

3.2 On the 8th of September 2016 I published the 6/9/16 email on my website "Kangaroo Court of Australia" as part of an article titled "Paedophile priest gets 3 months jail for raping 3 boys by NSW Supreme Court's Justice Hoeben" which is still on my website and no one has ever complained about it.

3.3 On the 3rd of February 2017 I verbally repeated part of the 6/9/16 email and article in court and I was charged with contempt of court. The hearing for contempt was heard on the 4th of May 2017.

3.4 On the 21th of June 2017 NSW Police raided my unit and took my computers.

3.5 On the 21st of June 2017 the NSW Police charged me in relation to the 6/9/16 email with the crime of breaching section 474.17 of the Criminal Code: "using a carriage service to menace, harass, or cause offence". Unknown to me, in September 2016 Chief Justice Tom Bathurst ordered senior court staff (CEO and Principle Registrar Chris D'Aeth and The Prothonotary Rebel Kenna) to have the police charge me for the email I sent on the 6th of September 2016 to all the judges of the NSW Supreme Court. The police charge was withdrawn by the CDPP on the 28th of March 2018 which was the date the hearing was meant to be. It was obviously withdrawn because it was malicious and protected political communication as per the 1997 High Court of Australia precedent Lange v ABC.

3.6 In June/July 2017 Seven Network and Seven West Media subpoenaed my computer and documents from the NSW Police and they copied my computer.

3.7 I filed a Notice of Motion challenging the validity of the subpoena.

3.8 On the 22nd of August 2018 I was sentenced to 18 months jail with a non-parole period of 13 months for the above contempt charge. I appealed and the sentence was reduced to 4 months fixed.

3.9 On the 13th of September 2018 Justice Rees tried to bully and intimidate me have a hearing for my notice of motion regarding the validity of Seven Network and Seven West Media's subpoena for my computer. I refused to participate as I was not in a position to properly representant myself as I was in jail. The bullying by Justice Rees included having jail staff threaten me which I assume was after they were threatened by Justice Rees or her staff.

3.10 On the 7th of December 2018, while I was still in jail, Justice Rees handed down a judgment and dismissed my Notice of Motion and gave Seven access to the copy of my computer. Justice Rees was well aware that Seven West Media and their owner Kerry Stokes have multiple SLAPP lawsuits against me and access to the computer would be used for all those lawsuits.

3.11 I was released from jail on the 21st of December 2018 and I filed an appeal against Justice Rees decision. I was refused a fee waiver by the registrar and they took over 4 weeks to notify me because they said the email was accidently left in the draft box and not sent. I appealed the decision against the fee waiver refusal and at this date I have never heard back from the court and Seven and Kerry Stokes lawyers have now had access to the copy of my computer.

3.12 I was before Registrar Leonie Walton on the 11th of March 2019 and she was very bullying in her manner against me. She refused to stand down from hearing the matter based on perceived bias given the content of evidence before the court and she should have at least referred the matter to the duty judge which she did not.

Part IV:

[A brief statement of the applicant's argument in support of the removal.]

4.1 NSW judges should not hear the matter given the evidence before the court in this matter which includes unchallenged allegations by me that 18 NSW judicial officers are paedophiles or suspected paedophiles. The evidence also includes unchallenged allegations Chief Justice Tom Bathurst is a paedophile. There is also documented evidence before the court that NSW Judges took bribes totaling $2.2 million from the Australian mafia which was reported by Fairfax Media and the ABC's Four Corners program in 2015. The $2.2 million bribe was confirmed as being a fact by Justice David Davies in court in December 2015.

4.2 Seven should never have been allowed to subpoena my computer from the police especially given the malicious police charge was dropped. The fact that Seven have now had access to a copy of my computer, for all their court cases against me, has totally tainted the court cases.

4.3 This matter is directly associated with the High Court of Australia matter s22/2019 which I have filed an Application for Special Leave to Appeal and both matters should be heard together.

Part V:

[Any reasons why an order for costs should not be made in favour of the respondent in the event that the application is refused.]

Seven West Media and Seven Network have abused the legal system over and over again since 2014 running numerous SLAPP lawsuits against me.

Part VI:

[A list of the authorities on which the applicant relies, identifying the paragraphs at which the relevant passages appear.]

Lange v Australian Broadcasting Corporation [1997] HCA 25, (1997) 189 CLR 520

R v Magistrates' Court at Lilydale; Ex parte Ciccone [1973] VR 122

Ebner v The Official Trustee in Bankruptcy [2000] HCA 63

Part VII:

[*The particular constitutional provisions, statutes and statutory instruments
applicable to the questions the subject of the application set out verbatim. If more
than one page in length, this Part should be attached as an annexure.*]
Common Law as per the precedents in the above authorities.

Dated: 8/5/19   9/5/19

[Applicant ~~or the legal practitioner~~
representing the applicant]

To: The Respondent
           Attn: Martin O'Connor – Addisons Lawyers – Level 12 / 60 Carrington
           St Sydney 2000

TAKE NOTICE: Before taking any step in the proceedings you must, within
14 DAYS after service of this application, enter an appearance in the office of the
Registry in which the application is filed, and serve a copy on the applicant.

The Applicant is represented by:
[*Firm name, address for service, telephone and facsimile numbers and email
address*]
or
The Applicant's address for service is:
Shane Dowling – 1/78b Ocean St, Bondi. Sydney NSW 2026
Ph: 0411238704
Email: shanedowling@outlook.com.au

On the 22nd of June 2020, the matter was set down for a directions hearing before Justice Kunc as I had applied for legal aid in December 2019 for the contempt hearing and we were waiting for a final decision from them to determine if they would pay for a lawyer to represent me. My initial application to legal aid was refused and it was again refused on appeal.

Justice Kunc should have set a hearing date at the directions hearing but he jumped ship as I think there was too much heat building on him as he was leaving a long trail of evidence of his corrupt conduct. Also, I told Justice Kunc that I said to the NSW police that he was a key suspect in the David Speers hoax phone call which I detail in chapter 19. Justice Kunc set the matter down for another directions hearing before the Registrar in the Equities List for a hearing date.

The hearing of the Notice of Motion for contempt is now scheduled for hearing on the 1st and 2nd of February 2021 to be heard by Justice Kate Williams.

Chapter 6

Paedophile priest gets 3 months jail for raping 3 boys by NSW Supreme Court's Justice Hoeben

At 11.35pm on the 6th of September 2016, I sent an email to all the judges of the Supreme Court of NSW naming 15 judges, 2 registrars and 1 magistrate as either known paedophiles or suspected paedophiles and raising the allegation of the $2.2 million judicial bribes by the Australian mafia.

I put them all on notice that I would be publishing an article making the allegations against them and I said in the email "I am writing to you all regarding the list of paedophile judges that I intended on making a formal complaint about to the AFP, Australian Crime Commission, NSW Crime Commission and Royal Commission into Child Sexual Abuse."

On the 8th of September 2016, I published the below article. In the article is the email I sent to all the judges of the Supreme Court of NSW on the 6th of September 2016. It is the email that sparked a huge backlash and the "get Shane Dowling campaign" that is still being run to this day by Chief Justice Tom Bathurst and the NSW judiciary.

No one has ever asked me to take down the article from my website as the email has always been protected because it is political communication and it is now also protected from by the defence of "absolute privilege" given it has been filed in court as evidence, including in the High Court of Australia. No one named in the email and article has ever denied the allegations I made against them.

I was motivated to write the article after I came across the Court of Appeal judgment where Father Robert Flaherty had his sentence reduced to 3 months jail for raping 3 boys. What made this even more scandalous is that it happened while the Royal Commission into Child Sexual Abuse had been in progress for a couple of years exposing hundreds of priests and others raping children and the judiciary continually failing victims.

When a judge gives a paedophile 3 months jail for raping 3 boys, the judges are not enforcing the law as they have a legal duty to do. The judges are knowingly breaking the law should be investigated by the police and sacked by the government.

One of the worst things about judges handing down judgment protecting paedophiles is the damage it does to the victims/survivors. The media reported the initial trial of Father Flaherty when he received a minimum six months and one of the victims was reported to be happy that at least Father Flaherty had been exposed. Another victim was bitterly disappointed with the lenient sentence which many victims are when criminals are given lenient sentences and they feel they have been let down again.

I remember reading the Father Flaherty Court of Appeal judgment and thinking to myself, in relation to three judges who handed down the decision and other judges who had also handed down decisions in favour of paedophiles, "Fuck you. Game on."

And I went to work writing the article to expose them and I sent the email to make sure I complied with defamation law as per the 1997 High Court of Australia judgment Lange v ABC.

The defamation law I had learned over the previous 2 years dealing with Kerry Stokes' SLAPP lawsuits came in handy.

Below is the article and email published on my website on the 8th of September 2016. Remember it is the email that motivated Chief Justice Tom Bathurst to drive hard for the police to jail me, but he failed. But he stitched me up on two other matters.

Paedophile priest gets 3 months jail for raping 3 boys by NSW Supreme Court's Justice Hoeben

I have seen some scandalous and corrupt judgements, but I can't remember any worse than paedophile catholic priest Father Robert Flaherty being sentenced in August 2016 to a non-parole period of 3 months jail for abusing and raping 3 boys. It is plainly obvious that the judges involved need to be investigated themselves.

I have collated a list of paedophile judges and suspected paedophile judges below and emailed the list to all the NSW Supreme Court judges giving them an opportunity to respond before I published their names. I am also in the process of sending a formal complaint to the relevant authorities regarding paedophiles in the judiciary and not all my evidence is in this article but I will focus on making a fair and reasonable case against the 4 judges in the Father Flaherty matter.

The rest of the evidence I will publish at the relevant time although I have published plenty before such as an article in 2014 titled: "*Premier Mike Baird & Chief Justice Bathurst fail to act on paedophile supporter Judge Garry Neilson*."

Paedophile Magistrate Peter Liddy – Jailed for 25 years in 2001

Most people find it hard to believe that there are paedophile judges but the first Australian judicial officer jailed was South Australian magistrate Peter Liddy who is still in jail today. It was reported in 2001:

"Former South Australian Magistrate, Peter Liddy, continues to make Australian legal history. In June he became the first Australian judicial officer convicted of child sex crimes. And today he was given a 25-year sentence – believed to be the longest sentence handed down to any paedophile. " (Click here to read more)

Paedophile Magistrate Peter Liddy

Father Robert Flaherty

In February 2016 Father Flaherty was jailed for 2 years and 3 weeks with a non-parole period of 6 months by the NSW District Court's Judge Richard Cogswell, SC for sexually abusing 3 boys. (Click here to read more)

The church had allowed Father Flaherty to move from parish to parish even though they knew he had abused boys.

As you would expect the prosecution appealed because the sentence was a joke. The appeal was heard in the NSW Court of Criminal Appeal by Justice Hoeben, Justice Price and Justice Simpson, with Hoeben being the senior judge. What did they do? They decreased the sentence to 2 years with a non-parole period of 3 months. (Click here to read the summary of the judgement)

Father Flaherty's lawyers did the big sob story that he suffered numerous health issues and only had 6 to 12 months to live. Half the criminals before the courts argue similar things and they don't get reduced sentences.

To put it in perspective how scandalous the Father Flaherty matter is, it is worth comparing it to another recent appeal involving Bega paedophile Maurice Van Ryn. Mr Van Ryn was sentenced to 7 years jail by Judge Clive Jeffreys for abusing 9 children. The court of appeal increased it to 13 years 6 months and said Judge Jeffreys judgment was: *so manifestly inadequate it amounted to "an affront to the administration of criminal justice"*. (Click here to read the full judgment) Just for the record the 3 appeal judges in the Van Ryn matter were Justice Leeming, Johnson and Hulme.

Compare the 13 1/2 years jail for Van Ryn to the 2 years jail with a non-parole period of 3 months for Father Flaherty and it is not too hard to work out something is terribly wrong. It seems to be when there is little media coverage the judges take advantage of it and do what they want as Van Ryn was very high profile, yet Father Flaherty did not get much media coverage for some reason.

Judges supporting paedophiles with grossly inadequate sentencing has been a long-term problem and can only mean one thing and that is there are numerous judges who are themselves, paedophiles. Former federal Senator Bill Heffernan said last year that he was in possession of a list of high-profile paedophiles which included judges that he received from a federal law enforcement agency and when judges hand down lenient sentences then those judges should come under suspicion until there is a public enquiry.

What makes the Flaherty matter even more scandalous is the fact that it has happened while there is a Royal Commission into Child Sexual Abuse in progress costing hundreds of millions of dollars and NSW Supreme Court judges have said we do not care and we are untouchable. But they are not untouchable from this website (KCA) naming them and the court of public opinion.

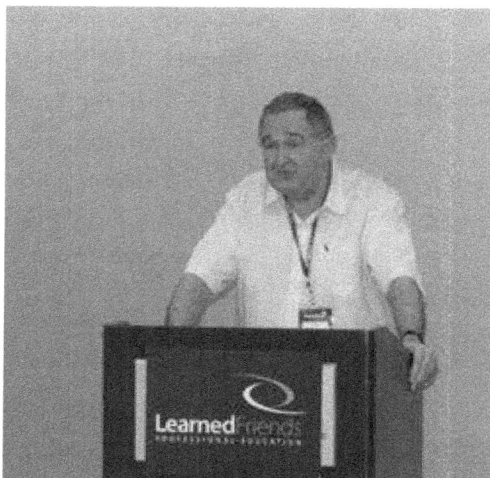

Justice Cliff Hoeben

Justice Cliff Hoeben, Chief Judge at Common Law, NSW Supreme Court

Below is the email I sent to Chief Justice Tom Bathurst and all of the other NSW Supreme Court judges.

From: Shane Dowling [mailto:shanedowling@hotmail.com]
Sent: Tuesday, 6 September 2016 11:35 PM
To: victoria_bradshaw@courts.nsw.gov.au;
chambers.president@courts.nsw.gov.au;
dorothy_yon@courts.nsw.gov.au;
maree_harland@courts.nsw.gov.au;
chambers.macfarlanja@courts.nsw.gov.au;

trish_beazley@courts.nsw.gov.au;
morna_lynch@courts.nsw.gov.au;
giorgina_kotevski@courts.nsw.gov.au;
jasmine_geary@courts.nsw.gov.au;
chambers.gleesonja@courts.nsw.gov.au;
chambers.leemingja@courts.nsw.gov.au;
lynn_nielsen@courts.nsw.gov.au; adam_zwi@courts.nsw.gov.au;
kim_pitt@courts.nsw.gov.au;
cheryl.scholfield@courts.nsw.gov.au;
karen_adams@courts.nsw.gov.au;
linda.head@courts.nsw.gov.au;
renee_ingrey@courts.nsw.gov.au;
carla_wilson@courts.nsw.gov.au;
maria_heraghty@courts.nsw.gov.au;
chambers.johnsonj@courts.nsw.gov.au;
margaret_gaertner@courts.nsw.gov.au;
katherine_moroney@courts.nsw.gov.au;
jacqui.gray@justice.nsw.gov.au;
chambers.breretonj@courts.nsw.gov.au;
lisa_freeman@courts.nsw.gov.au;
colleen_sutton@courts.nsw.gov.au;
bernadette_heywood@courts.nsw.gov.au;
kate_moore@courts.nsw.gov.au;
chambers.mccallumj@courts.nsw.gov.au;
sally_mccrossin@courts.nsw.gov.au;
carol_lloyd@courts.nsw.gov.au;
chambers.slatteryj@courts.nsw.gov.au;
anita_singh@courts.nsw.gov.au;
chambers.schmidtj@courts.nsw.gov.au;
sue_page@courts.nsw.gov.au;
maria_kourtis@courts.nsw.gov.au;
chambers.garlingj@courts.nsw.gov.au;
catherine_young@courts.nsw.gov.au;
margaret.smith2@courts.nsw.gov.au;
anne_cochrane@courts.nsw.gov.au;
barbara_ruicens@courts.nsw.gov.au;

megan_grace@courts.nsw.gov.au;
lauren_channells@courts.nsw.gov.au; chambers.beech-
jonesJ@courts.nsw.gov.au; poppy_xenakis@courts.nsw.gov.au;
sara_bond@courts.nsw.gov.au;
shari_williams@courts.nsw.gov.au

Subject: Paedophile Judge list to be sent to the AFP, Australian
Crime Commission, NSW Crime Commission and Royal
Commission into Child Sexual Abuse for investigation

Dear Chief Justice Bathurst, Justice Hoeben, Justice Price, Justice
Simpson other judges

I am writing to you all regarding the list of paedophile judges that
I intended on making a formal complaint about to the AFP,
Australian Crime Commission, NSW Crime Commission and
Royal Commission into Child Sexual Abuse. The list is below.

Known paedophiles

Chief Justice Tom Bathurst – NSW Supreme Court

Justice Clifton Hoeben – NSW Supreme Court

Justice Derek Price – NSW Supreme Court (He is also Chief
Judge of the NSW District Court)

Justice Carolyn Simpson – NSW Supreme Court

Judge Richard Cogswell – NSW District Court

Judge Garry Neilson – NSW District Court

Magistrate Doug Dick – NSW Magistrates Court

Suspected paedophiles

Justice Ian Harrison – NSW Supreme Court

Justice Lucy McCallum – NSW Supreme Court

Justice Peter Hall – NSW Supreme Court

Justice Michael Adams – NSW Supreme Court

Acting Justice Henric Nicholas – NSW Supreme Court (now retired)

Acting Justice Robert Hulme – NSW Supreme Court

Justice David Davies – NSW Supreme Court

Justice Peter Garling – NSW Supreme Court

Justice Stephen Campbell – NSW Supreme Court

Registrar Rebel Kenna – NSW Supreme Court

Registrar Christopher Bradford – NSW Supreme Court

If you are on the list and would like a right of reply to deny that you are a paedophile and argue that you should not be on the list, please email me by close of business Wednesday the 7th of September 2016. I will also likely publish the list on my website, if you would like me to publish a reply please send me one by 5pm Wednesday the 7th of September.

If you are not on the list but have evidence of paedophile judges, please contact me on the details below.

As we all know corruption in the NSW Courts is widespread and systemic. In July 2015 Fairfax Media and the ABC's Four Corners program reported that NSW judges had been bribed $2.2 million by the Mafia which was confirmed by Justice David Davies in December 2015. Maybe you have evidence that the above judges have also benefited from the Mafia bribes or other bribes. If you have evidence of judicial bribery, please contact me ASAP.

Regards

Shane Dowling

Email end

No one has responded just the same as they all shut their mouths last year when Fairfax Media and the ABC's Four Corners exposed NSW Judges for taking bribes of $2.2 million from the Mafia. (Click here to read more)

Summary

The Father Flaherty matter has happened in an environment where the NSW Attorney-General has claimed there will be harsher laws for child abusers:

"The New South Wales Government is planning to introduce life sentences for child sex offenders and paedophiles."

"NSW Attorney General Gabrielle Upton will introduce new legislation this week increasing the maximum sentence for sexual intercourse with a child under 10 from 25 years to life imprisonment." (Click here to read more)

And has happened where NSW Attorney General Gabrielle Upton also had *"two specialist judges appointed to the District Court to hear child sexual assault cases across the state."* (Click here to read more)

Doesn't seem like the NSW Attorney General Gabrielle Upton is achieving much.

In the next week or so I will make a formal complaint as I have flagged above but before then please email me or write in the comment section below any evidence that you might have regarding child abusers in the judiciary which I might add to the complaint.

End of article

The email above sent on the 6/9/2016 is what put a target on my back for Chief Justice Tom Bathurst and the court, but I didn't find out until the following year.

Chapter 7

"Known paedophile Chief Justice Tom Bathurst" calls the NSW police to jail journalist Shane Dowling for the crime of journalism

My hearing for the second Contempt of Court charge, for what I said in court on the 3/2/17, was on the 4th of May 2017. During the hearing, I raised the fact that no one had ever complained about the email I sent on the 6th of September 2016 or the article I published on the 8th of September 2016 naming judges as paedophiles or suspected paedophiles which was worse than what they claimed I said in court.

What they did next was to put pressure on the NSW police to raid my unit and charge me for the email, which happened on the 21st of June 2017. But the brief of evidence and witness statement that I received much later showed that the NSW Police, Federal Police and CDPP wouldn't charge me even though they had been in receipt of the complaint for about 9 months. Why? Because they obviously knew the email was a political communication which is protected under the Australian constitution as per the 1997 High Court precedent Lange v ABC.

The reason they put pressure on the NSW police to charge me was because without it their contempt charge against me was weakened given the same allegations they claimed I said in court were on my website and I had emailed all the judges who took no action.

After the police raid and charge on the 21st of June 2017, I published an article on the 24th of June 2017 titled "Journalist charged by police for asking questions about judicial corruption" as per below.

Journalist charged by police for asking questions about judicial corruption

On Wednesday, the 21st June I was charged by the NSW police for breaching telecommunication laws for an email that I sent in September 2016 to all the judges of the NSW Supreme Court asking questions and giving them an opportunity to respond to allegations which is nothing more than journalists do around the world every day of the week.

The police executed a search warrant on my unit while I was at work and took my computer and the spare one I have which the police said they will give back in about 10 days which has forced me to buy a new one. I went to the police station after work and was charged.

If I am found guilty, the repercussions are potently huge for every journalist in the country who emails questions to criminals or alleged criminals before they publish articles. The police officer who charged me even said that the area of law that I am being charged with is unsettled. In other words, he was not sure that there was a legal basis for charging me.

At this point, there is only one complainant and that is the NSW Supreme Court registrar Rebel Kenna although it was the Crown

Solicitor Ms Lea Armstrong who made the complaint on Rebel Kenna's behalf. They are also the 2 people who are overseeing a current Contempt of Court case against me in the NSW Supreme Court.

The charges are some 9 and 1/2 months after I sent the email, and the police said no one else has complained at this point but it is only 6 weeks since I raised allegations of criminal conduct against Rebel Kenna and Lea Armstrong in the NSW Supreme Court on the 4th May 2017. It makes it very obvious that Rebel Kenna's complaint is a retaliatory action against me raising her and Ms Armstrong's criminal conduct in court.

The email in question shows up in an article I published last year titled "*Paedophile priest gets 3 months jail for raping 3 boys by NSW Supreme Court's Justice Hoeben*" and the article was also filed in court on the 4th of May as part of my defence.

The court matter that was in court on the 4th of May is the contempt proceeding by the NSW Supreme Court called "*Prothonotary of the Supreme Court of NSW v Shane Dowling*". The Prothonotary is the head registrar for the court and it is my understanding that is Rebel Kenna so she would have known what I said about her in court on the 4th of May. Lea Armstrong was in court that day instructing the barrister so was also aware of the allegations I made against her and Rebel Kenna.

Background

On the 3rd of February 2017, the registrar of the NSW Supreme Court sought leave to have me charged for contempt for comments I made in court that day and I wrote an article about it titled: "*Chief Justice Bathurst has journalist charged with contempt for accusing him of corruption*" and said:

NSW Chief Justice Tom Bathurst instituted contempt of court proceedings against me for accusing him of corruption in court on Friday the 3rd of February 2017. The corruption is being a bribe-taker and paedophile which I have previously written on my website. Chief Justice Bathurst has used taxpayer funds and taken out a suppression order to conceal who has charged me with contempt and to conceal the fact that they are trying to hide the very serious allegations. (Click here to read more)

When I was finally charged in April, they dropped the claims against me for saying anything about Chief Justice Bathurst and: "*I was charged for contempt for allegedly calling a Justice Clifton Hoeben a paedophile and Registrar Christopher Bradford a suspected paedophile and a bribe-taker in court on the 3rd of February 2017. I have pleaded not guilty and deny the allegations against me.*" (Click here to read more)

Hearing on the 4th May 2017 – Justice Helen Wilson – Supreme Court of NSW

At the hearing, I pleaded not guilty and denied the allegations and also ran a defence that I was also protected by the implied freedom of political communication in the Australian constitution.

I wrote on the 11th of June in an article titled: "*Blogger charged with contempt ordered to serve Attorney-Generals with Notice of a Constitutional Matter*"

The pursuit of me by the Supreme Court of NSW for contempt has stepped up a notch with the court ordering me to serve all Australian Attorney-Generals with a Notice of a Constitutional Matter pursuant to section 78B of the Judiciary Act 1903.

Neither Clifton Hoeben or Registrar Christopher Bradford have filed an affidavit in the case nor have they denied the allegations that they say I made. They have also not charged me or complained about the allegations I made against them in an article last year titled "Paedophile priest gets 3 months jail for raping 3 boys by NSW Supreme Court's Justice Hoeben" even though I wrote to them and let them know I would be publishing the allegations. So, I take it they confirm that the allegations in the article are true and correct. (Click here to read more)

It is possibly the 11th of June article that was the trigger for Rebel Kenna and Lea Armstrong to make the retaliatory complaint to the police given I had pointed out no one had denied the allegations I had made against them in the article and email.

Rebel Kenna

The email complained about was sent to every judge of the NSW Supreme court on the 6th of September 2016 and the article with the email in it was published on the 8th September 2016. The article was about a paedophile priest receiving 6 months jail after abusing 3 boys and when it was appealed by the prosecutor because the sentence was scandalously inadequate instead of getting a longer sentence the judges reduced it to a minimum 3 months.

In the email, I made allegations against various judges and registrars for being paedophiles, suspected paedophiles and gave them the opportunity to respond before I published the article and let them know I would be publishing the email. Not one responded or denied the allegations, but they obviously received the email given Rebel Kenna's complaint.

The article and email also raised the issue of NSW judges receiving bribes of $2.2 million as reported by Fairfax Media and the ABC's Four Corners in 2015. (Click here to read more)

At no stage did anyone sent the email respond or deny the allegations. No one has ever contacted me to complain about the email or article. There have been no defamation threats or action. There has never been any Contempt of Court action.

Rebel Kenna's complaint to the police which was done via Lea Armstrong said the email made her physically sick. So why didn't she complain or take any action before?

I had previously made a complaint to the court of assault against Rebel Kenna and a court sheriff in 2015 and on the 4th of May

2017 I made a number of allegations against Rebel Kenna including:

1. Rebel Kenna colluded with a court sheriff to threaten and assault me while I was in court at the bar table representing myself on the 24th of August 2015 and I made a formal complaint to senior management of the court. (Click here to read more)

2. Every decision Rebel Kenna made at various directions hearings was in the favour of Kerry Stokes' barrister Sandy Dawson and Rebel Kenna was clearly acting corruptly.

3. I raised the article and email from last year in court on the 4th of May and while I did not expressly mention Rebel Kenna in relation to the article and email, she would have known she was named in them and would have been very annoyed that I had raised the email and article in court.

4. In court, on May 4th I raised the fact that previously in court when I was in front of Rebel Kenna for a directions hearing I asked her not to list a hearing before *"paedophile judge Garry Neilson"*. I said this a number of times and Rebel Kenna did not complain.

NSW Crown Solicitor – Lea Armstrong

NSW Crown Solicitors Office make compliant for Rebel Kenna

Why the NSW Crown Solicitor is making a complaint to the police on behalf of a public servant is very disturbing. Rebel Kenna should have been made to make the complaint herself. Why is the taxpayer paying for it?

One positive is that there is no suppression order on the charges against me or the article I published last year so it can be spoken about freely and it also shows how futile the suppression orders are in the contempt matter against me.

Telecommunications laws – CRIMINAL CODE ACT 1995 (Commonwealth)

The exact part of the Telecommunication laws that I have been alleged to have breached is section 474.17 of the CRIMINAL CODE ACT 1995. Using a carriage service to menace, harass or cause offence

(1) A person commits an offence if:

    (a) the person uses a carriage service; and

    (b) the person does so in a way (whether by the method of use or the content of a communication, or both) that reasonable persons would regard as being, in all the circumstances, menacing, harassing or offensive.

If Rebel Kenna was so offended, why didn't she make a complaint when I emailed her and the Supreme Court judges in September 2016. Why did Rebel Kenna start to be involved and continued to be involved in the prosecution of my contempt case? Why hasn't she sued for defamation, etc?

Threat to all journalists – Fairfax Media and Eddie Obeid

If I am found guilty of breaching section 474.17 of the telecommunications act for emailing questions, allegations and putting the parties on notice that I plan on publishing them that leaves the door open in the future for other journalists to be charged with the same crime.

In 2006 Fairfax Media and its journalists Kate McClymont and Anne Davies were found to have defamed former Labor Party MP Eddie Obeid by claiming he was corrupt and he tried to get a $1 million bribe. I am sure that Kate McClymont and Anne Davies would have emailed Eddie Obeid questions before they published and in a case like that there would have been nothing stopping Eddie Obeid from making a complaint to the police for breaching section 474.17 of the telecommunications act given the court found the allegations were defamatory. Any journalist could face charges just for asking questions. (Click here to read more)

As we all know Eddie Obeid is now in jail because he was corrupt when he was a politician.

Attack on Freedom of Political Communication and journalist's rights

This is a case of government officials using a police force trying to stop an Australian citizen's right to free speech and political communication. I make no apologies for criticising the courts and judges given their scandalous conduct. Former Chief Justice of High Court of Australia, Sir Anthony Mason said:

In Nationwide News Pty Ltd v. Wills, Mason CJ described scandalising as a 'well recognised form of criminal contempt' (at para 21) but suggested there was no contempt at common law 'if all that the defendant does is to exercise his or her ordinary right to criticise, in good faith, the conduct of the court or the judge' (at para 21).

He stated the judiciary should be open to criticism and cited US Supreme Court Justice Hugo Black stating in Bridges v. California in 1941:

The assumption that respect for the judiciary can be won by shielding judges from published criticism wrongly appraises the character of American public opinion. ... an enforced silence, however limited, solely in the name of preserving the dignity of the bench, would probably engender resentment, suspicion, and contempt much more than it would enhance respect (pp. 270-271). NATIONWIDE NEWS PTY. LIMITED v. WILLS [1992] HCA 46;

I've been issued with a court attendance notice for August which I assume is like a directions hearing and what the process is after that I am unsure. I had to buy another computer to see me through until I get my other one back from the police and I don't know if I would be keen on using the old one now.

This matter has a distance to go, but it is a battle well worth fighting. Just for the record, the police were fine with me writing this article. But in saying that when the police are raiding the homes of journalists and taking their computer, it should be disturbing for all Australians. Even more so when there was no need to as I had already told the court on May 4th that I had published the article and email and tendered it as evidence.

End of article.

The police charge was frivolous and vexatious and was later withdrawn by the CDPP. Not long after the police raid, the court gave Kerry Stokes and Seven West Media a copy of my computer via the NSW police although, with a legal challenge by me, they didn't get access until 2019.

Lea Armstrong who is mentioned above as the NSW Crown Solicitor was promoted to a judge of the Supreme Court of NSW in October 2018 by NSW Attorney General Mark Speakman which was just 2 months after she helped stitch me up for jail.

Chapter 8

Three Australian Prime Ministers protecting paedophiles and their protectors: John Howard, Tony Abbott and Scott Morrison

In recent years hundreds of millions of dollars have been spent by the federal government and state governments on various enquiries regarding paedophiles. The biggest enquiry was the federally funded Royal Commission into Institutional Responses to Child Sexual Abuse, but the Victorian government had the "Inquiry into the Handling of Child Abuse by Religious and Other Organisations" which published a report in 2013. NSW had a smaller Inquiry focused on child abuse cover-ups by the Catholic Church and police in Newcastle, which published its report in 2014.

So, it's extremely disappointing to see two former Australian Prime Ministers, John Howard and Tony Abbott, publicly support

Cardinal George Pell who was a convicted paedophile at the time. John Howard also wrote a letter of reference for Pell for his sentencing after he was convicted of sexually abusing two boys. And Tony Abbott visited George Pell in jail after his conviction.

George Pell, who was convicted in December 2018, was set free by the High Court of Australia and had his conviction quashed, in April 2020, on a technicality that doesn't pass the pub test.

But the Royal Commission into Institutional Responses to Child Sexual published their unredacted report in May 2020 which found that George Pell had perjured himself under oath and covered-up the sexual abuse of hundreds of children. They had kept the redacted parts of the report secret since 2017 while police investigated Pell and then he faced criminal charges. George Pell also played a part in moving paedophile priests from parish to parish, knowing full well they would abuse more children. Tony Abbott and John Howard have continued to publicly support Pell.

On the day the Royal Commission published the unredacted report, many commentators made obvious observations like the one below by journalist Anthony Klan on Twitter:

Anthony Klan ✅
@Anthony_Klan

Oh dear. Pell is officially a pedophile enabler. All those who covered for him, and attacked journalists and victims on his behalf, are also, by extension, pedophile enablers.

1:39 PM · May 7, 2020 · Twitter Web App

65 Retweets   **152** Likes

I published an article on the 2nd of March 2019, which was before Pell was released by the High Court, titled "Australian paedophile support ring, which includes 2 former PM's, out themselves in their support of George Pell". The article is below, but you will need to visit my website to watch the videos on it.

Australian paedophile support ring, which includes 2 former PM's, out themselves in their support of George Pell

In the last week 2 former Australian Prime Ministers, John Howard and Tony Abbott, have confirmed they supported George Pell before and after he was convicted of being a paedophile. The only person I know who would support a paedophile is another paedophile. So, with that and the other evidence below, the question that has to be asked is if Howard and Abbott are paedophiles themselves.

In 2015 former Liberal Party Senator Bill Heffernan said in parliament that he had a police list of 28 paedophiles, which included a former Prime Minister and current judges, that was leaked to him by a law enforcement body. This was not refuted by the Attorney-General or former Attorney-Generals who it was also claimed had seen the list. In fact, no one in government or anywhere else ever denied the list existed.

George Pell and Tony Abbott

Then this week 2 former Prime Ministers, Tony Abbott and John Howard, gave their full-support for convicted paedophile Cardinal George Pell which included John Howard writing a letter of reference (see the letter below) for Pell to try to get him a lesser jail sentence. At the very least it should make you wonder if at least one of them is a paedophile although Tony Abbott was the Prime Minister at the time Bill Heffernan raised the list in parliament so that would rule him out as the "former Prime Minister" named on the list.

"In the photo, Catholic priest Gerald Ridsdale (left, in sunglasses and hat) walks to court, accompanied by his support person (Bishop George Pell, then an auxiliary bishop in Melbourne), when Father Ridsdale was pleading guilty to his first batch of criminal charges in May 1993 for sexually abusing children. But no bishop accompanied the victims, who felt deserted by the church leaders."

Even though we didn't know at the time it turns out Pell was supporting his fellow paedophile in court and obviously didn't care less for the victims. But the picture alone says Pell was a grub for supporting Father Ridsdale in court and Prime Ministers, and any person with self-respect should have nothing to do with Pell.

I published an article in 2015 titled: "Who is the former Australian Prime Minister and judges who are paedophiles?" and said:

There is enough detail in Senator Heffernan's allegations to make them very credible. Some of the details are:

1. The list *"formed part of police documents that had been "signed off" by Gary Crooke, QC, the former senior counsel assisting NSW's Wood royal commission into police corruption in the 1990s. Mr Crooke declined to comment when contacted by Fairfax Media on Tuesday."*

2. The list includes a former Australian Prime Minister, judges, members of the legal fraternity and others.

3. *"Every Commonwealth attorney-general since Philip Ruddock had seen the list"*. This seems to have been confirmed by Philip Ruddock and Former Labor Attorney-General Mark Dreyfus.

4. Senator Heffernan *"accused former royal commissioner Justice James Roland Wood of refusing to investigate lawyers who had allegedly attended a Kings Cross "boy brothel".* (Click here to read more)

5. The name of the club was Costellos and was a known "boy brothel" attended by members of the Sydney legal fraternity. (Click here to read more)

6. Former Royal Commissioner Wood denied the allegations by Senator Heffernan, but not outright. *"Mr Wood could not recall if the alleged list had been raised at the 1995 commission but said: "I reject that we failed to investigate anyone that fell within our terms of reference."* That is a very weak denial by Mr Wood and allows him plenty of wriggle room to change his story later down the track if needed. (Click here to read more)

(Click here to read the full 2015 article: "Who is the former Australian Prime Minister and judges who are paedophiles?"

Below is the video of Senator Bill Heffernan on 19th October 2015 making the allegations in parliament:

FEDERAL POLITICS
ALLEGATIONS A FORMER PM IS A PEDOPHILE ⦀❸NEWS

0:00 / 0:30   HD

Below is a picture of former Australian Prime Ministers and it would be one of them who is on the police list:

Former Prime Ministers – October 2015

In September 2013 I wrote the below in an article:

"Tony Abbott and George Pell have a history of working together in politics. Before the 2004 election, Tony Abbott gave an infamous interview on the ABC's Lateline where he was caught lying and deceiving in relation to a meeting with George Pell.

A couple of days after the meeting George Pell was a signatory to a letter criticising the Labor Party. " (Click here to read the article) Below is the video showing Tony Abbott lying.

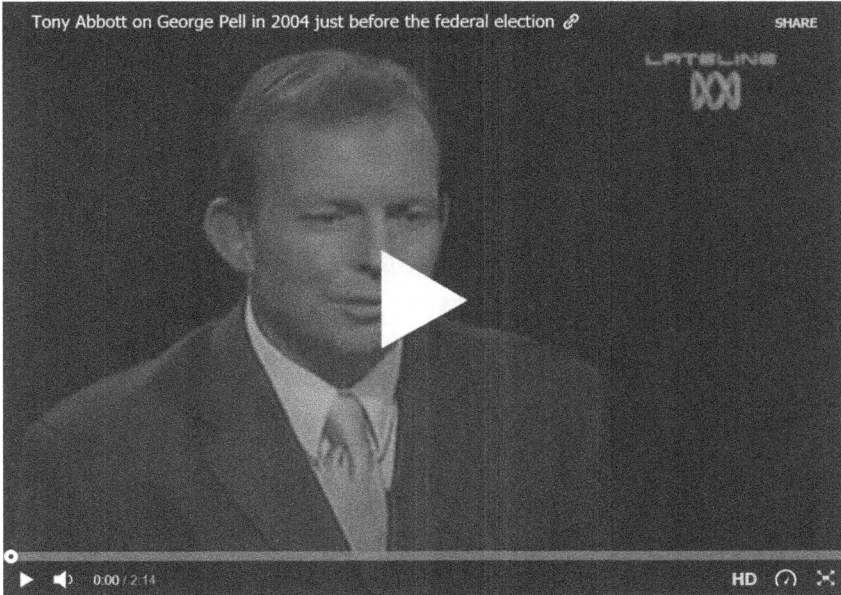

Tony Abbott on George Pell in 2004 just before the federal election   SHARE

LATELINE

0:00 / 2:14   HD

On Wednesday (26/2/19) Tony Abbott did an interview with radio announcer Ben Fordham and ducked and weaved, like he did in the previous video from 2004, when asked if he had spoken to George Pell after he was convicted of being a paedophile. Eventually, Abbott answered yes, but his ducking and weaving says a lot. The interview is below.

Abbott called Pell on day
verdict was revealed

0:00 / 0:53   HD

Below is the letter that former Prime Minister John Howard sent to George Pell after he was convicted of being a paedophile to be used as a reference in court to try to help Pell get a reduced sentence. As far as I am concerned the letter is about as scandalous as it gets and shows what contempt John Howard has for survivors of abuse.

Hon John Howard OM AC

26 February 2019

His Honour Chief Judge Kidd
County Court
MELBOURNE VIC 3000

Your Honour

Re George Cardinal Pell

This character reference is provided in the context of charges being dealt with in relation to Cardinal Pell.

I am aware he has been convicted of those charges; that an appeal against the conviction has been lodged and that he maintains his innocence in respect of these charges. None of these matters alter my opinion of the Cardinal.

I have known Cardinal Pell for approximately thirty years. We first became acquainted when he was, I think, an Assistant Bishop in the Archdiocese of Melbourne. Inevitably we became better known to each other after he became Archbishop of Melbourne and, later still, Archbishop of Sydney.

Cardinal Pell is a person of both high intelligence and exemplary character. Strength and sincerity have always been features of his personality. I have always found him to be lacking hypocrisy and cant. In his chosen vocation he has frequently displayed much courage and held to his values and beliefs, irrespective of the prevailing wisdom of the time.

Hon John Howard OM AC

Cardinal Pell is a lively conversationalist who maintains a deep and objective interest in contemporary social and political issues.

It is my view that he has dedicated his life to his nation and his church.

Yours sincerely

(John Howard)

John Howard's reference for paedophile George Pell to try to help reduce his sentence is almost identical to Tony Abbott's reference for accused paedophile Priest Father John Nester in 1997 to try to help him get his conviction overturned. I wrote an article in 2013 titled "*Tony Abbott and his friend Cardinal George Pell. Perceived bias for the Royal Commission into child sex abuse*" and said:

Tony Abbott – reference for accused paedophile Priest Father John Nester in 1997

Father John Nestor and Tony Abbott both attended the Sydney's St Patrick's Seminary in the 1980s when Mr Abbott was planning on becoming a Priest.

Father Nester *"was a priest in the Wollongong diocese in NSW when he was charged with the indecent assault of a 15-year-old altar boy in 1991."*

"Father Nestor was convicted in Wollongong Local Court on February 18, 1997, and sentenced to 16 months in jail, with the magistrate describing the case as a "gross breach of trust"."

"In court, the priest admitted he had – while dressed in boxer shorts and a singlet – slept on mattresses on a floor in the presbytery with the boy and his younger brother sometime between June and September 1991."

On appeal in October 1997, the conviction was overturned. But Father Nester was never allowed to return as a priest.

"The then-Wollongong Bishop, Philip Wilson, now Catholic Archbishop of Adelaide, advised Fr Nestor in writing "significant additional material that I have received ... has been a cause of worry concerning your suitability for a further pastoral appointment in this diocese or any other"."

"Fr Nestor appealed to the Vatican's Congregation for the Clergy, which decreed he be reinstated."

"But in February 2001, the Wollongong diocese appealed and the decree was overturned." (Click here to read more)

During the course of those proceedings, Tony Abbott who was then a Federal MP gave a reference in court for Father Nester.

"Tony Abbott insisted on providing a character reference for a Catholic priest later struck off the clergy list by the Vatican following a child abuse case, the former priest says."

"Mr Nestor told AAP at his home in rural NSW that Mr Abbott agreed to provide the character reference in 1997 after being approached by his barrister."

"When the lawyer approached Tony Abbott, he said look, I know you're a parliamentary secretary and you may feel that because of your position you don't want to get involved in this case'."

"Tony said, no, I'm coming down,'. He insisted on coming down and giving the reference, because he's a man of integrity." (Click here to read more)

Tony Abbott told the court Father Nester was *"An extremely upright and virtuous man. I guess one of the things that I liked very much about John when I first met him, was his maturity, intellectual, social, emotional he was, to that extent I guess, a beacon of humanity at the Seminary"* (Click here to read more)

In an interview in March this year, the victim questioned why Tony Abbott gave evidence:

"the alleged victim, who asked not to be named, said Mr Abbott should not have provided a character reference for Mr Nestor."

"I was not aware of who Tony Abbott was at the time," he said.

"While I do not necessarily believe that he has done anything wrong, in hindsight it may have been better if he had not involved himself in the matter."

It is understood Mr Abbott communicated with Mr Nestor twice after the court cases, but has had no contact with him for almost 15 years.

"In 1997, Mr Abbott provided a reference for Mr Nestor in an open court. He was subsequently acquitted by a District Court judge," a spokesman for Mr Abbott said.

The alleged victim queried why Mr Abbott hadn't stayed in contact with Mr Nestor.

"If someone was of such good character, why has contact not been kept?" he asked.

He said Mr Abbott's reference may have been a factor in Mr Nestor's successful appeal.

"Certainly a character reference from a member of parliament would hold some sway, no doubt about it," he said.

"It probably did play a big part, but there were other things that played a bigger part. For example, John Nestor never gave evidence at the trial. He was never cross-examined."

He said his case should be examined by the royal commission into child sex abuse. (Click here to read more)

The Nester case and Tony Abbott's involvement at the very least show poor judgement by Tony Abbott given Nester was ultimately struck off as a Priest. (Click here to read the article)

As far as I know, the Royal Commission didn't review the Father Nester case. In summary, Tony Abbott supported alleged paedophile Father Nestor and now supports George Pell even after he has been convicted of sexually abusing children. The fact that Tony Abbott tried to conceal his support for Pell shows he knows what he is doing is wrong.

George Pell's lies on 60 Minutes in 2002 – We now know that George Pell was a paedophile overseeing what compensation the Church would give survivors and doing what he could to make sure the police never became involved in any of the cases of abuse by Priests as per the below video.

A few others such as Rupert Murdoch's News Corp and their journalists have also been supporting Pell and in doing so have stuck their hands up saying they are members of the Australian paedophile support ring. Exactly what Murdoch and News Corp have been up to could end up being exposed in court as the Victorian CDPP has apparently said they intend on following through with contempt charges against some of their journalists for breaching suppression orders and sub judice laws.

I think the ultimate fallout from this matter will be far-reaching covering the church, the judiciary, politics and the media.

It's a disgusting thought that a former Australian Prime Minister could be a paedophile, but the possibility can't be dismissed. What can be said for a fact that since George Pell's conviction a high-profile paedophile support ring has outed itself in the Australian media and some parts of Australian politics and it needs to be investigated.

End of article

In the above article which I published in 2013, I mentioned "The then-Wollongong Bishop, Philip Wilson, now Catholic Archbishop of Adelaide". In March 2015 Philip Wilson was charged with concealing a serious offence regarding child sexual abuse in the Hunter region concerning a different matter to the one above. He was convicted in May 2018 but appealed and was acquitted in December 2018. He is no longer the Archbishop of Adelaide.

Our current Prime Minister Scott Morrison and his wife Jenny spent time in 2019 helping promote Hillsong Church pastor Brian Houston promote his church while Mr Houston is under investigation by the NSW police for covering up his father's sexual abuse of children. It's not believable that Scott Morrison and his wife did not know about the police investigation. I wrote an article on the 13th of July 2019 titled "NSW Police confirm PM Scott Morrison's mate Hillsong's Brian Houston still under investigation for concealing paedophile father" as per below.

NSW Police confirm PM Scott Morrison's mate Hillsong's Brian Houston still under investigation for concealing paedophile father

Prime Minister Scott Morrison and his wife were on stage leading prayers in front of 21,000 people on Tuesday night (9/7/19) with the Hillsong Church's Brian Houston who is still under investigation by the NSW police for concealing the sexual abuse of children by his father Frank Houston.

In 2014 while giving evidence at The Royal Commission into Institutional Responses to Child Sexual Abuse Brian Houston admitted he knew his father had abused children and he had failed to report it to the police so it is not a fact that is in dispute or a fact that Scott Morrison wouldn't know.

There are many reasons, which I outline below, why Scott Morrison should have never been on stage with paedophile protector Brian Houston who is under investigation by the NSW police.

I emailed questions to the Prime Minister as per below but he has refused to answer but the NSW police did respond to my email (as below) on Wednesday (10/7/19) and confirmed that they are still investigating Brian Houston which was first reported by the media in November 2018 by Channel 9. Why didn't Nine follow-up with the police as I did? Maybe it is because Nine's Chairman is former federal treasurer Peter Costello who is also a mentor to Scott Morrison and who has also led prayers at the Hillsong annual conference.

I sent the below email to the NSW Police Media Unit on Wednesday at 5.04pm (10/7/19)

From: SHANE DOWLING
Sent: 10 July 2019 17:04
To: xxxx@police.nsw.gov.au
Subject: Media request: Brian Houston Hillsong Church

Dear Sir/Madam

I am a journalist and have a question in relation to Brian Houston who is the founder and a pastor at Hillsong Church.

Can you please confirm whether or not the NSW Police are still investigating Brian Houston from the Hillsong Church in relation to his handling of the sex crimes committed by his father Frank Houston or any other crimes?

Regards

Shane Dowling

Kangaroo Court of Australia

I received the below response from the NSW Police Media unit at 5.13pm on Wednesday (10/7/19)

From: xxxxx <xxxxxxxx@police.nsw.gov.au> **On Behalf Of** #PMU
Sent: 10 July 2019 17:13
To: SHANE DOWLING
Subject: Re: Media request: Brian Houston Hillsong Church [DLM=For-Official-Use-Only]

Regarding your inquiry,

The matter continues to be investigated by officers attached to The Hills Police Area Command.

No further comment will be made while the investigation is ongoing

Regards,

Media Unit
NSW Police Force

Given it was widely reported in November 2018 that Brian Houston was under investigation by the NSW police, why didn't any other media report that this week given Prime Minister Scott Morrison was on stage with Houston? All the other media could have done what I did and contacted the NSW police to see if Brian Houston was still being investigated.

There are many questions:

- What is an Australian Prime Minister doing on stage with someone under investigation for criminal offences?

- Why are the Australian Prime Minister and his wife Jenny normalising child sexual abuse by being on stage with Brian Houston and supporting him and his church?

- Is Prime Minister Scott Morrison interfering with a police investigation given he would have to know that his appearance with and support of Brian Houston would put pressure on the police not to charge Brian Houston?

- Why have no other media reported that Brian Houston is still under investigation by the NSW police? Are the media now too scared to upset the government given the government's threats to jail journalists?

Jenny Morrison, Scott Morrison and Brian Houston at Hillsong Church on Tuesday night (9/7/19)

Jeffrey Epstein

American billionaire and convicted paedophile Jeffrey Epstein was arrested in America on Saturday (6/7/19) and it has been all over the media since showing Epstein with his friends such as former President Bill Clinton and current President Donald Trump. The point about Epstein is that he was arrested 4 days before Scott Morrison was on stage with Brian Houston and Morrison would have seen all the bad press for the politicians associated with Epstein. So, why did Morrison risk going on stage with Houston given he is under investigation by NSW police for concealing the sexual abuse of children by his father? It's worth noting that the Epstein matter also involves an alleged cover-up.

In the below video Scott Morrison answers questions from Brian Houston at the Hillsong Church conference on Tuesday (9/7/19).

It costs $370 for a ticket to the annual Hillsong conference, so supporting God isn't cheap.

Former federal treasurer and current Nine Entertainment Chairman Peter Costello at Hillsong Church in 2005. Nine Entertainment own Channel 9 and papers such as The SMH and The Age etc.

Many other politicians attended the Hillsong Church conference with Peter Costello in 2005: "NSW Premier Bob Carr and federal ministers Alexander Downer, Kevin Andrews and Peter Dutton, as well as NSW Christian Democrats MP Fred Nile, Liberal MP David Clarke and other state parliamentarians as they wanted the votes. (Click here to read more) Other than Scott Morrison, I don't think as many politicians went this year with Brian Houston under investigation by the Police.

Hillsong Church – Brian Houston and the Frank Houston cover-up background

Brian Houston and his wife Bobbie started the Hillsong Church in 1983 and originally called it the Hills Christian Life Centre. It is like a franchise of the Assemblies of God. Brian's father Frank was also a pastor in New Zealand and Australia.

In 1999 the mother of a victim referred to as AHA at the Royal Commission and who later outed himself on 60 Minutes as Brett Sengstock made a complaint to the church. The church covered it up and the Child Abuse Royal Commission was critical of Brian Houston, his conduct in dealing with the abuse and failing to report it to the police.

Wikipedia says there were up to 9 victims:

"Although Brian Houston was legally obligated to report the crime, he did not do so. The victim (Brett Sengstock) later testified to the Royal Commission into Institutional Responses to Child Sexual Abuse that Frank Houston offered him AU$10,000 as compensation at a McDonald's in the presence of Hillsong Church elder Nabi Saleh. During an internal church investigation, Frank Houston eventually confessed to the crime. The commission also heard that he was involved in the sexual abuse of other children in New Zealand."

"A further internal investigation by Assemblies of God in Australia, in conjunction with the Assemblies of God in New Zealand, found six additional child sexual abuse allegations, which were regarded as credible." (Click here to read more)

Brian Houston said in an interview in 2016 that he didn't know how many victims there were. Why hasn't he and Hillsong tried to find out?

Sixty Minutes reported in November 2018, as per the below video, that Brett Sengstock tried to sue the Assemblies of God for compensation but they refused to pay anything and claimed that they were not liable as Frank Houston never worked for them when Brett Sengstock was abused. That is the same routine the Catholic Church has used for decades to deny survivors compensation. Surely a God-fearing multi-millionaire like Brian Houston could have given Brett Sengstock some compensation.

At the annual conference for Hillsong Church, Scott Morrison said: "Australia needs more prayer and more love". What about the victims and survivors of Frank Houston's sexual abuse? Why didn't the Prime Minister mention them? (Click here to read more)

Scott Morrison would have been fully aware that the Australian Media would report his attendance at the Hillsong Church conference and his support for the church and Brian Houston and what he said. So, Morrison was, in reality, preaching to all Australians and sending a powerful message to the police who are investigating Brian Houston not to charge him otherwise they will embarrass the Prime Minister.

I sent the below email to the Department of the Prime Minister and Cabinet on Friday (12/7/19) at 1.29pm and have not had a response at this time.

From: SHANE DOWLING
Sent: 12 July 2019 13:29
To: media@pmc.gov.au
Subject: Media request regarding Prime Minister Scott Morrison

Dear Sir/Madam

I am a journalist and have 8 questions in relation to Prime Minister Scott Morrison and his relationship with Brian Houston who is the founder and a pastor at Hillsong Church.

It was reported in the media that Prime Minister Scott Morrison and his wife were on stage with Brian Houston at the Hillsong Church conference on Tuesday the 9th of July 2019 and it has also been reported that Prime Minister Scott Morrison regards Brian Houston as a mentor.

The questions are:

1. Can you please confirm if Prime Minister Scott Morrison was aware that the NSW police are currently investigating Brian Houston for covering up the sexual abuse of children by his father, Frank Houston?

2. Can you please confirm if Prime Minister Scott Morrison was aware that the Royal Commission into Institutional Responses to Child Sexual Abuse found that both the New South Wales executive and the national executive of the Assemblies of God failed to follow its complaints procedure when handling the allegations?

3. Can you please confirm if Prime Minister Scott Morrison was aware that the Royal Commission also found both executives failed to appoint a contact person for the victim (referred to as AHA), did not interview AHA about his allegations, did not interview Frank Houston, and did not record any of the steps it took?

4. Can you please confirm if Prime Minister Scott Morrison was aware that the Royal Commission also found neither the national executive nor Brian Houston referred the allegations to police, and the Royal Commission determined Houston "had a conflict of interest in assuming responsibility for dealing with AHA's allegations because he was both the National President of

the Assemblies of God in Australia and the son of Mr Frank Houston, the alleged perpetrator"?

5. Can you please confirm if Prime Minister Scott Morrison was aware that Brian Houston, who was then the national president of the Assemblies of God, confronted his father with the allegations in 1999 and the preacher confessed?

6. Can you please confirm if Prime Minister Scott Morrison was aware that Brian Houston called a meeting of the national executive, and relinquished the chair, but remained present during discussions on the allegations and disciplinary actions against his father?

7. Can you please confirm if Prime Minister Scott Morrison was aware that the Assemblies of God executive began investigations later discovering a further eight alleged victims of Frank Houston? But did not to make them public telling its churches in a letter from Brian Houston there was "no reason" for it to be announced as others may use it to further their agendas?

8. Can you please confirm if Prime Minister Scott Morrison was aware that Brian Houston defended his failure to go to the police, despite having no doubt it was criminal conduct?

Can you please respond by 5pm today (Friday 12/7/19) in case I have further questions. My deadline for publication is 5pm Saturday the 13th of July 2019.

Regards

Shane Dowling

Kangaroo Court of Australia

The evidence against Brian Houston and the Hillsong Church of covering up paedophile Frank Houston's abuse of children has been around a long time and most of my questions to the Prime

Minister came from an article on the Royal Commission in 2015 (Click here to read). So, it's impossible for Prime Minister Scott Morrison to say he didn't know and explains why he refused to answer my questions.

Brian Houston and his family also gave an interview in 2016 on The Inside Story program and it is worth watching the part where they discuss Frank Houston because all they seem to care about is themselves and what impact it had on them. There was no discussion on what they would do for the victims and Brian Houston is caught out giving two different reasons why he didn't go to the police, one version for the show and another version when he was in the witness stand at the Royal Commission.

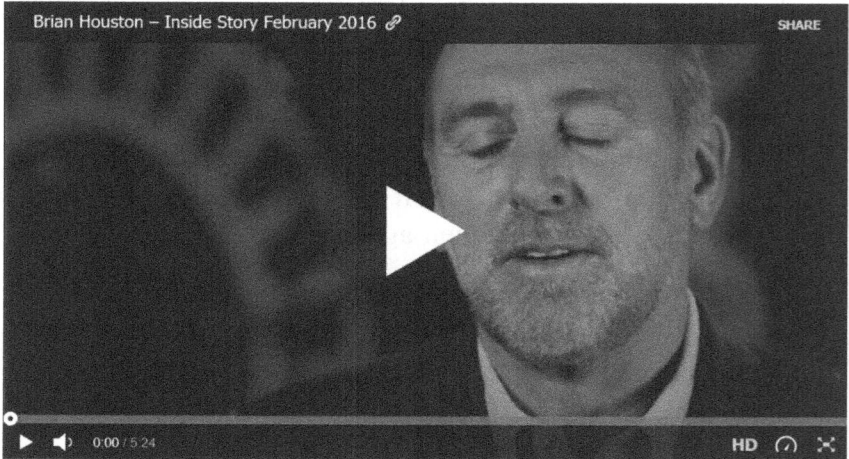

Brian Houston – Inside Story February 2016

Why do Liberal Party Prime Minister's support paedophiles and their protectors such as former PM John Howard writing a letter of reference for convicted paedophile George Pell to use at his sentencing hearing and former PM Tony Abbott also publicly supporting George Pell after he was convicted? (Click here to read more)

Is Scott Morrison interfering in a police investigation? Or trying to influence a police investigation like John Howard did with George Pell?

In 2004 Frank Houston died and at his funeral service was the then Deputy Police Commissioner Andrew Scipione who later became Police Commissioner and is said to be friends with Brian Houston. Houston gave evidence in 2014 at the Royal Commission, where he admitted failing to go to the police in relation to the sexual abuse of children by his father. Apparently, the police started looking at the issue given the evidence at the Royal Commission but did nothing because of a lack of evidence but reopened the matter about the same time as the Sixty Minutes story went to air.

Sixty Minutes didn't have the same trouble the police did in getting plenty of evidence for their report in November 2018. It's worth noting that Andrew Scipione didn't retire as Police Commissioner until March 2017.

One of the saddest things about this issue is that thousands of survivors were promised compensation after The Royal Commission into Institutional Responses to Child Sexual Abuse ended in 2017 and the government set up the National Redress Scheme but after 12 months only 5% of applications have been processed. I think Scott Morrison should be focused on fixing that rather than helping Brian Houston promote himself and the Hillsong Church.

There is a tonne of evidence to charge Brian Houston with concealing a serious indictable offence, yet he hasn't been charged. Why? It makes you wonder if much will happen with the police investigation given the Prime Minister gave Brian Houston the green light on Tuesday at the Hillsong conference.

Make no mistake, Prime Minister Scott Morrison knew Brian Houston is still under investigation by the police and Morrison knew it was highly inappropriate for him to be at the Hillsong Church on Tuesday night (9/7/19) helping promote it. But Morrison knows that he gets a lot of votes from the Hillsong Church and his local church which is linked to Hillsong so in a situation like this Morrison believes that votes count more than doing what is ethical and moral. I'll keep on following up on this story.

End of article

On the 5th of October 2019, I wrote an article titled "Hillsong Church Pastor Brian Houston perjured himself at the Child Sex Abuse Royal Commission. The evidence." which is below.

Hillsong Church Pastor Brian Houston perjured himself at the Child Sex Abuse Royal Commission. The evidence.

Hillsong Church Pastor Brian Houston clearly and blatantly perjured himself at the Child Sex Abuse Royal Commission when he was in the witness stand under oath in 2014. The reason for Brian Houston's perjury was that he was trying to cover-up the fact that he and the Australian Christian Churches (ACC) covered-up the sexual abuse of children by Brian's father Frank Houston.

Brian Houston is currently under investigation by the NSW police for concealing the sexual abuse of children by his father. The NSW police confirmed this in an email to me on the 10th of July 2019 after Scott Morrison was on stage with his good friend Brian Houston helping him promote the Hillsong Church. (Click here to read more)

Below I'll focus on three blatant lies that Brian Houston told when he was in the witness stand under oath.

1. Brian Houston lied about getting legal advice in relation to his father's sexual abuse of Brett Sengstock.

2. Brian Houston lied about why he never went to the police about his father's sexual abuse of children.

3. Brian Houston lied about calling Brett Sengstock on the phone and claiming Brett Sengstock said he did not want the police involved. (Brett Sengstock is given the name AHA by the Royal Commission in the documents)

I've spent the last few days going through the witness statements and transcript on the website for the Royal Commission into Institutional Responses to Child Sexual Abuse for Case Study 18: Australian Christian Churches. There are a lot more lies than just those three, but they are especially important and obvious lies.

Background

I won't write all the details, but you can read Brett Sengstock's witness statement by clicking here.

Brett Sengstock was sexually abused as a child in the 1970's by Frank Houston, who was the father of Hillsong Church founder Pastor Brian Houston. In 1999 the Church's management and Brian Houston were made aware of Frank Houston abusing Brett Sengstock which Frank Houston admitted to his crimes when confronted.

On the 16th of September 1999 Brett Sengstock was sent a letter on behalf of Church management advising him that:

The secular courts is not the way, I believe to go but to the church where I believe you will receive a fair hearing. I will stand with you Brett I for I believe you.

If you feel you can't I would urge you to seek ministry for your healing for you can rise up, put this awful incident behind you and be the man that God wants you to be.

I trust Frank also confesses this awful deed, repents for sinning against God, receives forgiveness, is disciplined and rises to a higher place in God because this blight on his character has been dealt with. (Click here to see the letter)

The letter to Brett Sengstock from the Church management telling him that the "secular courts" "was not the way to go" to solve his problem was in effect also saying don't go to the police and keep your mouth shut so the Church can cover it up.

Frank Houston was never sacked when he admitted to abusing Brett Sengstock. He was allowed to resign. Brett Sengstock says when he spoke to Brian Houston in 1999 he was told: **"You know, it's your fault all of this happened. You tempted my father."**

In 2014 the Royal Commission into Institutional Responses to Child Sexual Abuse heard evidence into Brett Sengstock's abuse and the failure of Brian Houston and the Church management to go to the police etc which the final report criticised and the report is the foundation of the current police investigation. (Click here to read the final report)

Above is Hillsong Church Pastor Brian Houston giving evidence during the Royal Commission into Institutional Responses to Child Sexual Abuse hearings in Sydney, Thursday, Oct. 9, 2014. In the top left corner is his father, paedophile Frank Houston.

Brian Houston lied about getting legal advice in relation to his father's sexual abuse of Brett Sengstock. (First lie)

Keith Ainge gave evidence at the Royal Commission because he was National Secretary of the Assemblies of God Australia

(AOGA) from May 1995 to May 2011 (AOGA became Australian Christian Churches (ACC) in 2007) when Frank Houston's sexual abuse of children was exposed. Keith Ainge said in his witness statement at paragraph 14:

"We did consider whether we needed to compulsorily report the offence to police. However, my recollection is that legal advice had been obtained, and this advice was to the effect that the complainant could report the matter to police given his age, and **that there was no obligation on the National Executive to report the matter to police. I do not recall where the legal advice came from, or who sought the legal advice.**" (Click here to read the full witness statement)

No lawyer in Australia would have given that advice, which makes it obvious why he can't remember "where the legal advice came from." Every lawyer will tell you that if you know a crime has been committed you have a legal obligation to report it to the police. The cover-up was in full swing from the start.

In the transcript below when Keith Ainge gave evidence in the witness stand at the Royal Commission, he pointed the finger straight at Brian Houston for directing the cover-up.

Keith Ainge – Transcript page 9275 (Click here to read the transcript)

Q. And that you were relying on what Brian Houston said to you about the complainant not wanting it to go to the police; is that correct?
A. Correct.
Q. And you had not had the matter assessed by an independent person?
A. That's correct.
Q. And you had not had an independent person appointed to deal with the complainant?
A. That's correct.
Q. On that basis, you determined that there was no need to refer

the complaint to the police?

A. That's correct.

Brian Houston gave evidence in the witness stand at the Royal Commission in relation to talking to a lawyer which was pure perjury. He claims he only knew the first name of the lawyer and they haven't been able to find him since. He obviously didn't try too hard.

Brian Houston – Transcript page 9331

Q. You were concerned about what would happen with your father in criminal proceedings, weren't you, and you spoke to a barrister about that?

A. I went to see, not a barrister – a lawyer.

Q. Who did you speak to?

A. Pardon?

Q. Who did you speak to?

A. Well, a family friend took me there. The lawyer's name was **– the lawyer's name was Graham. I can't remember his last name.** I think he was at Mallesons. And we have been in contact with Mallesons and they have no record of that meeting.

Q. Have you spoken to the lawyer concerned directly?

A. I think we may have tried. I'm just looking at my associate. I think we may have tried, but the answer is no.

It is ridiculous and obvious perjury by both Brian Houston and Keith Ainge. Keith Ainge says the board of directors had legal advice that they didn't need to go to the police but he doesn't know where it came from and Brian Houston says he only knows the first name of the lawyer he received legal advice off and he now can't find the lawyer.

Brian Houston made no mention of meeting with the lawyer in his witness statement so it looks like to me that under pressure in the witness stand he made up the lie about the meeting with the lawyer and that's why he said he couldn't remember the lawyer's second name. ([Click here and see page 9383 of the transcript](#))

Brian Houston lied about why he never went to the police about his father's sexual abuse of children. (Second lie)

Brian Houston gave evidence below saying he didn't go to the police because Brett Sengstock was 35 or 36.

Brian Houston – Transcript page 9315

Q. At that stage, you certainly knew that very serious allegations had been made against your father?
A. Yes, I did.
Q. And that the allegations were likely to be criminal conduct of one sort or another?
A. **Yes, I did. I didn't have any doubt that it was criminal conduct.**
Q. Why didn't, at that stage, you go to the police and tell them what you had been told?
A. On that day, right there?
Q. Yes.
A. Well, all of the information I was being given by different people was that the man is 35, 36 years of age and if he decides to go to the police, he can, or if anyone else decides to go to the police, they can. If we were talking about someone – if this complaint was about someone who was under 18 then and there, I'm absolutely certain we would have reported it to the police. We would have made sure that's where it went. Rightly or wrongly, I genuinely believed that I would be pre-empting the victim if I were to just call the police at that point.

Brain Houston again gave evidence below saying he didn't go to the police because Brett Sengstock was 35 or 36.

Brian Houston – Transcript page 9327

Q. Did you think at that stage, "This is the time that it needs to be referred to the police"?
A. No.

Q. Why was that?

A. Because he was 35, 36 years of age and I genuinely believed that it was his prerogative to do that. And I most certainly never, ever did, or tried to, suggest that nobody should go to the police. I knew, for the five years my father was still alive, there was every possibility that he would be charged.

If Brian Houston didn't go to the police because Brett Sengstock was 35 or 36, then why does Brian Houston come up with another reason below?

Brian Houston lied about calling Brett Sengstock on the phone and claiming Brett Sengstock said he did not want the police involved. (Third Lie)

Later on, giving evidence, Brian Houston says he didn't go to the police because Brett Sengstock said he didn't want the police involved

Brian Houston – Transcript page 9340

Q. You say that in that telephone call, Brett Sengstock said, "I don't want to go public. I don't want to go to the police. I don't want my identity public."

A. Yes.

Brian Houston said in his witness statement at paragraph 38 (Click here to read the witness statement) (In the witness statement the redaction starts off referring to Brett Sengstock as AHI then changes it to the correct pseudonym AHA)

At paragraph 38 Brian Houston claims he phoned Brett Sengstock after he first heard about the allegation and that Brett Sengstock said to him "I don't want to go public about the abuse or go to the Police.

At paragraph 41 Brian Houston says, "I believed that it was the prerogative of Brett Sengstock to make a report to the police if he wished since he is an adult. I did not dissuade from making a report to the police."

But Brett Sengstock told the Royal Commission different:

Brett Sengstock – Transcript page 9081

Q. As you may know, Pastor Houston has given a statement to the Royal Commission. He says that he first became aware of the allegations in late October and he says that, at about that time, you had a conversation with him in which you said to him, "I don't want to go public. I don't want to go to the police. I don't want my identity public." Does that sound correct or incorrect to you?
A. Incorrect.
Q. What is incorrect about it?
A. I don't recall the call at any stage whatsoever.
Q. So, it's incorrect because you can't remember it, or you think it's unlikely you said something like that?
A. It is unlikely.
Q. Why is it unlikely?
A. Because the things that he would have said in it. I had very little to do with Brian Houston other than the statement that he gave before in regards to the money, and I wanted nothing more to do with him.

Brian Houston made up a phone call so he could say that Brett Sengstock told him he didn't want the police involved, Houston made up a meeting with the lawyer (or the lawyer told him to go to the police so Houston now says he can't find the lawyer) and Houston made up the excuse of not going to the police because Brett Sengstock was 35 or 36. The reason Houston didn't go to the police was that he was protecting his tax-free business, the Hillsong Church, and his father and couldn't care less about the children sexually abused by his father.

In late 2000 Brian Houston and the management of the Assemblies of God in Australia knew there were rumours of other victims of Frank Houston who had been sexually abused as children. In 2000 Brian Houston and the Assemblies of God in Australia held a Special Executive Meeting on the 22nd

November 2000 at Hillsong Church, Castle Hill. which the minutes of the meeting said in part:

Brian Houston outlined the accusations that have been raised against Frank Houston, in relation to inappropriate sexual behaviour with boys around 33 years ago.

Brian outlined the actions of the New Zealand executive in investigating rumours of inappropriate behaviour involving Frank Houston and between two and five people. They are meeting from the 26th of November to discuss further action. (Click here to see the minutes of the meeting)

Brian Houston and the Church's management gave various reasons why they didn't go to the police when they found out about Frank Houston's abuse of Brett Sengstock. But what is their excuse for not going to the police when they found out there were many more victims? The only logical answer is that they were lying and always in cover-up mode from the start and had no intentions of ever going to the police and did what they could to make sure the police didn't find out because they wanted to protect their tax-free cash cows, the Churches. Their game plan was identical to the cover-ups they would have seen happening at other Churches.

Key evidence that Hillsong Church Pastor Brian Houston gave at the Child Sex Abuse Royal Commission in 2014 is not supported by other evidence and it's certain that Brian Houston committed perjury.

After looking at the evidence and transcript one thing is a known fact, there is a powerful prima facie case to charge Brian Houston with concealing the child sex abuse by his father Frank Houston and there is no excuse for why the NSW Police have not charged Brian Houston and it points to another police cover-up.

In 2004 Frank Houston died and at his funeral service was the then Deputy Police Commissioner Andrew Scipione who later became Police Commissioner and is said to be friends with Brian

Houston which I believe at least tells part of the story of why Brian Houston has never been charged.

Brian Houston by his own admission never went to the police about his father's sexual abuse of children even though he admitted he knew it was a criminal offence so there is no reason why the police can't charge him.

Brian Houston apparently sent a letter to some media threatening them with defamation a week or so ago. Houston's not in a position to threaten anyone as a defamation court case would again shine the light on him concealing his father's crimes.

Slowly but surely every lie that Brian Houston has told in covering up his father's crimes is being exposed and every time that happens questions will be asked why Scott Morrison is his friend and openly supporting Brian Houston while he is under investigation by the police.

End of article

On the 28th of November 2019, I published an article titled "NSW Police refuse to deny PM Scott Morrison has interfered in the investigation into paedophile protector Brian Houston" which is below.

NSW Police refuse to deny PM Scott Morrison has interfered in the investigation into paedophile protector Brian Houston

The NSW police are refusing to deny political interference by Prime Minister Scott Morrison in the police investigation of his good friend and mentor Brian Houston, who is under investigation for concealing his father's sexual abuse of children.

The email I sent to the NSW Police yesterday (27/11/19) is below but I will quickly outline some of the background and a previous email I sent to the police which puts into context why it is important that the police answer the latest questions I have put to them.

Background

I have previously written about Brian Houston perjuring himself at the Child Sex Abuse Royal Commission when he was in the witness stand under oath in 2014 (Click here to read more) and I published the below video showing Brian Houston's lies which are also relevant to this article.

The NSW police have been investigating Brian Houston for a long time but still haven't charged him despite his open admissions as per the below video.

Hillsong Church Pastor Brian Houston caught lying...

I emailed the NSW Police on the 10th of July 2019 and asked them if they were still investigating Brian Houston for covering up his father's sexual abuse of children which had been reported in November 2018. I sent the email and had a response 9 minutes later confirming they were still investigating Brian Houston as per below.

I sent the below email to the NSW Police Media Unit on Wednesday at 5.04pm on Wednesday (10/7/19)

From: SHANE DOWLING
Sent: 10 July 2019 17:04
To: xxxx@police.nsw.gov.au
Subject: Media request: Brian Houston Hillsong Church

Dear Sir/Madam

I am a journalist and have a question in relation to Brian Houston who is the founder and a pastor at Hillsong Church.

Can you please confirm whether or not the NSW Police are still investigating Brian Houston from the Hillsong Church in relation to his handling of the sex crimes committed by his father Frank Houston or any other crimes?

Regards

Shane Dowling

Kangaroo Court of Australia

I received the below response from the NSW Police Media unit at 5.13pm on Wednesday (10/7/19)

From: xxxxx <xxxxxxxx@police.nsw.gov.au> **On Behalf Of** #PMU
Sent: 10 July 2019 17:13
To: SHANE DOWLING
Subject: Re: Media request: Brian Houston Hillsong Church [DLM=For-Official-Use-Only]

Regarding your inquiry,

The matter continues to be investigated by officers attached to The Hills Police Area Command.

No further comment will be made while the investigation is ongoing

Regards,

Media Unit
NSW Police Force

This was a huge problem for Prime Minister Scott Morrison, given the night before he was on stage in front of 22,000 people at the Hillsong conference with Brian Houston promoting the Church. I published an article on the 13th of July titled "NSW Police confirm PM Scott Morrison's mate Hillsong's Brian Houston still under investigation for concealing paedophile father." (Click here to read more)

In September 2019 it was reported that Scott Morrison tried to take Brian Houston on his visit to the USA and Washington, but the White House rejected Brian Houston. (Click here to read more)

On Tuesday (26/11/19) news broke that Prime Minister Scott Morrison had phoned the NSW Police Commissioner to ask about a police investigation into federal MP Angus Taylor which had only been announced a few hours earlier.

The police started "an investigation into the origins of an altered document used to attack the Sydney lord mayor, Clover Moore." (Click here to read more)

And a few hours later Scott Morrison was on the phone to the NSW Police Commissioner. The ABC reported:

"Federal Opposition Leader Anthony Albanese believes Mr Morrison crossed a line by calling Commissioner Mick Fuller after it was revealed police launched an investigation into an allegedly forged document used by Energy Minister Angus Taylor's office in a political attack against Sydney's Lord Mayor Clover Moore." (Click here to read more)

Scott Morrison and Police Commissioner Fuller previously claimed to be neighbours and friends but are now trying to downplay their friendship.

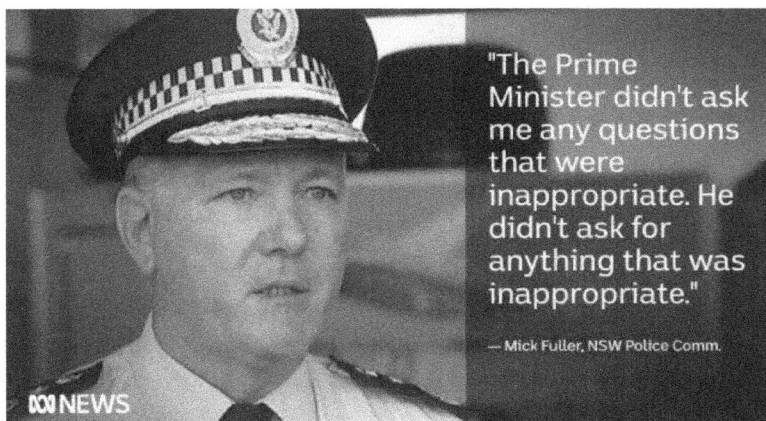

"The Prime Minister didn't ask me any questions that were inappropriate. He didn't ask for anything that was inappropriate."

— Mick Fuller, NSW Police Comm.

Putting two and two together it became obvious to me that if Prime Minister Scott Morrison phoned the NSW police to stick his nose into a police investigation into federal MP Angus Taylor, then it is almost certain he would have also done the same for his good friend and mentor Brian Houston. So, I sent the below email to the NSW police media unit (27/11/19):

From: SHANE DOWLING
Sent: 27 November 2019 13:33
To: xxxxx@police.nsw.gov.au
Subject: Media request

Dear Sir/ Madam

Given Prime Minister Scott Morrison called NSW Police Commissioner Mick Fuller on Tuesday the 26th of November 2019 to discuss the police investigation into federal MP Angus Taylor only a few hours after the police investigation had been announced.

1. Has Scott Morrison at any stage also called Commissioner Fuller or any other police officer to discuss the police investigation into Hillsong Church Pastor Brian Houston?

2. Has anyone from Scott Morrison's office ever contacted anyone in the NSW police to discuss the police investigation into Hillsong Church Pastor Brian Houston?

Can you please respond by the close of business today so I can publish?

Regards

Shane Dowling

Kangaroo Court of Australia

At the time of writing this article, I haven't had a response from the police but they normally respond in a matter of minutes as the previous email shows so it looks like the cover-up is in full swing. I'll follow-up in the near future.

Prime Minister Scott Morrison has always refused to answer questions about his attempt to take Brian Houston to the White House. But Scott Morrison had to have known at least since November 2018 that Brian Houston is under investigation by the NSW police yet he still jumped on stage at the Hillsong Church in July 2019 with Brian Houston and also tried to take him to Washington in September 2019.

Scott Morrison just hopping on stage with Brian Houston and trying to take him to Washington would have put the investigating police in NSW under pressure to drop the charges against Brian Houston because they wouldn't want to embarrass the Prime Minister. That alone I think shows Scott Morrison is prepared to use his position as PM to interfere in a police investigation when it suits him for his own benefit.

Taking everything into account, what is the chance that Scott Morrison has spoken to the NSW police either directly or indirectly via his staff to interfere in the Brian Houston police investigation? Almost certain I would say, and the police wouldn't deny it when I emailed them.

End of article

The NSW Police never responded to the second email above.

Chapter 9

Doing jail for Kerry Stokes, Channel 7 and the Jane Does

On the 2nd of February 2017 lawyers for Jane Doe 1 and Jane Doe 2 emailed me a Notice of Motion to have me charged for contempt for failing to take down an article naming them in the Tim Worner / Amber Harrison / Seven fraud, sex and drug scandal. On the 10th of August 2017, I was sentenced to four months in jail and released on the 9th of December 2017. I wrote an article on the 4th of March 2018 which outlines the details below:

Doing jail time for Kerry Stokes, Channel 7 and the Jane Does

Last year I spent 4 months in jail after refusing to abide by another dodgy suppression order issued in the Tim Worner / Seven / Amber Harrison sex, drug and fraud scandal and continued to name 2 other women in the scandal whom the court gave the pseudonyms Jane Doe 1 and Jane Doe 2.

The suppression order and subsequent contempt charge was paid for by Kerry Stokes' Seven West Media on behalf on Jane Doe 1 and Jane Doe 2 who are an on-air TV personality at Channel 7 and a well-known actress. The irony is that the women's names are still on my website and numerous other websites and no one has said anything.

It was about standing up to dodgy suppression orders and exposing the fraudulent use of shareholder's funds and the corruption

Writing the article that got me into trouble was never about whether or not the 2 women had a sexual relationship with Tim Worner. It was about whether they were involved in using shareholder's funds to help facilitate the relationship and whether shareholder's funds were used for their benefit or to shut them up as was the case with Amber Harrison.

Amber Harrison admitted she had been given a $10,000 bonus off her lover and Seven CEO Tim Worner for no justifiable reason and had been paid $100,000's to shut her mouth about the affair. Seven said they paid Amber Harrison over $400,000 for her to shut her mouth. And then there were $millions of shareholder's funds spent on legal fees against Amber Harrison and others to conceal the truth.

So, the question has to be asked is how much more money has Tim Worner spent on other alleged sexual partners at Channel 7. None of the women I have named have signed affidavits denying they had sexual relationships with Tim Worner as Amber Harrison has alleged but they were happy to send me to jail and their frivolous and vexatious SLAP defamation lawsuit against me continues.

They were named in a legal document which was submitted to the Australian Human Rights Commission and I had a right to name them and there was never any exceptional circumstance which was required by law to say I couldn't name them.

And I had lost count of the number of dodgy suppression orders and non-publication orders Stokes and his companies had taken out against myself and others, so I had decided to take a stand.

Just think of all the celebrities being named in sex scandals recently such as Geoffrey Rush, Craig McLachlan and Don Burke. None of them have been able to get suppression orders, so why have Jane Doe 1 and Jane Doe 2? It's because of judicial bribery for dodgy suppression orders. Kerry Stokes' Seven paying for the Jane Doe defamation case and contempt case against me is not about protecting them. It is about protecting Seven's CEO Tim Worner. So, Kerry Stokes and the Seven board had me jailed to protect Tim Worner.

By the women hiding behind the pseudonyms it does damage to the reputation of all the women at Channel 7 as "a well-known on-air host at 7 and a well-known actress at 7 allegedly had sexual relationships with Tim Worner" is all over the internet. And it was on the internet before I ever named them.

The process and the jails

I had never been to jail before and had no criminal record before last year's 4-month stint. I'll post a separate article in relation to Justice Ian Harrison's scandalous judgment.

The biggest thing about jail is the initial shock of thinking you'll be in a dodgy jail like the Surry Hills holding cells with no sunlight for your whole sentence but after that boredom is the main issue.

I was jailed on the 10-8-17 and the standard routine for jail in NSW is that you first go to the Surry Hills holding cells which are at the police station for 2 to 5 days. I spent 3 days and 2 nights there. From there I went to Penrith holding cells for 3 days which I think is at the courthouse. At neither place do you get to see any sunlight. The Surry Hills holding cells are regarded as the worst jail in the state.

From there I went to Parklea jail, which is a remand jail. From memory, I arrived there on the 16/8/17. Prisoners there are either waiting to be sentenced or classified and sent to their prison to do their sentence. For example, I was given a C1 classification which is minimum security. I would have been given a C2, but I still had further court matters, so they gave me the C1.

Parklea is a maximum-security jail and you are allowed out of the cells for about 6 hours a day from roughly 9am to 3pm. At least once a week on a Tuesday it would be an all-day lock-in. Sometimes there might be a few lock-ins during the week.

A few months before I arrived there was a video that a former prisoner uploaded to the internet showing himself using a mobile phone, having drugs and a weapon in jail which gained widespread media attention and because of that there would be regular searches of the cells which the prisoners called ramps.

I never saw any fights but heard from others there were a few. Overall, the prisoners are mainly concerned about doing their sentence and getting out.

Then on the 14th of September, I was sent to the Outer Metropolitan Multi-Purpose Correctional Centre (OMMPCC). It was a lot more relaxed than Parklea and we were allowed out of our cells for a couple of hours longer each day. Most of the inmates had 12 months or less to go, though some had up to 4 years or so remaining. The offences were also fairly minor driving, drug offences and AVO breaches etc. Others had longer sentences of up to 10 years but had been in for quite a while and because of their good behaviour had worked their way down from a maximum-security jail to a minimum-security jail.

Because of the type of offence I was convicted of I was sent to a minimum-security jail which is a lot better than the maximum-security jails.

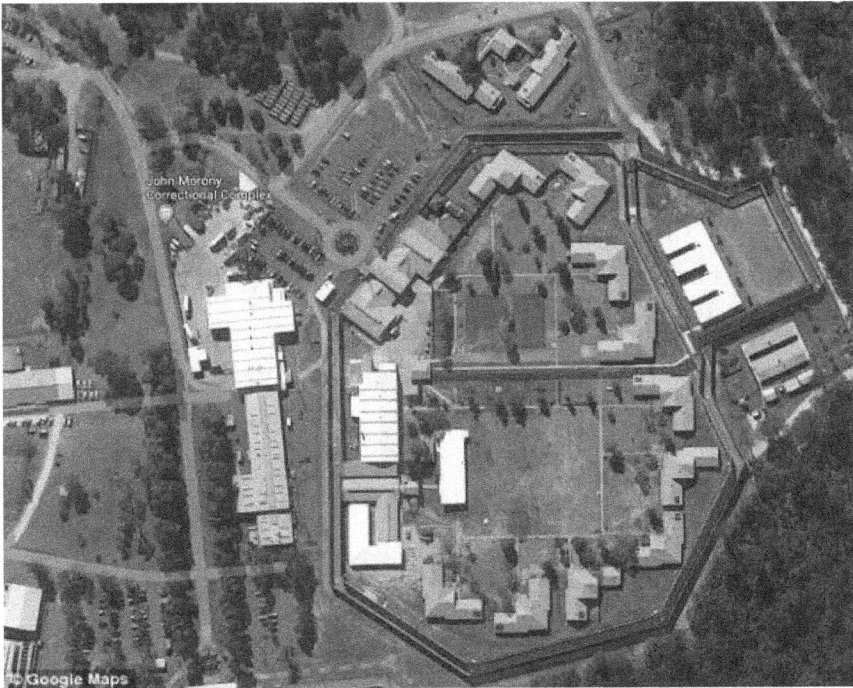

Above is the Outer Metropolitan Multi-Purpose Correctional Centre, which is commonly called John Morony 2. There is another male and female jail just out of picture.

If you look at the picture above the very bottom green building is where I lived for the last 3 months of my 4-month sentence. It was called "I Wing" and housed 25 inmates. There were 10 others Wings inside the jail and 2 outside the jail called the Honour Houses, which you can see right at the top of the picture.

The inmates living in the Honour Houses had to have impeccable good behaviour records and most had normal type jobs they went to during the day and then went back to the Honour House at night. They also got weekend leave and other benefits.

The jail had various jobs for inmates such as the laundry, ground maintenance both inside and outside the jail and the upholstery shop making lounges etc. I worked in the Printshop for about the last 7 weeks of my sentence.

It says on their website:

The John Morony Correctional Complex is located 5 km south of Windsor, a town 56km to the north west of Sydney.

The complex houses

- the **John Morony Correctional Centre**, a medium security correctional centre for remand and sentenced male offenders

- the **Outer Metropolitan Multi-Purpose Correctional Centre**, a minimum-security correctional centre for men and

- **Dillwynia Correctional Centre**, a minimum/medium security correctional centre for women.

I can genuinely say all the guards at the jails that I was at and dealt with were good and treated people well.

Hells Angels and Brothers for Life etc

In NSW the jails generally only have one or two bikie gangs per jail. For example, Parklea jail is a Hells Angels jail and so was OMMPCC. Outside of jail, they might have bad reputations but inside jail, they are like everyone else in that they just want to do their time and go home. The same with the BFL. I got along with them fine.

When Australian media are having journalists jailed to close down free speech and stop journalists exposing corruption every Australian should be concerned

People sit here in Australia criticising other countries and their abuses of human rights and their treatment of journalists who expose corruption. We might not be at the level of killing journalists which we read about happening in Russia, but we do jail them as I can attest.

Looking forward

I would have preferred not to have gone to jail but I have no regrets and like everything, in life, you always should look at the positives. I managed to lose 10 kg with plenty of exercise and I'm back eating a normal breakfast which I had stopped doing about ten years ago and feel better for it. And we all know the saying "if it doesn't kill you, it makes you stronger."

There were a lot of funny characters in jail and I met a lot of good people who had just made mistakes in life. It was also good to see how positive some were even though they had a few years to go.

Yes, there are a lot of bad people in jail but by and large, they are in the maximum-security jails doing long sentences. It is like another inmate said to me not long after I first arrived: *"Most of the people are in jail because of the wrong split-second judgement they made. It was a would've, could've or should've moment and they made the wrong call."* For me, it was taking a stand against corrupt suppression orders and judicial corruption and I would like to think my time in jail helped shine a light on it to at least some degree.

I have other court matters coming up which relate to free speech and political communication and hopefully I can avoid more jail time. Then there are also Kerry Stokes' ongoing frivolous and vexatious defamation matters to deal with. But I can see a light at the end of the tunnel and win, lose or draw one of the goals of this website is to blaze a trail in dealing with judicial corruption for others to learn from who will hopefully go on to do bigger and better things to hold people in power to account. And I think this website site is achieving that, at least to some degree.

End of article

Chapter 10

Being charged for contempt by the Supreme Court of NSW

On the 3rd of February 2017, I went to court and by the end of the day, the court had taken the initial step to having me charged with Contempt of Court. I published an article about it a few days later on the 5th of February titled "Chief Justice Bathurst has journalist charged with contempt for accusing him of corruption" as per below.

Chief Justice Bathurst has journalist charged with contempt for accusing him of corruption

NSW Chief Justice Tom Bathurst instituted contempt of court proceedings against me for accusing him of corruption in court on Friday the 3rd of February 2017. The corruption is being a bribe-taker and paedophile which I have previously written on my website. Chief Justice Bathurst has used taxpayer funds and taken out a suppression order to conceal who has charged me with contempt and to conceal the fact that they are trying to hide the very serious allegations.

I taped the proceedings on Friday, which is below, for my own safety given previous threats and intimidation in court by the judicial officers and others including Registrar Rebel Kenna and a Court Sheriff in 2015. (Click here to read more)

It is a classic case of trying to bastardise, bully and intimidate a whistleblower especially given the allegations have been on my website for a long time which they are well aware of and the fact that I have put them on notice that I will be making a complaint to the relevant authorities.

Justice Clifton Hoeben, Chief Judge at Common Law and Registrar Christopher Bradford are the 2 other applicants in the matter. Chief Justice Bathurst is prosecuting his own case in his own court and doesn't want anyone to know.

These are the same allegations that I have made against Chief Justice Bathurst over the last few years on my website and allegations that I have emailed directly to Chief Justice Bathurst and the other Supreme Court judges for a response before I published. (Click here to read more) Chief Justice Bathurst has never sued me for defamation nor have any of the other judges because they would have to do it in their own name and be exposed to the media.

In court Friday 3/2/2017

I was in court Friday for the frivolous defamation case by Jane Doe 1 and Jane Doe 2 and they have filed 2 notices to have my defence struck out and have me charged with contempt which is separate to the contempt charge that Chief Justice Bathurst has instigated.

The matter was before Registrar Bradford, and after an argument, was transferred to the duty judge. I gave Bradford a mouthful, and he said he would take it further which he has along with Chief Justice Bathurst and Justice Hoeben who I also named as per the video below. Bathurst is the Chief Justice and he is the one who controls the court and he is the ultimate decision-maker.

Chief Justice Bathurst has instituted proceedings via the Jane Doe 1 and Jane Doe 2 defamation case against me which is being run by Kerry Stokes' Seven West Media. Bathurst's name or the other applicant's names do not appear on the paperwork anywhere, and with the suppression order I am not meant to tell anyone.

What Chief Justice Tom Bathurst has done is sneaky, dodgy and corrupt as it gets.

Chief Justice Tom Bathurst

I have written a lot of articles on judicial corruption and a couple that support the key allegations are raised below.

Bribes

In 2015 Fairfax Media and the ABC's Four Corners reported that the Mafia had bribed NSW judges $2.2 million. Nothing has ever been done and Tom Bathurst who is the head judge for NSW never said anything although Justice David Davies shot off his mouth in court and confirmed it when I was there. (Click here to read more)

Paedophiles in the judiciary

On the 8th of September 2016, I wrote an article titled *"Paedophile priest gets 3 months jail for raping 3 boys by NSW Supreme Court's Justice Hoeben"* and said:

Father Robert Flaherty

In February 2016 Father Flaherty was jailed for 2 years and 3 weeks with a non-parole period of 6 months by the NSW District Court's Judge Richard Cogswell, SC for sexually abusing 3 boys. (Click here to read more)

The church had allowed Father Flaherty to move from parish to parish even though they knew he had abused boys.

As you would expect the prosecution appealed because the sentence was a joke. The appeal was heard in the NSW Court of Criminal Appeal by Justice Hoeben, Justice Price and Justice Simpson with Hoeben being the senior judge. What did they do? They decreased the sentence to 2 years with a non-parole period of 3 months. (Click here to read the article)

This is relevant in regards to what I said about Justice Hoeben in court last Friday. It is also relevant because I published the article on the 8/9/16 and emailed the judges and Registrar Bradford and the next day I was in court, 9/9/16, which is the first video below.

This has happened at the same time that Australia is spending billions on a Royal Commission into Child Sex Abuse that will end up costing billions trying to fix the damage done to many lives:

"The royal commission estimated the total cost of redress for 60,000 abuse survivors, including administration costs, at $4.3 billion" (Click here to read more)

Justice Hoeben and the others including Chief Justice Bathurst who heads the court should be made to front the Royal Commission and explain themselves. While Bathurst is there he might want to tell everyone why the NSW Judicial Commission, which he is President, is protecting paedophile judge Garry Neilson?

Videos

The first video was filmed in court on the 9th of September 2016. I asked Registrar Bradford to transfer the matter to the duty judge, given that I have written on my website that he is a bribe-taker and suspected paedophile. He refused.

Video 1 – I have also published the below 2 videos on YouTube as one video – (Click here to watch)

The second video below was filmed on Friday the 3rd of February 2017. A few minutes before the below video was recorded, I asked Bradford to transfer the matter to the duty judge and gave him a mouthful. He threatened to get the Court Sheriff and have me removed. The other party's lawyers weren't there as proceedings had just started, so I backed off and waited for the other party's lawyer and then approached the bench again at about 9.05am. There were about 50 lawyers and barristers in the room for the directions hearings.

Video 2

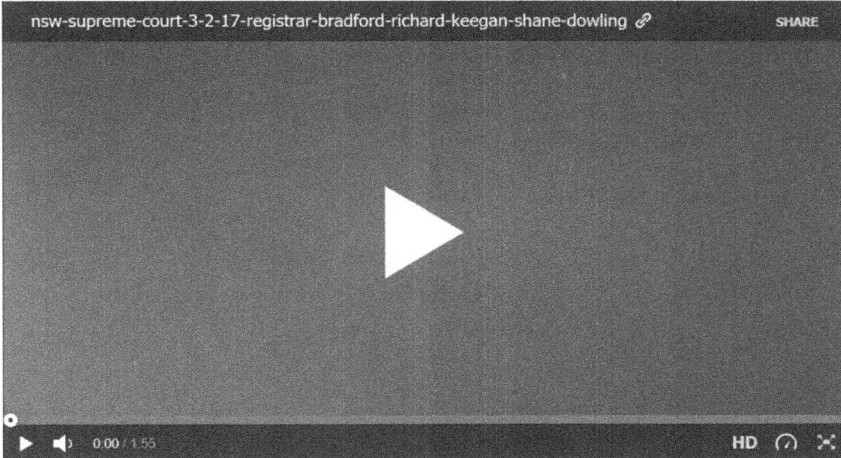

nsw-supreme-court-3-2-17-registrar-bradford-richard-keegan-shane-dowling   SHARE

▶ 🔊 0:00 / 1:55   HD ⌒ ✕

Registrar Bradford has aided and abetted Kerry Stokes numerous times in dragging out a <u>frivolous and vexatious defamation case</u> that has gone for almost 3 years. He is as dodgy as they come.

All courts should be live-streamed to the internet which would greatly cut down judicial corruption and corruption in the wider community.

What I said in court on the 3/2/17

Bradford already knew on what basis I wanted the matter transferred given I raised it a few minutes before and also raised it last year in the first video. He should have never been anywhere near the case.

I also said in court that Justice Clifton Hoeben a few months ago gave a paedophile priest 3 months jail. The only person I know who would give a paedophile priest 3 months jail is another paedophile. He's "an absolute grub".

At the end, Registrar Christopher Bradford implied I was a grub, so why hasn't he been charged with scandalous conduct? I said, "it's on my website" Bradford replied "every grub can have a website" I responded, "well you must have one too".

What they really don't like is that I humiliated them with the truth in front of fifty-odd lawyers and barristers who were in court for the directions hearing.

Disappearing on the court lists

Kerry Stokes lawyers have been threatening everyone and anyone who writes about the Tim Worner sex scandal and got some help from the court as per the below picture.

There is a suppression order not to name the 2 applicants Jane Doe 1 and Jane Doe 2, and that is it. Journalists can report everything else, including my name. (Click here to read more). Yet the court actually suppressed the whole case on the court lists, so nothing showed up. The hearing time and place should have shown up on the court's website the day before the directions hearing which it didn't and also up to 3 weeks before on the NSW Courts website which it wasn't there earlier in the week. When I got to court, I found out why as it says 35 (case suppressed) below.

		Friday 3 February 2017	
Registrar C Bradford		**Law Courts Building**	
		Court 9C Queens Square Sydney	
32	Jane Melanie Behrens by her tutor David Frederick Behrens v Dr William Herlihy 2016/00321946	Directions (Professional Negligence Registrar)	09:00 AM
33	Michael Bruce Egerdie v Renukadas Sakalkale 2016/00322037	Directions (Professional Negligence Registrar)	09:00 AM
34	Bilal Bilal v State of New South Wales 2016/00357353	Directions (Common Law Registrar)	09:00 AM
35	(case suppressed) 2016/00383575	Directions (Common Law Registrar)	09:00 AM

Bradford and the court staff said it was an error. Yeah, right. It is the media who mainly use the list and given that the last hearing in December got national coverage it certainly helps to make sure the media don't know when the hearings are. Kerry Stokes has a lot of pull when he is getting help from the courts. I write this because it is part of the overall corruption and many readers have told me how they were never notified about court dates and had judgments made against them etc.

How many times have Chief Justice Bathurst and/or other judges done this before?

I have named and shamed corrupt judges, magistrates and Crown Prosecutors such as Director of Public Prosecutions Lloyd Babb SC and Margaret Cunneen and I am obviously on their hit list and they will try anything to get me. But all they have done is exposed themselves. I am entitled to an opinion and have freely expressed that in court which they know I have done previously on my website and raised some parts in court.

There is a clear High Court of Australia judgment that supports what I have done and said and that is Coleman v Power which is also promoted on the NSW Judicial Commission's website. Apparently, none of them have heard of it. I didn't abuse the registrar; I made a number of statement of facts and voiced my opinion.

Then there is also the truth defence. If my allegations were baseless, they could have and would have sued me for defamation long ago.

You don't have to agree with everything I say but a fair-minded person would agree that Registrar Bradford should not have been anywhere near the case and I am entitled to voice my opinion. A fair-minded person would also agree there needs to be a public inquiry in the whole affair especially given that Chief Justice Tom Bathurst is now in the middle of it as a litigant using taxpayer's funds for an attempted secret hearing to persecute a whistleblower.

Court hearing and court orders

Jillian Caldwell, Special Counsel for Crown Solicitor, left a message on my mobile phone at 2.02pm (3/2/17) saying she would be going to court in the afternoon to get a suppression order. She didn't invite me to go but just to call her if I want. I returned the call at 6.11pm but it went to voicemail although I assume, they received the message because a few minutes later I was emailed the court orders at 6.17pm.

The Court orders that:
(1) Under s10 of the Court Suppression and Non Publication Orders Act 2010 the contents of Exhibit 1 be prohibited from disclosure other than from the parties, except without leave of the Court, until further order.
(2) The Court further orders that:
Pending further order, pursuant to the Court's inherent power, publication of the following is suppressed (save for the proper purposes of the proceedings and any related contempt proceedings):
(a) the content of allegations made by Shane Dowling ('the defendant') before Registrar Bradford of the Supreme Court in open court on 3 February 2017 ('the allegations');
(b) that Mr Bradford and judges of the Supreme Court of New South Wales were the subject of the allegations; and
(c) that the allegations were made.
(3) Stand over the balance of the Notice of Motion to 3:30pm Wednesday, 8 February 2017. (Click here to read the court orders)

If they had of checked my website like I said in the video they would know I was immediately in breach of the court orders because I have been writing about judicial corruption for a number of years and have regularly named Chief Justice Bathurst, Justice Clifton Hoeben and Registrar Christopher

Bradford. This includes what I said in court on Friday, which automatically puts me in contempt of the court orders. (3/2/17) (Click here to read more)

They are also going to charge me with contempt:

4. Pursuant to Part 55 r.11(1) of the Supreme Court Rules 1970, that the Prothonotary apply by motion, or commence proceedings, for punishment for contempt in relation to the defendant's conduct. (Click here to read the Notice of Motion)

I can't make it on the 8th as I have to work. Given what I said in court is on my website and has been for ages, there is no justification for the suppression order or short notice. The duty judge Justice Beech-Jones who set the date was also the duty judge in the morning when I was before him for directions and he knew I was self-represented, had to work and had limited funds. And he knew I already had a hearing booked for the next Friday, which he set directions for. It is scandalous and I will email the prosecutor Jillian Caldwell and try for a time the following week.

The above is the outline of my defence and shows no cause of action and what a scandal it is that Chief Justice Tom Bathurst, Justice Clifton Hoeben and Registrar Chris Bradford can use taxpayer's money to hide their corruption and crimes and want to do it with a wide-ranging suppression order.

I wonder if the Attorney-General Gabrielle Upton and newly appointed Premier Gladys Berejiklian are aware of the contempt proceedings by Chief Justice Bathurst and did they approve it or do they claim there is a separation of powers and they had no idea?

What has happened above is a major positive because it is clear evidence of corruption and abuse of power by Chief Justice Bathurst and the judiciary and exposing it is what this website is about.

I'll put updates in the comment section if anything major happens over the next few days as things may move fast if they think they can get away with it. So, check back.

End of article

I was formally charged for contempt in April 2017. They had filed a summons on the 27th of March 2017 and tried to sneak into court without me being there, but I caught them. I published an article on the 8th of April about what happened titled "Free speech and political speech is being suppressed in Australia by the NSW Supreme Court" as per below.

Free speech and political speech is being suppressed in Australia by the NSW Supreme Court

Suppression orders are being used to gag anyone and everyone in NSW and Victoria to conceal corruption. This week I was formally charged with contempt by the NSW Supreme Court. I can't tell you everything because they put suppression orders on it, but it relates to me making statements regarding judicial corruption involving 2 judges and a court registrar.

So, the bottom line is the judges have used their own court to put suppression orders on their own case. It doesn't get any more corrupt than that. Back in February when the ball first started rolling for a contempt case against me I wrote an article telling people what had happened and they have also charged me with contempt because I told people which they say breached the first suppression order they took out in February.

I won't breach the court orders in this article to show how dodgy it is and show you what news will look like in the future if they are allowed to get away with their abuse of suppression orders.

It looks like I am about to be persecuted for my political beliefs because I'm trying to do something about judicial corruption. You always have to look on the positive and that is if they do try to persecute me, which they have already started with the court case, it will help highlight just how corrupt the judges are and how badly they need to be reined in.

Free speech and political speech in Australia

If you raise issues of government corruption or corruption within government departments, you are protected from prosecution. The reason you are protected is because it is political speech.

Beginning with a series of cases in 1992, the High Court has recognised that freedom of political communication is implied in the Australian Constitution. This freedom 'enables the people to exercise a free and informed choice as electors'. (Click here to read more)

Coleman v Power (2004) 220 CLR 1 is a High Court of Australia case that deals with the implied right to freedom of political communication found in the Australian Constitution.

"They accepted that communications alleging corruption of police were protected by the implied right to freedom of political communication. They also accepted that political communication could include insults. Further, they noted that insulting words were a well-known tradition in Australian politics from "its earliest history"." (Click here to read more)

Not only does it cover alleging corruption by police but any government employee including judges.

Three previous issues that I have raised are the widespread use of ex parte hearings (secret hearings), dodgy suppression orders and a paedophile priest getting 3 months jail after abusing 3 boys. All these issues need to be investigated by authorities, are clearly political speech, and raise issues of government corruption.

Most of the articles on this website are political speech in that they deal with government in one way or another.

Suppression orders – Only allowed in exceptional circumstances

I covered suppression orders in a recent article and how *"Australia is facing a national scandal regarding dodgy suppression orders"*. (Click here to read the article)

It has recently been brought to my attention that even law firms have had enough of judges issuing suppression orders with no regard for the law.

Two lawyers from Melbourne firm Marque Lawyers recently published a paper titled *"This is why open justice is broken"* and said:

"Suppression orders are infringing too far on open justice. New research from Victoria highlights some pretty scary trends. Suppression orders are often too broad, lack appropriate end points, are unclear in their terms, beyond the scope of the court's powers, and made without sufficient explanation of their necessity." (Click here to read more)

The judges need investigating for illegally issuing suppression orders.

Background – (Click here to read the previous article setting out much of the background)

I have been getting bounced around the NSW Supreme Court since April 2014 with various defamation proceedings by Kerry Stokes. He has also instituted contempt proceedings against me twice for breaching dodgy suppression orders. The first time in 2014 I was found guilty and fined $2000 but it was so corrupt and a clear conspiracy to have me falsely charged that the NSW Justice Department said they would not enforce the fine when I complained.

The second time was this year via the defamation case known as Jane Doe 1 and Ors v Shane Dowling which is being paid for by Seven West Media and controlled by Kerry Stokes. I was found guilty in March of breaching another dodgy suppression order and are waiting for a sentencing hearing. Before the sentencing hearing goes ahead, we are waiting for a judgment by Justice Lucy McCallum on whether the suppression order should have been issued in the first place as I have challenged it. A decision by Justice McCallum could have an impact on any sentence. The reality is it is a huge scam.

Current contempt case – (Click here to read the vague summons with the statement of charges) (Click here to read the suppression orders)

They tried to have the contempt matter dealt with without even telling me which is unbelievably corrupt.

The court registrar took the initial step in instituting contempt proceedings against me in February but I had not heard anything about it since except for a short administrative email on Monday the 27/3/17 giving me a document from February. There was no mention that they had instituted the contempt proceeding.

I only found out because I checked the court listing for the next three weeks on the NSW Courts website and seen a listing titled "Prothonotary of the Supreme Court of New South Wales v Shane Dowling 2017/94322" which was listed before the Duty judge on Tuesday the 4th April and I assumed they instituted the contempt matter but was not sure as they had not contacted me to tell me anything. So, I emailed the judge the night before and complained that I had not been given any notice and did not know what it was about as I have not been served any paperwork.

On Tuesday, it was then set down for a directions hearing on Thursday the 6th of April. I was served the summons by email and then served by a process-server on Wednesday the 5th of April, which is the day after it was originally meant to be heard.

Why didn't they notify me earlier? Because they wanted a default judgment in their favour? How corrupt is the Crown Solicitor Lea Armstrong?

Lea Armstrong – Crown Solicitor

Lea Armstrong in the NSW Crown Solicitor which put simply is a government law firm with over 350 staff which does legal work for other government departments. She is personally running the matter against me and was in court on Thursday instructing the barrister. Her name appears on the court documents.

Corrupt Crown Solicitor – Lea Armstrong

I wonder why someone who heads up a legal firm of 350 people is personally dealing with my matter? And why has she acted so corruptly?

Justice Christine Adamson

Right on cue the judge hearing the directions hearing on Thursday, Justice Christine Adamson, gave the prosecution barrister everything she wanted and gave me nothing.

Justice Christine Adamson (Far left – sitting) – 2003 – When she was a barrister.

Where the conduct of judicial officers is going to be decided there should be an interstate judicial officer brought in to hear the matter so there is no perceived bias. The prosecuting barrister even said that but argued against an interstate judge. I asked for an interstate judge to hear the case, but Justice Adamson refused, which makes the whole hearing a scandal. There will be a judge hearing a matter that involves the conduct of his or her own mates from the NSW Supreme Court.

Justice Adamson also put a suppression order on their evidence filed. What have they got to hide? I asked for any possible suppression orders to be argued for or against early next week, but Justice Adamson refused. She also forced me to agree to a hearing date when I had only received all the paperwork and evidence while we were in court.

They're certainly gunning for me for either a big fine or jail, it seems. Will I become a political prisoner in Australia so they can try to conceal judicial corruption? They are not after me for anything I have done. It is what I have said they don't like and the fact that I won't shut up even with their dodgy suppression orders. The battle above is very much about free speech and political speech in Australia.

The contempt matter is set down for hearing on the 4th May 2017 in the NSW Supreme Court.

End of article

On the 15th of April 2017, I made a formal complaint to law enforcement agencies and published an article titled "Judicial corruption complaint made to the Federal Police, Crime Commission & others" as per below.

Judicial corruption complaint made to the Federal Police, Crime Commission & others

I made a formal complaint of judicial corruption to the Australian Federal Police as per the below email. The complaint would put me in breach of suppression orders that are meant to stop me from speaking about the corruption, but the suppression orders are invalid as they breach my constitutional right to political speech. Political speech covers government corruption including judicial corruption which has been ruled on by the High Court of Australia.

I have also made complaints to the NSW Crime Commission, The Royal Commission into Institutional Responses to Child Sexual Abuse and others. The below email is exactly as I sent it (with a few corrections) although I have added the video and it is a follow-up from two previous articles. (Click here and here to read the previous articles)

From: SHANE DOWLING
Sent: Saturday, 15 April 2017 3:19 PM
To: 'andrew.colvin@afp.gov.au' <andrew.colvin@afp.gov.au>;
'commissioner@afp.gov.au' <commissioner@afp.gov.au>
Subject: Formal Complaint judicial corruption

Dear Commissioner Andrew Colvin – Australian Federal Police

I publish a judicial corruption website called Kangaroo Court of
Australia and I have been charged with contempt of court for
allegedly calling Justice Clifton Hoeben a paedophile and
Registrar Christopher Bradford a suspected paedophile and a
known bribe-taker which is set down for hearing on the 4th May
at 10am in the NSW Supreme Court in Sydney. (See
attached Summons and Particulars of Charge document)

This is a major cover-up attempt which includes but is not limited
to: Suspected bribery, money laundering, paedophilia, using a
carriage service to harass and intimidate and conspiracy to have
someone falsely charged.

There is a video of what was said in court and the charges are not
factually correct, be that as it may, the court has put suppression
orders on the matter so that I cannot say what the exact charges
are and I cannot name Justice Hoeben, Registrar Bradford and
Chief Justice Tom Bathurst who was also mentioned in the video
which was filmed in court. (Click here to see the video)

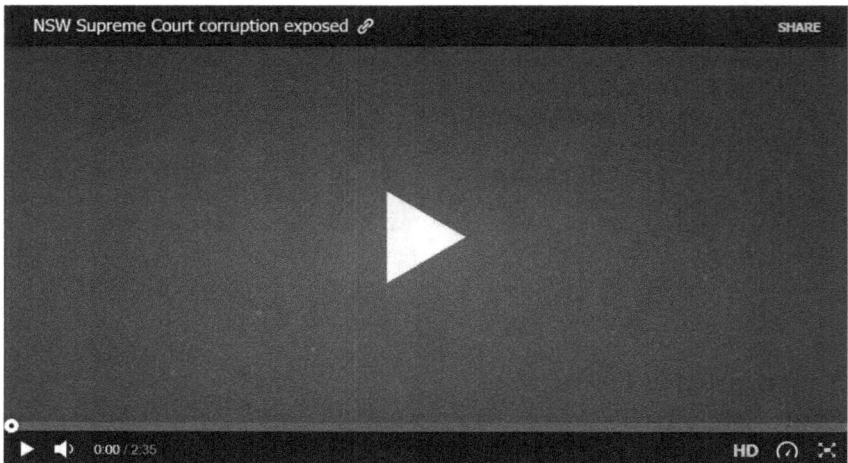

NSW Supreme Court corruption exposed 🔗   SHARE

▶ 🔊   0:00 / 2:35   HD ⌒ ⤢

(If you would like to download the video click where it says Share on the top right-hand corner of the video then click on "Original File" or H.264 (MP4).)

The net effect of the suppression orders is that you have judges of the NSW Supreme Court taking out suppression orders in their own case to cover it up from public scrutiny of allegations of bribery and paedophilia as per the charges against me which is about as corrupt as it gets.

Background

Whistleblowing

What is happening is a clear and blatant attempt to silence a judicial corruption whistleblower using illegal means.

Judicial bribery – In 2015 Fairfax Media and the ABC's Four Corners published stories stating that NSW Judges had been bribed $2.2 million by the Mafia. (Click here to read more) This has never been fully investigated but obviously should have been.

Judicial corruption – In Victoria and NSW judges are continually and illegally issuing suppression orders with no justification and having ex parte hearings with no justification. One can only assume that in many of those cases money is changing hands given the judges do not justify their decisions yet know they must. (Click here to read more)

Judicial paedophilia – In 2015 Senator Bill Heffernan claimed in Parliament on Tuesday (19/10/15) that he has a police list of 28 prominent people that includes a former Prime Minister and current judges that are suspected of being paedophiles. (Click here to read more) In 2016 a paedophile priest was given only 3 months jail for sexually abusing 3 boys which is scandalous and requires an investigation. (Click here to read more)

Multiple jail threats if I keep on whistleblowing – using a carriage service to harass and intimidate.

I have received multiple threats of jail if I keep on whistleblowing. I even received a threatening call late at night. I made a complaint to the NSW Crown Solicitor but have not received a response. At the time I made the complaint to NSW Crown Solicitor Ms Lea Armstrong I did not know she was the instructing solicitor in the matter against me which I am now aware.

The complaint is below and was sent on the 2/4/17.

Dear Ms Lea Armstrong – NSW Crown Solicitor

I am currently being pursued by the NSW Supreme Court for contempt of court which is being handled by Jillian Caldwell (Special Counsel for Crown Solicitor) in your office, which you may or may not be aware of. The matter has been afoot since February and further background information can be found in the attached email.

I wish to make a formal complaint in relation to a threatening phone call that I received from a male who identified himself as being from the Crown Solicitors office or the Solicitor General's office. When I took the call, I had no doubt the person was calling from your office. What happened is below:

"At 8.11pm on Tuesday the 14/2/17 I received a call on my mobile phone from an unknown number from a male who identified himself as calling from the Crown Solicitors office or the Solicitor General's office. He gave me a name, but I forget what it was. I told him he should not be calling me that time of night and that he could have called me today or tomorrow. He said he would call back tomorrow and asked me if the mobile was the best number. I asked what it was about, and he said that if I did not take down the 2 videos on my website that Registrar Bradford would have me incarcerated as he was very upset. He also said I should apologise to Registrar Bradford."

"I went off at him and said he should not be calling me that time of night about it. He again said that Registrar Bradford was very upset. I said to call me tomorrow and hung up."

"At 4.25pm on Wednesday the 15/2/17 I received a missed call from an unknown number."

I have a few questions:

1. *Can you confirm if anyone in your office called me at 8.11pm on Tuesday the 14/2/17? Can you confirm if Jillian Caldwell is aware of anyone calling me?*

2. *If it was someone in your office can you please tell me their name and position?*

3. *Given that it is possible that several federal laws and state laws have been breached (E.g. 474.17 Using a carriage service to menace, harass or cause offence) can you advise of what action you will take?*

4. *What next step do you suggest I should take?*

Can you please respond ASAP?

Regards

Shane Dowling

I find it very disturbing that the Crown Solicitor Ms Lea Armstrong has not responded to the above email complaint and I would like you to investigate the threatening phone call.

The suppression orders

The suppression orders are invalid as they impede my constitutional right to political speech. The judges who issued the suppression orders would know this as it is a well-known precedent: Coleman v Power (High Court of Australia 2004). In the precedent, Coleman was handing out flyers alleging police corruption and called the police corrupt and slimy lying bastards. One of the police he alleged was corrupt (Power) arrested Coleman and charged him with using "insulting words" under the Vagrancy Act. Coleman was found guilty but when it ultimately went to the High Court the "Vagrancy Act" was found to be invalid in the situation. The High Court found talking about police corruption is political speech and laws cannot restrict political speech as it is a person's constitutional right. The High Court also found talking about any government corruption including judicial corruption was political speech and protected.

The point is, in my matter the judges and people prosecuting the matter would know the Coleman v Power precedent makes the suppression orders invalid and are trying to cover the whole matter up from public scrutiny with invalid suppression orders.

The court has also failed to bring in an interstate judge to hear the matter that is required when the conduct of a judge is under question, which it clearly is in this matter given the charges against me. This is another part of their attempt to cover the matter up.

I have a lot more detailed evidence and await the opportunity to give a full statement to any investigating officer.

Regards

Shane Dowling

Sending the complaint is a start. I'll keep on following up. People ask me what they can do to help. Well, feel free to send a complaint yourself to the AFP at the above email addresses as they are public servants and are meant to work for us and every voice counts.

End of article

Chapter 11

Filing and serving a Notice of a Constitutional matter

This chapter is a bit technical but put simply I basically argued I had a constitutional defence to what they claimed I said in court and which they claim was a contempt of court.

I denied the allegation but certainly said it on my website, and it is still there to this day and they have never asked me to take it down as there is no legal basis to do so.

Justice Helen Wilson issued orders a few days after the hearing on the 4th of May 2017 ordering me to file a serve a Notice of a Constitutional matter and I published an article on the 11th of June 2017 titled "Blogger charged with contempt ordered to serve Attorney-Generals with Notice of a Constitutional Matter" as per below.

Blogger charged with contempt ordered to serve Attorney-Generals with Notice of a Constitutional Matter

The pursuit of me by the Supreme Court of NSW for contempt has stepped up a notch with the court ordering me to serve all Australian Attorney-Generals with a Notice of a Constitutional Matter pursuant to section 78B of the Judiciary Act 1903.

This article is an update as to where the proceedings are at and also to drive home that the suppression orders put on the matter should never have been issued.

I was charged for contempt for allegedly calling a Justice Clifton Hoeben a paedophile and Registrar Christopher Bradford a paedophile and a bribe-taker in court on the 3rd of February 2017. I have pleaded not guilty and deny the allegations against me.

I have used numerous precedents in my defence but the main one is Lange v ABC 1997 (HCA). (Click here to read more) The bottom line to the Lange v ABC High Court of Australia precedent is that laws that infringe on political communication are invalid. Political communication includes political corruption and also includes communication regarding government employees and judges are government employees.

The prosecution in effect argued in court that judges are above the law and what is said in court is not covered by the freedom of political communication as per Lange v ABC 1997 (HCA).

Put simply my defence is: 1. I didn't say what they claim. 2. What I did say is protected by the implied freedom of political communication in the Australian Constitution. and 3. Even if I did say what they claim I would also be protected by the implied freedom of political communication in the Australian constitution.

The hearing for contempt was heard on the 4th of May and with further time allowed to file and serve further written submissions the matter has dragged on until this point. Now I have served the Attorney-Generals it could possibly be drawn out another month or two depending on a number of variables. (Click here to read my further submissions) and (Click here to read the further submissions of prosecution)

I regard this as a positive step whether or not the Attorney-General's intervene as it shows that there should never have been a suppression order given it is now confirmed there is a political argument to be had and laws that infringe on political communication are invalid.

Background

I have written about this a number of times and if you are new to this story, you can read the background by clicking on the below links to previous articles:

Chief Justice Bathurst has journalist charged with contempt for accusing him of corruption – 5/2/2017

Free speech and political speech is being suppressed in Australia by the NSW Supreme Court – 8/4/2017

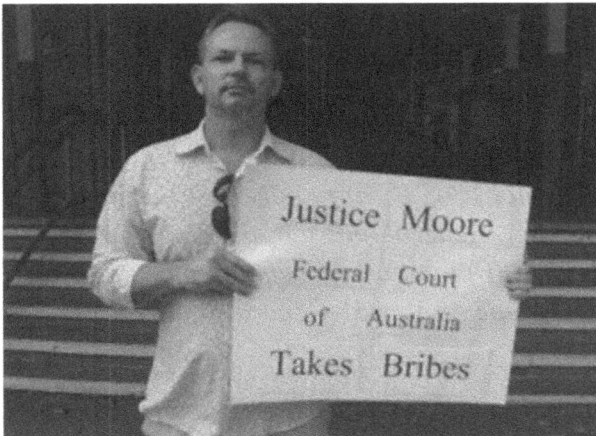

The above photo was taken in 2008 and is on the front of my book "Love Letter from the Bar Table" Justice Michael Moore was made aware of the photo as I filed it as part of an affidavit. He never charged me with contempt or even threatened to. So why am I now being charged for saying that Registrar Christopher Bradford takes bribes?

Neither Clifton Hoeben or Registrar Christopher Bradford have filed an affidavit in the case nor have they denied the allegations that they say I made. They have also not charged me or complained about the allegations I made against them in an article last year titled "*Paedophile priest gets 3 months jail for raping 3 boys by NSW Supreme Court's Justice Hoeben*" even though I wrote to them and let them know I would be publishing the allegations. So, I take it they confirm that the allegations in the article is true and correct.

JUDICIARY ACT 1903 – SECT 78B – Notice to Attorneys-General (Click here to read more)

The below quote is on the Australian Government Solicitor's website and explains how a Notice of a Constitutional matter works:

The Australian Government can become involved in constitutional litigation in either of 2 ways. First, the Government may be a party in its own right, where proceedings have been commenced by or against it. Second, the Commonwealth Attorney-General has a right to intervene on behalf of the Government in cases raising constitutional issues.

The Judiciary Act 1903 (Cth) requires parties in such cases to give the Attorney-General notice of the constitutional issues (under section 78B) to allow a decision to be made on intervention by each Attorney-General (under section 78A).

In relation to possible interventions, AGS's role includes considering notices given under the Judiciary Act and, in consultation with the Commonwealth Solicitor-General and other interested agencies, advising the AGD on whether the Attorney-General should intervene. This year AGS reviewed 259 notices given under s 78B of cases raising constitutional law issues.

The Attorney-General intervened under s 78A at the hearing of 9 cases in the High Court and 1 case in each of the Family Court, Victorian Supreme Court and Western Australian Court of Appeal and was a respondent to an appeal to the High Court where he had intervened in the court below.

AGS also advises the Australian Government on all submissions on constitutional law issues that are put to courts on behalf of Commonwealth agencies. This is to ensure that these submissions are accurate and apply Commonwealth constitutional policy consistently. (Click here to read more)

Responses from the Attorney-Generals

Justice Helen Wilson issued orders giving me until the 7th of June to serve the State and Federal Attorney-General's the section 78B Notice of a Constitutional Matter. (Click here to see the Notice of a constitutional Matter that I sent to the A-Gs) The Federal Government have responded as per the below letter:

AGS

Australian Government Solicitor
4 National Circuit, Barton ACT 2600
Locked Bag 35, Kingston ACT 2604
T 02 6253 7000 DX 5678 Canberra
www.ags.gov.au

Canberra
Sydney
Melbourne
Brisbane
Perth
Adelaide
Hobart
Darwin

9 June 2017

Mr Shane Dowling

By email: shanedowling@outlook.com.au

Dear Mr Dowling

PROTHONATARY OF SC OF NSW v DOWLING, Shane – NSWSC – CLU – 78B

We act for the Commonwealth Attorney-General and acknowledge receipt of your letter dated 9 June 2017 giving him notice pursuant to s 78B of the *Judiciary Act 1903* of a constitutional issue in the above proceeding.

We will write to you again when a decision has been made on the question of intervention.

Yours sincerely

Australian Government Solicitor

And the Queensland government responded saying that they will not intervene at the moment but if it gets to the High Court of Australia, they will reconsider intervening. (Click here to read the QLD Government's letter)

At this point, the other States and Territories have not made a decision about intervening.

Issues raised by the Notice of a Constitutional Matter

The constitutional questions raised in my case and my viewpoints are:

1. Is what is said in court protected by the freedom of communication on matters of government and politics as per Lange v ABC (1997) HCA?

A. Yes. As per Lange v ABC (1997) HCA and Nationwide News Pty. Limited v. Wills [1992] HCA 46; (1992) etc.

2. Is criticism and/or allegations of corruption against Judicial officers protected by the freedom of communication on matters of government and politics as per Lange v ABC (1997) HCA?

A. Yes. As per Lange v ABC (1997) HCA, Nationwide News Pty. Limited v. Wills [1992] HCA 46; (1992), Theophanous v Herald & Weekly Times Ltd (1994) 182 and Coleman v Power [2004] HCA 39; 220 etc.

3. Are suppression orders issued by a court invalid if they infringe on the freedom of communication on matters of government and politics as per Lange v ABC (1997)?

A. Yes. As per Lange v ABC (1997) HCA, John Fairfax Publications Pty Limited v the Attorney General for New South Wales [2000] NSWCA 198 and Nationwide News Pty. Limited v. Wills [1992] HCA 46; (1992) etc.

4. Are proceedings for contempt invalid if they infringe on the freedom of communication on matters of government and politics as per Lange v ABC (1997)?

A. Yes. As per Lange v ABC (1997) HCA, John Fairfax Publications Pty Limited v the Attorney General for New South Wales [2000] NSWCA 198 and Nationwide News Pty. Limited v. Wills [1992] HCA 46; (1992) etc.

Confirmation that there should have never been a suppression order on the matter

The High Court of Australia has handed down numerous precedents making it very clear that any laws that infringe on political communication are invalid.

So, the question that needs to be asked when deciding if there should or shouldn't be suppression orders on this matter are: Is what is being argued in the case a political issue? The answer is blatantly yes because the court has ordered me to serve all the Attorney-Generals with the section 78B Notice of a Constitutional Matter and any argument regarding the constitution is political. And the prosecution agreed that I should serve the notice, so they are not disputing it is a political matter.

The suppression orders say I can't repeat what I said in court and I can't name the judges and registrar which I have done in this article and the previous articles and that has resulted in another charge for contempt. Yep, another contempt charge for me breaching a suppression order that should not have been issued because it infringes my freedom of political communication which for example is doing nothing more than letting the followers and readers of this website know about the corruption that is happening in court.

Why the Attorney-Generals should intervene

All the Attorney-Generals should intervene given it is a case involving judges of a court prosecuting their own case and putting a suppression order on it to protect their names and trying to conceal what happened which is a national scandal. What the judges don't like is me calling them out for being the criminals they are. And they are too scared to sue me for defamation because they would lose or even if they won their reputations would be destroyed as the public would see that they are not fit to be judges.

The Attorney-Generals should also intervene because new media like this website and social media are not scared of reporting judicial corruption as the old media are so the judges are trying to intimidate new media in an attempt to conceal judicial corruption. This has to be stopped.

Ultimately this case needs to end up in the High Court to give it a final resolution because it has the potential to have a far-reaching impact. If judicial corruption and what is said in court is determined to be outside the protection of the implied freedom of political communication in the constitution, then who and what else is also outside the law?

End of article

Chapter 12

Police raid and being charged by the NSW Police for the federal crime of "using a carriage service to menace, harass or cause offence"

As soon as I sent the email on the 6th of September 2016, which is in the introduction of the book, the Supreme Court of NSW staff made a complaint to the NSW Police on the instructions of Chief Justice Tom Bathurst but I didn't know that at the time. I was charged by the police in June 2017 for sending the email, but it wasn't until December 2017 that I found out all the details of what had been happening behind the scenes. In the next few chapters, I will explain why it took me so long to find out that the court was trying to stitch me up for some jail time, but for this chapter, I'll focus on what happened.

I know what happened behind the scenes after I sent the email because when the NSW police did eventually charge me, I received a brief of evidence a few months afterwards. The brief of evidence was gold as it helped my case is a big way, but the charge was discontinued later by the Commonwealth Director of Public Prosecutions.

Below is the article I published on the 16th of December 2017 titled "Chief Justice Tom Bathurst behind judicial paedophile and bribery cover-up evidence shows" which was just after I got out of jail after doing the 4 months jail for breaching the suppression orders in the Jane Doe matter.

Chief Justice Tom Bathurst behind judicial paedophile and bribery cover-up evidence shows

Court evidence filed by NSW Police has the witness statement of NSW Supreme Court registrar Chris D'Aeth which shows Chief Justice Tom Bathurst has conspired with others since September 2016 trying to jail journalist Shane Dowling for making judicial paedophile and bribery allegations against 15 judges, including Bathurst, in an article he published in September 2016. The article is titled "*Paedophile priest gets 3 months jail for raping 3 boys by NSW Supreme Court's Justice Hoeben*" and also part of the police's brief of evidence. (Click here to read more)

It was not until over 9 months later in June 2017 that Shane Dowling was charged by NSW police for an email sent to the judges giving them an opportunity to respond to the allegations before he published the article. The email is part of the article.

The brief of evidence tendered to the court has the below witness statement of Chris D'Aeth and at paragraph 10 he talks about Chief Justice Bathurst's involvement and the subsequent referral to the Commonwealth Director of Public Prosecutions in September 2016. As Tom Bathurst is the Chief Justice it would have been his decision to refer the matter to the CDPP.

Based on the statement of Chris D'Aeth, and what I know, the CDPP decided to take no action except to refer it to the Federal Police who also decided to take no action. It is only after 2 further complaints to the NSW Police (February then either May or June 2017) did they act.

The NSW police were trying to prosecute the matter but given it is a federal offence that potentially has a jail term over 12 months the Magistrate took it out of the police's hands and said the CDPP has to prosecute the matter. The police didn't seem to be happy about them losing control, but I was.

The allegations have gone unchallenged by all of the judges named by Mr Dowling in the article, but Registrar Rebel Kenna did ultimately make a retaliatory complaint which led to the police charge.

What is very disturbing is that while Chief Justice Tom Bathurst was secretly trying to have Shane Dowling jailed Mr Dowling was jailed for 4 months by Chief Justice Tom Bathurst's Supreme Court in an unrelated freedom of speech matter.

The judge who jailed Mr Dowling, Justice Ian Harrison who is also named in the email and article, said at the hearing in February 2017 that Mr Dowling wouldn't be going to jail but when he sentenced Mr Dowling in August 2017 he gave Mr Dowling 4 months jail. Did Chief Justice Tom Bathurst intervene?

Perceived bias

Whether Tom Bathurst intervened is not something that needs to be proved to determine perceived bias and did Mr Dowling get a fair hearing and would Mr Dowling ever get a fair hearing in the future in the NSW Supreme Court given Chief Justice Tom Bathurst's continued attempts to have Mr Dowling jailed

The court shouldn't be dealing with any matters involving Shane Dowling (me) anymore and certainly shouldn't be sending Mr Dowling to jail.

Paedophile judges

There is no doubt there is a bribery racket in the NSW courts and a paedophile ring/protection racket. In the last few weeks alone Sydney magistrate Graeme Curran has been charged with historic child sex offences (Click here to read more) and District Court Judge John North gave a paedophile a suspended sentence and protected him by suppressing his name. (Click here to read more) Justice North needs to be sacked then fully investigated.

Kerry Stokes' involvement

Seven West Media's lawyers have been working overtime trying to get access to the police evidence. One has to assume that Seven's owner Kerry Stokes is worried there is evidence in the police file that he is involved in the judicial bribery and/or paedophile ring as I have written numerous articles accusing him of judicial bribery which he has never denied.

The police witness statement of Chris D'Aeth, CEO and Principal Registrar of the Supreme Court of NSW, is below.

STATEMENT OF A WITNESS

In the matter of:	Threatening email
Place:	Day Street Police station
Date:	02/02/2017

Name:	Chris D'Aeth

STATES:

1. This statement made by me accurately sets out the evidence that I would be prepared, if necessary, to give in court as a witness. The statement is true to the best of my knowledge and belief and I make it knowing that, if it is tendered in evidence, I will be liable to prosecution if I have wilfully stated in it anything that I know to be false, or do not believe to be true.

2. I am 41 years of age.

3. I am the executive director and principal Registrar for the Supreme Court of New South Wales. I have been performing this role within the Supreme Court in Sydney since October 2015.

4. My duties include primarily administration of court processes, liaison with Judicial officers and the department of Justice.

5. On the 6th September 2016 I was forwarded an email from Rebel KENNA – Prothonotary of the Supreme Court of New South Wakes. This email was titled 'FW: Paedophile Judge list to be sent to the AFP, Australian Crime Commission , NSW Crime Commission, and Royal Commission into Child Abuse for Investigation.

6. I read this this email and I thought it was deeply offensive to the persons listed within the email. I note the email to was addressed to Judges and registrars of the Supreme Court.

7. The email contained information regarding the recipients being either known or suspected paedophiles. I noted that the email was sent from Shanedowling@hotmail.com. I recognised the name Shane Dowling from the courts, he has emailed the courts on previous occasions. I was also aware of a website he controls called Kangaroo Court of Australia. I am aware that

Witness:		Signature:	
Name:	David COLLARD	Name:	Chris D'AETH
Date:	02/02/2017	Date:	02/02/2017

this webpage contains information about the courts and judicial registrars. It is a blog that he runs and controls.

8. On the 8th September 2016 I forwarded this email to Jillian CALDWELL – Special Counsel for the Crown Solicitor. Contained within the email to Jillian I wrote to her requesting the email be reviewed and advice on steps forward. I have since forwarded this email trail to Detective Senior Constable Kristian JURIC of Sydney City Local Area Command.

9. On the 20th September 2016, I received and email reply from Julian Caldwell. This email was sent with an attachment which was a 21 page document regarding advice regarding the email from Shane Dowling.

10. On the morning of the 21st September 2016, I discussed the advice given by Jillian with Chief Justice , The Honourable Tom Bathurst AC. After this discussion I sent Jillian another email requesting that the matter be sent to the commonwealth DPP for consideration.

11. Jillian replied to this email, After this I am aware that Jillian wrote to the Commonwealth DPP regarding this matter. The email trails regarding our conversation have been forwarded to Detective Kristian JURIC.

12. On the 26th September 2016, I received an email from Jillian, attached was a letter from the Commonwealth DPP indicating the matter had been referred to the AFP for further investigation. I have forwarded this email and attachment to Detective JURIC.

13. I PROUCE EMAILS SENT TO JILLIAN CALDWELL.

David Collard
2/2/17.

CHRIS D'AETH
2/ /17

The police and CDPP have failed twice to file and serve a full brief of evidence and things such as other witness statements, interview transcript and the emails referred to above at paragraph 13 etc are still missing. The CDPP now have until January 16, 2018, to file all their evidence and the matter is set down for hearing on the 28th March 2018.

When the matter was in court on the 12th December 2017 the CDPP wanted a 6-week adjournment to "consider the charge". The magistrate said no. I think they are working in with the Supreme Court and up to some dirty tricks. They should do the right thing and withdraw the charge.

I have no doubt that the reason the CDPP and Federal Police never took action in 2016 is because they had legal advice that I had not breached any laws which makes it hard for them to follow through now.

End of article

Below is the article I published on the 24th of March 2018 titled "Big freedom of speech / political communication win with CDPP to drop criminal charges against journalist Shane Dowling" which was a few days after I received a letter from the Commonwealth Director of Public Prosecutions (CDPP) notifying me the charge would be discontinued and below that is the follow-up article.

Big freedom of speech / political communication win with CDPP to drop criminal charges against journalist Shane Dowling

Trumped-up criminal charges of using a carriage service to menace, harass or cause offence, in relation to an email I sent in 2016 will be dropped against journalist Shane Dowling (me) the Commonwealth Director of Public Prosecutions (CDPP) has announced. This is a huge win for free speech and political communication.

The (CDPP) advised me on Wednesday (21/3/18) at 5.26pm that they will be withdrawing the criminal charges against me in relation to the email that I sent to the Supreme Court accusing judicial officers of being known paedophiles or suspected paedophiles and raising judicial bribery allegations. It was a trumped-up charge that police statements by court staff show was being driven by Chief Justice Tom Bathurst.

Bloggers are jailed around the world for standing up for freedom of speech which I personally experienced last year and the authorities were trying to line me up for more jail time with this beat-up charge.

The withdrawal of the charge is the conclusion to the article I posted a few days ago titled "NSW Chief Magistrate Judge Graeme Henson protects his paedophile mate Chief Justice Tom Bathurst and 17 others" which related to the Local Court refusing my subpoenas for witnesses and documents and an application for an interstate Magistrate to hear the matter.

I wrote in the previous article:

The NSW police charged me in June 2017 for an email that I sent in September 2016 accusing 16 Judicial Officers and 2 Registrars of being known paedophiles or suspected paedophiles and raising the $2.2 million Mafia bribe of NSW judges.

The email in question shows up in an article I published last year titled *"Paedophile priest gets 3 months jail for raping 3 boys by NSW Supreme Court's Justice Hoeben"* and the article was also filed in court on the 4th of May as part of my defence.

Late last year (2017) evidence came to hand via a police statement of CEO and Principal Registrar of the Supreme Court of NSW Chris D'Aeth that Chief Justice Tom Bathurst was the driving force to have me charged and jailed and I wrote an article titled: *"Chief Justice Tom Bathurst behind judicial paedophile and bribery cover-up evidence shows"* (Click here to read the article)

Legal Aid

Legal Aid did pay for lawyers to represent me, but they did absolutely nothing, so I went back to representing myself which ended up being the right move. But that's a story in itself which I will cover another time.

Below is the letter that was emailed to me by the CDPP Wednesday afternoon.

CDPP

Australia's Federal Prosecution Service

Commonwealth Director
of Public Prosecutions

Locked Bag A4020, Sydney South
1235
Level 10, 175 Liverpool Street
Sydney NSW 2000
DX 11497, SYDNEY DOWNTOWN

Telephone **(02) 9321 1100**
Facsimile (02) 9264 8241
www.cdpp.gov.au

Your Reference:

Our Reference: SC17100331

21 March 2018

By Email: shanedowling@outlook.com

Shane Francis Dowling
Unit 7/4 Park Parade
BONDI NSW 2026

Dear Mr. Dowling

Matter of Shane Francis DOWLING
Local Court Proceedings 2017/186138

I refer to the above matter which is listed for hearing on 28 March 2018.

I advise that this Office has considered the brief of evidence in accordance with the *Prosecution Policy of the Commonwealth*. A decision has been made to discontinue the charge against you.

When the matter is called for mention on 28 March 2018, a prosecutor from this office will appear to have the proceedings formally discontinued.

A copy of this correspondence has been provided to the Registry of the Downing Centre Local Court.

Yours faithfully

Andrew Doyle
Assistant Director
Illegal Imports and Exports
and Human Exploitation and Border Protection

cc: Downing Centre Local Court Registry
        dclc@justice.nsw.gov.au

The letter says the proceedings will be formally discontinued on Wednesday the 28th of March. You can read the Prosecution

Policy of the Commonwealth by clicking here. How sending an email is part of the Illegal Imports and Exports and Human Exploitation and Border Protection is beyond me. The actual charge was breaching the *Criminal Code Act 1995* section 474.17 — using a carriage service to menace, harass or cause offence.

If I had been found guilty every journalist in the country who has sent criminal allegations to people giving them an opportunity to respond before they published would have been in trouble. Giving someone an opportunity to respond before publishing is important for a defence in any possible defamation claim. (See Lange v ABC, High Court 1997)

An example would be Fairfax journalist Kate McClymont who has written about jailed former politician Eddie Obeid and helped put him in jail. In 2006 Eddie Obeid sued Fairfax and Kate McClymont for defamation and won. If Obeid could have charged McClymont for using a carriage service to menace, harass or cause offence he would have and if I had been convicted then criminals in the future would charge journalists.

Another example is the recent book by ABC journalist Louise Milligan, The Rise and Fall of Cardinal George Pell. The book makes claims that George Pell abused children, which if true would mean he is a paedophile. Louise Milligan or her publishers would have sent the claims to George Pell first and given him the opportunity to respond, otherwise, they would leave themselves open to defamation claims. Once again if Pell could have charged Milligan for using a carriage service to menace, harass or cause offence he would have.

Free speech and political communication

The case against me was futile from the start and there are clear precedents that showed what I said in the email was political communication because I raised issues of government corruption which is protected by the Australian constitution. (See Lange v ABC, High Court 1997)

How much taxpayer's money was wasted and what will the repercussions be for those involved in the stitch-up?

Chief Justice Tom Bathurst is meant to be an expert in the law, and he knew all along he was conspiring to have an innocent person charged and jailed. He has been trying to have me jailed since at least September 2016 and I have no doubt he was involved in having me jailed last year for 4 months.

The charges won't be formally discontinued until Wednesday so not much will happen until after then. But I suspect there would be some worried people because I will be doing everything possible to make sure someone is held to account.

I have also been found guilty for contempt for something else I said in court in February 2017 and breaching suppression orders they put on it, but I cannot say much as there are bail conditions that mean if I breach the suppression orders again I'll go back to jail. I am due to be sentenced on the 6th of April 2018 but that might change as I am trying to have the suppression orders reviewed first. Once again, I have no doubt that Chief Justice Bathurst is the driving force behind it.

The question that needs to be answered is how much of taxpayer's money has been wasted by Chief Justice Tom Bathurst trying to stitch me up for jail time. The dodgy attempt to jail me has involved the NSW police investigation and raid on my unit, the Federal police, numerous Supreme Court staff, staff from the NSW Crown Solicitors Office and the Commonwealth Director of Public Prosecutions and the Local Court staff as well as Legal Aid people who represented me etc. The cost of Chief Justice Bathurst's and the NSW Supreme Court's "get Shane Dowling" obsession has cost taxpayers at least $200,000 would be my guess and the number is still climbing. And then there is the reputational damage which will only start to be felt now the charges are to be withdrawn.

It's only a battle in the war, but it is a good battle to have won. Everyone who has supported this website can take some credit for having the charges dismissed, so thanks for that.

End of Article

Below is the article I published on the 2nd of April 2018 titled "CDPP formally drop criminal charges against journalist Shane Dowling in free speech case" when the police charge was formally dropped in court.

CDPP formally drop criminal charges against journalist Shane Dowling in free speech case

Criminal charges against me for an email I sent as a journalist to all the NSW Supreme Court judges raising allegations of judicial paedophilia and bribery in September 2016 were formally dropped by the Commonwealth Director of Public Prosecutions (CDPP) on Wednesday (28-3-18) at the Downing Centre Local Court in Sydney. I can now reveal the extent of the beat-up charge with the dodgy witness statements that suggest backdated police statements, lies by those involved and a conspiracy to have me falsely charged.

It was a clear-cut case of a conspiracy to have someone falsely charged based on the prosecutions own evidence where the NSW Police were told by the Federal Police and CDPP in late 2016 / January 2017 that no crime had been committed yet the NSW Police eventually charged me anyhow under pressure from Chief Justice Tom Bathurst.

But their plan came unstuck when the police prosecutor was told by a Magistrate in the Sydney Local Court in September 2017 that the CDPP would have to take over the matter and the Magistrate quoted a Supreme Court precedent ruling that federal laws that are indictable offences need to be prosecuted by the CDPP. That is the reason the charge was withdrawn as the CDPP could not go back on their original advice that no crime had been committed.

Out of the 18 judicial officers that I named as being paedophiles and suspected paedophiles only one ever gave a police statement and that was the lowest ranking person in Registrar Rebel Kenna. Her police statement was dated 6 months after I sent the email and six months after the initial police complaint. So, what took them so long?

The withdrawal of the charge only leaves 2 possibilities, and that is what I said in the email in 2016 is true or at least partly true or what I said in the email is political communication which invalidates all other laws as outlined in the 1997 High Court precedent Lange v ABC. Whatever the case the NSW Police who charged me and Chief Justice Tom Bathurst who pushed to have me charged knew that they were breaking the law when I was charged as no crime had been committed.

In this article, I'll focus on the timeline of who knew what and when and some of the lies which raise many questions. This is a follow-up article to last week's post (Click here to read).

Background

I have written numerous emails to the court making allegations of judicial paedophilia and bribe-taking and they never complained, so why did the 6th of September 2016 email rattle them so much? A couple of examples of previous emails are:

26th November 2015 – I sent an email to Chief Justice Tom Bathurst and Attorney-General Gabrielle Upton regarding a criminal investigation that I was conducting relating to a judicial paedophile ring and bribery ring. The email was also sent to all judges of the NSW Supreme Court, AFP Commissioner Andrew Colvin and ICAC etc. (Click here to read the email) The email started:

"Dear Chief Justice Tom Bathurst and Attorney-General Gabrielle Upton I am currently conducting a criminal investigation into the bribing of NSW judges and a judicial paedophile ring. The bribes have come from the Mafia, Kerry

Stokes, Ryan Stokes and others. One known paedophile, Judge Garry Neilson, has received protection from the Judicial Commission of NSW which is headed up by you Mr Bathurst." (Click here to read the email)

19th August 2016 – I sent an email to Registrar Bradford letting him know that I would be publishing an article accusing him of taking bribes from Kerry Stokes. (Click here to read the email) (Click here to read the article)

The timeline of events as outlined in the witness statements.

The most interesting thing about the timeline and police statements is the fact that Chief Justice Tom Bathurst went police shopping to find someone who would charge me when he had obviously been told that the CDPP and Federal Police wouldn't charge me because no crime had been committed.

6th September 2016 – Tuesday – 11.35pm – I sent an email to NSW Supreme Court judges accusing 18 judicial officers of being paedophiles or suspected paedophiles and raising issues of bribery: The email started off:

"I am writing to you all regarding the list of paedophile judges that I intended on making a formal complaint about to the AFP, Australian Crime Commission, NSW Crime Commission and Royal Commission into Child Sexual Abuse. The list is below."

"As we all know corruption in the NSW Courts is widespread and systemic. In July 2015 Fairfax Media and the ABC's Four Corners program reported that NSW judges had been bribed $2.2 million by the Mafia which was confirmed by Justice David Davies in December 2015. Maybe you have evidence that the above judges have also benefited from the Mafia bribes or other bribes. If you have evidence of judicial bribery, please contact me ASAP." (Click here to read more)

6th of September 2016 – (Source: Chris D'Aeth police statement) Registrar Rebel Kenna forwarded my email to Chris

D'Aeth, CEO and Principal Registrar of the Supreme Court of NSW. This seems odd as I sent the email at 11.35pm so it's hard to see Rebel Kenna checking her email that late at night and then forwarding it on. Maybe it just a mistake by Chris D'Aeth.

8th September 2016 – I published an article titled "Paedophile priest gets 3 months jail for raping 3 boys by NSW Supreme Court's Justice Hoeben" which included a copy of the email from the 6th of September.

8th September 2016 – (Source: Chris D'Aeth police statement) Chris D'Aeth forwarded my email from the 6th September to Jillian Caldwell, Special Counsel for the Crown Solicitor asking for advice.

8th of September 2016 – (Source: Detective Kristijan Juric police statement paragraph 4) Detective Senior Sergeant Day handed a report from the NSW Crown Solicitors Office to Detective Kristijan Juric regarding an alleged telecommunications offence in relation to the email I sent.

Detective Kristijan Juric makes no mention of the CDPP who the matter was later sent to by Chris D'Aeth via his instruction to Jillian Caldwell. Detective Kristijan Juric also fails to mention the AFP which the CDPP forwarded the matter too.

Detective Juric's statement jumps from a complaint on the 8th of September 2016 at paragraph 4 to paragraph 6 where he says:

"6. During my subsequent enquiries I contacted the Crown Solicitors Office of NSW to obtain contact details of persons named in the email and article. As result of these enquires on the 8th of March 2017, Rebel Kenna attended Sydney City Police Station and supplied a statement."

So, what did Detective Juric do from the 8th of September 2016 until the Kenna witness statement on the 8th March 2017? Did he contact the 17 others on the list and why didn't they give police statements? It makes no sense why a complaint was made to the

CDPP and Federal Police only days after the complaint was handed to NSW Police Officer Detective Kristijan Juric.

What might make sense is if the complaint was made first to the NSW Police and they said it was a federal crime and needed to go to the CDPP or AFP. Then the CDPP and AFP made a decision that no crime had been committed and then the NSW Police were pressured into charging me because the CDPP and AFP refused to do so. But only one of the 18 named as paedophiles and suspected paedophiles, Rebel Kenna, would make a complaint. I think it is likely that Rebel Kenna was pressured to make a complaint.

During my arrest, Detective Kristijan Juric said I could face other charges when they contact the others named in my email. Which means from the 8th of September 2016 until the 21st of June 2017 they had not contacted anyone else named in the email with the obvious question of why not.

9th of September 2016 – I was in court for a mention before Registrar Christopher Bradford. I asked Bradford to stand down given I had published on the internet that he is a suspected paedophile and known bribe-taker which I recorded on video. Registrar Bradford refused to stand down. (Click here to watch the video)

20th September 2016 – (Source: Chris D'Aeth police statement) Chris D'Aeth receives an email with a 21-page document attached from Jillian Caldwell giving advice regarding the email.

21st September 2016 – (Source: Chris D'Aeth police statement) Chris D'Aeth discusses advice given by Jillian Caldwell with Chief Justice Tom Bathurst. After the discussion, Chris D'Aeth sends Jillian Caldwell an email asking that the matter be sent to the CDPP for consideration.

26th September 2016 – (Source: Chris D'Aeth police statement) Chris D'Aeth receives an email from Jillian Caldwell saying she had been emailed by the CDPP and they had referred the matter to the Australian Federal Police for further investigation. I never heard from the AFP or the CDPP.

2nd February 2017 – (Source: Chris D'Aeth police statement) Chris D'Aeth writes a witness statement for the NSW Police. The fact that the NSW Police were back involved must mean the AFP and the CDPP had refused to charge me with any crime.

3rd February 2017 – At court on Friday the 3rd of February 2017 I said something in court and was later charged and found guilty for contempt and for breaching suppression orders that were put on the matter. The contempt matter was heard on the 4th of May 2017. I can't say what for as there are suppression orders on it and one of my bail conditions while I wait for sentencing is that I cannot breach the suppression orders again.

8th March 2017 – (Source: Rebel Kenna police statement 8-3-17) Rebel Kenna makes a police statement.

4th May 2017 – The hearing for the contempt was held before Justice Helen Wilson. I was later ordered to serve all Attorney-Generals a Notice of a Constitutional Matter.

One of my key arguments was that I had emailed the court in September 2016 accusing 18 judicial officers of being paedophiles or suspected paedophiles and raised bribery allegations but none of them had complained and I had also published the email in an article in September 2016 and they hadn't complained about that either.

21st June 2017 – I was charged by the NSW police for breaching telecommunications laws for the email that I sent in September 2016 to all the judges of the NSW Supreme Court asking questions and giving them an opportunity to respond to allegations which is nothing more than journalists do around the world every day of the week. The police executed a search warrant on my unit while I was at work and took my computer and the spare one I had which the police said they would give back in about 10 days which forced me to buy a new one. I went to the police station after work and was charged.

I thought the police charge was clearly related to me raising the fact that they had not complained about the email in court on the 4th of May during my defence for contempt. The police said that they had received a complaint from the Crown Solicitors Office which I remember as taking that they received a complaint from the CEO Leah Armstrong who at that stage had carriage of my case. Lea Armstrong stood down from having day-to-day carriage after the police charge.

The arresting police officer made a number of statements that seemed odd. He said that the area of law that I had been charged with was "unsettled". In other words, he was unsure whether or not I should have been charged. The police fact sheet says I make "derogatory and defamatory comments about people on my website". How would the police know? I have never been found guilty of defamation.

Conspiracy to have someone falsely charged:

CRIMES ACT 1914 – SECT 41

Conspiracy to bring false accusation

(1) A person commits an offence if:

(a) the person conspires with another person:

(i) to charge any person falsely with an offence; or

(ii) to cause any person to be falsely charged with an offence; and

(b) the offence referred to in paragraph (a) is an offence against a law of:

(i) the Commonwealth; or

(ii) a Territory. (Click here to read more)

I was charged with "using a carriage service to menace, harass or cause offence," which is a Commonwealth offence and is contained in section 474.17 the Criminal Code Act 1995. (Click here to read more)

The fact that the charge was withdrawn raises the obvious question of why I was charged in the first place. Only one complainant out of 18 when the police said they would be approaching the others. That in itself says I should not have been charged.

When looking at the facts of the matter it is easy to see why the AFP and the CDPP refused to charge me in the first place and why the CDPP withdrew the charge. Everything the NSW police did was dodgy.

The witness statements:

Detective Senior Constable Kristijan Juric – (Click here to read his witness statement)

Why did Detective Kristijan Juric do nothing from the 8th September 2016 when he first received the complaint until March the 8th 2017 when he took a witness statement from Rebel Kenna? Why did he wait until the 21st June to raid my unit and arrest me especially given Rebel Kenna claims she was concerned for her safety after I sent the email on the 6th of September 2016?

Chris D'Aeth – CEO and Principal Registrar of the Supreme Court of NSW – (Click here to read his witness statement)

I wrote an article last year titled: "*Chief Justice Tom Bathurst behind judicial paedophile and bribery cover-up evidence shows*" which starts off:

Court evidence filed by NSW Police has the witness statement of NSW Supreme Court registrar Chris D'Aeth which shows Chief Justice Tom Bathurst has conspired with others since September 2016 trying to jail journalist Shane Dowling for making judicial paedophile and bribery allegations against 15 judges, including Bathurst, in an article he published in September 2016. The article is titled "Paedophile priest gets 3 months jail for raping 3 boys by NSW Supreme Court's Justice Hoeben" and is also part of the police's brief of evidence. (Click here to read more)

Registrar Rebel Kenna – Prothonotary of the NSW Supreme Court – (Click here to read her witness statement)

The contempt that Rebel Kenna and the others have for the law is amazing when they are meant to be the ones enforcing it. The bail conditions that I had told a story in themselves. (Click here to see the bail conditions for the police charge)

Condition 4 was: "The defendant not assault, molest, harass, threaten or otherwise interfere with Rebel Kenna, or with a person with whom she has a domestic relationship". I have never threatened her nor was I ever going to so that condition is a bad joke. I don't know for sure, but I get the impression that is a standard type of bail condition when someone has made a complaint against you.

But Kenna's affidavit doesn't stack up especially at paragraphs 4, 7 and 8.

At paragraph 4 she says my conduct was so bad one day she had to have me removed by a court sheriff. What she doesn't say it that is the day I complained I was assaulted by her and the court sheriff and if I was so bad why did she allow me back in the court and why didn't she transfer the matter to another registrar or duty judge as I requested?

At paragraph 7 Kenna says she was so scared that she has *"amended how I travel to and from work in case Dowling is watching me"* and that she checks the court lists to see if I have a matter listed so she can avoid going outside or near the court and *"I have even taken my name off the electoral roll so that my residential address is more difficult to find"*. What total dribble.

If Kenna was so worried about me why did she wait from when I sent the email on the 6th of September 2016 until the 8th of March 2017 to make a statement to the police? Why did the police wait from the 6/9/16 until the 21st June 2017 to charge me if Kenna was so worried about her safety? Why didn't they contact me earlier and take out a restraining order of some type?

Rebel Kenna is a compulsive liar which her police statement shows. What Kenna might be worried about is if I saw her I might start asking her questions while recording it with my mobile phone which I have done many times before to others such as barrister Sandy Dawson and lawyer Richard Keegan etc. And then published it on the internet.

At paragraph 8 Kenna tries to make out I am stalking her. She says that she is aware that I have been sending emails to Jillian Caldwell seeking to find information about her. All I wanted to know is if Rebel Kenna is the Prothonotary and is she the one instructing the solicitors against me in the contempt charge because if she was it is highly inappropriate given the assault complaint I made against her.

One question for Kenna is also why did Chris D'Aeth make his police statement on the 2nd of February 2017 and Rebel Kenna made her police statement on the 8th of March 2017? Wouldn't the complainant always make their police statement first? It's more evidence to suggest they were trying to stitch me up.

The same people who had me found guilty of Contempt of Court by Justice Helen Wilson for what I said in court on the 3 February and breaching suppression orders they put on the matter are the same people who have been trying to have me jailed since I sent the email to the court on the 6th of September 2016.

In the police charge that has been withdrawn the key players were Chief Justice Tom Bathurst, Rebel Kenna, Chris D'Aeth and NSW Crown Solicitor Lea Armstrong.

The contempt matter is called the *"Prothonotary* of the Supreme Court of NSW v Shane Dowling". The Prothonotary is Rebel Kenna who was the complainant in the police matter. Chief Justice Bathurst was the key driver of the police charge and is the head of the Supreme Court which found me guilty of contempt. Lea Armstrong who oversaw the complaint to the police was personally handling the contempt matter until her role with the police was exposed after the police charged me in June 2017.

Police acting corruptly and as a personal crime gang for the judges

The police raided my unit and took my computers and then gave them to the Supreme Court who is now trying to give a copy of my computer to Kerry Stokes and Channel 7 which I am forced to fight. The police charge has been dropped, but the fight is not over yet although they are on the run.

End of article

In March 2018 the police charge was dropped as it was baseless in the first place and they knew it but they jailed me in August 2018 for the contempt matter for what I said in court on the 3rd of February 2017 and for breaching suppression orders they put on it. The suppression orders no longer exist as there was no legal basis for them.

Chapter 13

Royal Commission into Institutional Responses to Child Sexual Abuse - The judiciary protecting paedophiles

On the 22nd of April 2017, I published an article titled "Child Abuse Royal Commissioner Justice Peter McClellan outlines failures of judges and prosecutors" as per below.

Child Abuse Royal Commissioner Justice Peter McClellan outlines failures of judges and prosecutors

In a speech on the 13th of April 2017 the Chairman of the Royal Commission into Institutional Responses to Child Sexual Abuse, The Hon Justice Peter McClellan AM, raised issues regarding the failure of judges and prosecutors to do their jobs properly and therefore fail victims of child sex abuse.

Justice Peter McClellan is also an NSW Supreme Court judge and it is almost unheard of for judges to criticise their fellow judges, so it is a big call. And as I have reported in the last few posts, it is not just members of the public that are raising issues of judicial failings and corruption. Many members of the legal fraternity are also raising issues themselves as the problem is now out of control.

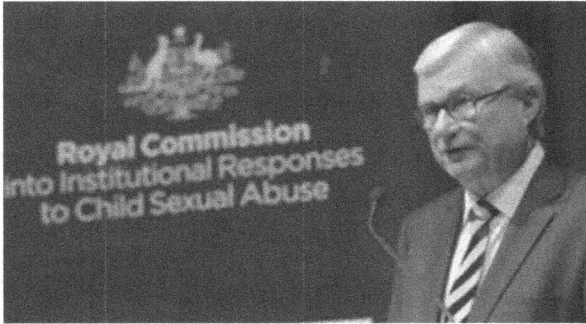

Justice Peter McClellan AM

How widespread is child abuse in Australia?

The Child Abuse Royal Commission has documented facts and figures which cannot be disputed that demands action with judicial reform and a broader inquiry into the Australian judiciary.

The Royal Commission Chairman Justice Peter McClellan has given 2 recent speeches in March and April 2017 that outline failings by judges and prosecutors in child abuse cases. (Click here and here to read more)

From the SMH:

Thousands of institutions have been implicated in allegations of child sexual abuse, according to new data released by a royal commission.

As the Royal Commission into Institutional Responses to Child Sexual Abuse commences its final public hearing, chairman Justice Peter McClellan has urged child protection reform and proper redress for victims.

The $500 million inquiry is Australia's longest royal commission, starting in 2013 and due to finish with a final report to the federal government in December.

In his opening remarks to the hearing, Justice McClellan said governments and institutions needed to focus on redress and regulatory changes, "designed to ensure that so far as possible no child is abused in an institutional context in the future".

"Survivors have waited too long for an effective response to their suffering and the future protection of Australian children must be given the highest priority," he said.

Justice McClellan and five commissioners have heard the testimony of more than 6500 child sexual abuse survivors in private sessions, with another 2000 people still awaiting a meeting.

Data gleaned largely from private sessions found there were more than 4000 institutions where alleged abuse of children occurred.

Counsel assisting the commission Gail Furness SC told the inquiry the statistics are likely to represent a fraction of child sexual abuse survivors. (Click here to read more)

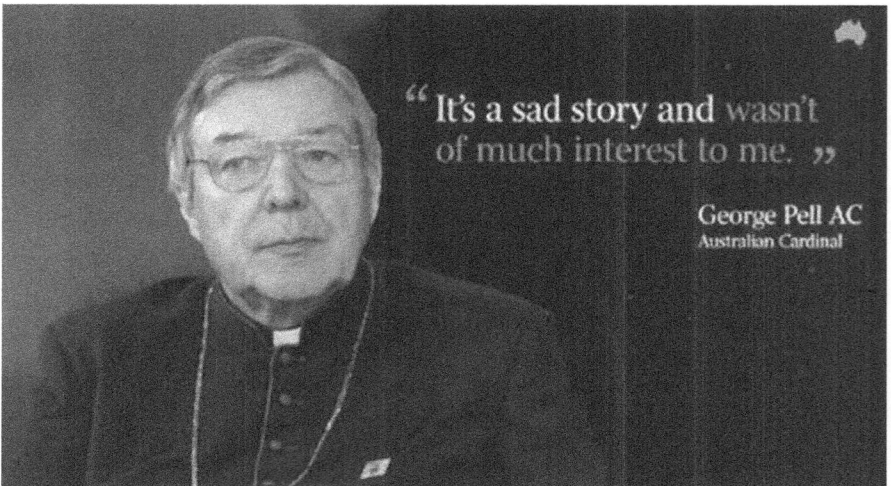

" It's a sad story and wasn't of much interest to me. "

George Pell AC
Australian Cardinal

The previous picture is Cardinal George Pell and his infamous line while giving evidence at the Royal Commission about paedophile priest Gerald Ridsdale abusing children *"It's a sad story, and it wasn't of much interest to me."* (Click here to read more)

Sentencing – *"More child sexual assault cases in court but fewer convictions: Justice Peter McClellan"*

Light sentences for people convicted of historical sexual offences against children could "undermine community confidence in the administration of justice", the chairman of the Royal Commission into Institutional Responses to Child Sexual Abuse will tell a conference of leading legal professionals. (Click here to read more)

Nothing could be truer. One of the most-read articles on this website is titled *"Paedophile priest gets 3 months jail for raping 3 boys by NSW Supreme Court's Justice Hoeben"*. The reason it is so well-read is that it does scandalise the courts when criminals such as paedophile priests get almost no sentence at all and the general public can't believe it is true.

10-year minimum sentence

Compare the 3-month sentence for the paedophile priest in NSW with the precedents in South Australia where the starting point is 10 and 12 years as quoted by Justice Peter McClellan and it shows what a scandal a 3-month sentence is:

In R v D a majority of the South Australian Court of Criminal Appeal held that heavier sentences should be imposed for child sexual abuse matters. They held that unlawful sexual intercourse with children under 12, when there are multiple offences committed over a period of time, should attract as a starting point a head sentence of about 12 years subject to a guilty plea, co-operation with the police, genuine contrition and other mitigating factors. In relation to unlawful sexual intercourse with children over 12 the starting point should be a head sentence of about 10 years imprisonment. Doyle CJ considered the court should take this course 'because of the seriousness of the crime in question, and because of its prevalence.' (Click here to read more)

Justice McClellan said that light sentences *"undermine community confidence in the administration of justice"* and I said basically the same thing in court, only stronger language, and I get charged with contempt of court. (Click here and here to read more) I wonder if Justice McClellan will now be charged with contempt of court?

Some of the recommendations flagged by Justice Peter McClellan for his final report to the Federal Government are:

As part of its criminal justice work the Commission is considering whether oversight or review mechanisms for ODDPs are necessary in the Australian context and, if so, what they might look like.

The Commissioners consider that all Australian DPPs should be able to implement a number of minimum requirements. Those requirements are:

1. *The adoption of comprehensive written policies for decision-making and consultation with victims and police.*

2. *Ensuring that all policies are publically available and published online.*

3. *Provision of a right for complainants to seek written reasons for key decisions.* (Click here to read more)

The failure of judges and prosecutors in this area of law is duplicated across most if not all areas of law and that is why a Royal Commission into the Australian judiciary is long overdue. Obviously, it is a Royal Commission that would need oversight from non-judges and non-lawyers if it was to get to the truth.

We need better review processes of decision-making by law enforcement agencies such as the Australian Federal Police

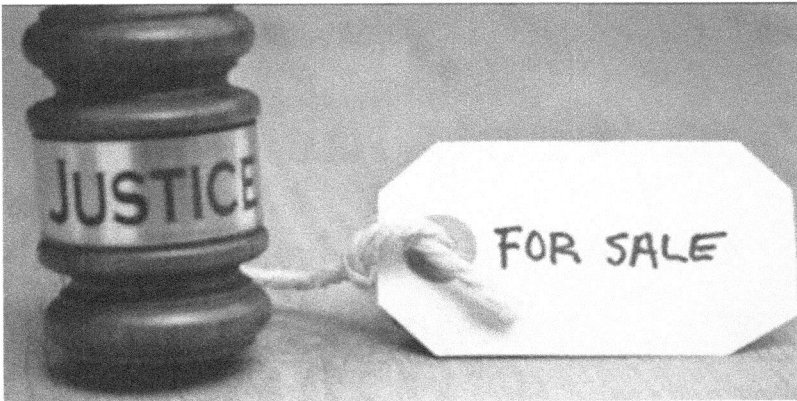

The Child Abuse Royal Commission is a great example because it is well-funded and has been going since 2013 and reports are well researched. The documented findings show without doubt the failings of the judiciary, law enforcement agencies and prosecutors to do their jobs.

This extends to federal parliament that is badly in need of a Federal ICAC to deal with federal corruption as the Federal Police regularly fail to charge politicians and federal government employees who have broken the law.

Times are changing fast and social media is empowering people to have oversight of all government decisions to some degree, but we can still do a lot better. The Australian judiciary and law enforcement agencies are operating well below public expectations in doing their jobs, so we need a major overhaul.

End of article

Chapter 14

NSW Police protecting paedophiles

In 2012 NSW police officer Detective Chief Inspector Peter Fox who was based in Newcastle blew the whistle on police failing to investigate paedophiles in the Catholic Church. This was similar to complaints heard later at the Royal Commission into Institutional Responses to Child Sexual Abuse in relation to the police failing to investigate complaints of child sexual abuse.

In November 2012 a Special Commission of Inquiry was set up to investigate Peter Fox's claims. The inquiry was headed up by Margaret Cunneen who at the time was a Deputy Senior Crown Prosecutor in the NSW Office of the Director of Public Prosecutions and she published a report in 2014.

The hit was put on the inquiry even before it started as Margaret Cunneen is a well-known paedophile protector who perjured herself at the Royal Commission into Institutional Responses to Child Sexual Abuse when she was forced to give evidence in relation to her protecting a paedophile who faced charges in Queensland.

It was also well-known that Margaret Cunneen is and has been friendly with corrupt police officers. But more on Cunneen in a minute.

In was reported in an article in the SMH in May 2014 titled "Special Commission of Inquiry: 'Hero' officer Peter Fox branded a liar" that:

The "hero cop" whose explosive claims about NSW Police handling of Catholic Church child abuse helped spark a royal commission, has been branded a liar in a report handed to the state government on Friday.

Detective Chief Inspector Peter Fox claimed that a police investigation into child sexual abuse allegations in the Catholic diocese of Maitland-Newcastle was a "sham" and asserted there was a "Catholic mafia" in the NSW Police that covered up crimes.

It went on to say: *The Special Commission of Inquiry into whether the Catholic Church covered up or NSW Police failed to properly investigate paedophile priest activity found there was no evidence to support Chief Inspector Fox's claims.*

The 750-page report by Commissioner Margaret Cunneen found that Chief Inspector Fox had "developed what amounted to an obsession about both the Catholic Church and alleged conspiracies involving senior police".

It found that evidence he provided to the commission was "implausible" and "deliberately untruthful". It also found that he was prone to "exaggerate aspects of his evidence". "The commission formed the view that Fox had engaged in conduct that was inconsistent with the integrity required of a police officer," the report noted.

In July 2014 Margaret Cunneen was in the witness box at the Royal Commission into Institutional Responses to Child Sexual Abuse trying to justify the dodgy legal advice she gave in 2004 that helped alleged paedophile Scott Volkers walk free. I watched it live and it was obvious to me she was blatantly perjuring herself and her evidence had no credibility.

On the 19th of April 2015, I published an article titled "Prosecutor Margaret Cunneen lies to hide friendship with killer Roger Rogerson etc" as per below.

Prosecutor Margaret Cunneen lies to hide friendship with killer Roger Rogerson etc.

Crown Prosecutor Margaret Cunneen is a compulsive liar who has been caught out badly contradicting herself in separate interviews with News Corp and Fairfax Media. In this article, we will also have a closer look at Cunneen's dodgy background which includes 1. Connections to major criminals such as Roger Rogerson 2. Helping alleged paedophiles such as Scott Volkers walk free and 3. The phone taps that will likely bring her undone.

Margaret Cunneen and her supporters are in crisis mode at the moment and trying to lie their way out of the problem but are only digging a bigger hole for themselves. They thought they had a win in the High Court against ICAC on Wednesday and that would be the end of it. (Click here to read more) That came unstuck Thursday (16/4/15) morning when it was revealed by the SMH that the ICAC investigation into Cunneen was sparked by *"Intercepted phone calls by a multi-agency taskforce investigating organised crime"*. They were investigating Cunneen's friend Stephen Fletcher and some of the calls must have mentioned Cunneen. (Click here to read more)

Interviews with Fairfax Media and The Australian and the big contradictions in answers

In 2011 Margaret Cunneen gave an interview with journalist Kate McClymont at the Sydney Morning Herald (SMH) and gave certain answers in relation to her personal association with major criminal Roger Rogerson. In February this year, Cunneen gave an interview with 2 journalists from The Australian and gave a different answer. (Click here to read)

This was not a one-off lie. Cunneen has also been caught lying about her relationship with Stephen Fletcher who has had criminal charges recommended against him and was paying off over 10 NSW Police officers to use their betting accounts. (Click here to read the Police Integrity Commission report – Operation Montecristo) One has to wonder, given Fletcher was paying the Police officers to use their betting accounts, was he also paying them for anything else more sinister?

Stephen Fletcher and Margaret Cunneen

Margaret Cunneen lied about her relationship with Fletcher in 2011 and implied she would have nothing to do with him again. But last year Fletcher went on holidays with Cunneen's son Stephen Wyllie and his girlfriend Sophia Tilly after the infamous car crash. So why is Cunneen lying? The ABC last year reported Stephen Fletcher was Margaret Cunneen's long-term boyfriend.

Convicted criminal Roger Rogerson and Margaret Cunneen

Margaret Cunneen helping convicted criminal and former corrupt police officer Roger Rogerson profit from his crimes at a book signing. Mr Rogerson is currently in jail awaiting trial for murder. Margaret Cunneen should be investigated as to why she is associating with criminals and helping a criminal profit from his crimes. Margaret Cunneen is a Deputy Senior Crown Prosecutor in NSW. For further information see: Kangaroo Court of Australia at: http://kangaroocourtofaustralia.com

Roger Rogerson is a former corrupt police officer and is in jail awaiting trial for murder. He is a major league crook and always has been. When he was a police officer, he took bribes to protect every type of criminal from murderers to drug dealers. He was kicked out of the force in 1986. Rogerson was charged in the late 1980s for drug dealing and attempted murder amongst other crimes and he has killed at least one person and probably more, not counting his current charge. (Click here to read more)

So, the question is: Why was Margaret Cunneen at Roger Rogerson's book signing helping him profit from his crimes in 2009?

When asked about it in 2011 Cunneen said: "*But I know Roger independently. I've known him since he was a detective ... He was never convicted of anything while he was a police officer.*" (Click here to read more)

Is Cunneen for real? Roger Rogerson is and was a major criminal and she should have never been anywhere near him and she knows it. In February this year Cunneen had changed her story to that she decided not to:

"continue to snub people who have gone to prison and paid their debt to society. I, and other prosecutors who attended, thought it important that prosecutors don't subscribe to lifelong punishment." (Click here to read more)

What dribble! She is trying to hide her scandalous friendship with Rogerson. But her answer raises some very serious questions such as: Who were the other prosecutors who attended the book signing? and: Is the prosecutor who is currently trying to convict Roger Rogerson of his murder charge one of the prosecutors who attended his book signing as a fan? Has Cunneen ever used her position to leak information to Rogerson or helped him in any way?

Based on what Margaret Cunneen told the journalists about the other prosecutors being at the book signing then all the staff at the Office of the Director of Public Prosecutions need investigating by ICAC just to be safe.

Scott Volkers

In 2004 Margaret Cunneen gave extremely dodgy legal advice that helped the Queensland Director of Public Prosecutions justify not reinstating charges against swimming coach Scott Volkers on paedophile charges. The Queensland DPP could not justify why the charges were dropped against Scott Volkers in the first place and needed dodgy legal advice to make sure he was not charged again otherwise the Queensland DPP would be looking very stupid if not corrupt.

Scott Volkers was accused of abusing 3 girls between the ages of 12 and 14, but charges were dropped in 2002. He was re-investigated by police, but the QLD DPP decided not to charge him again.

Margaret Cunneen's gave some scandalous advice that attacked the evidence of the girls and said: *"a conviction would be difficult to achieve because the girls were unlikely to have had developed breasts and thus the groping allegations would be difficult to substantiate."* (Click here to read more)

and: *"She also questioned whether a female abuse victim could have experienced an orgasm while being abused."*

"It is difficult to accept that Gilbert could have been sufficiently relaxed for orgasm to occur," Ms Cunneen wrote in legal advice to the Queensland DPP.* (Click here to read more or watch the 7.30 Report interview)

Margaret Cunneen's advice was disgraceful and there was obviously no legal or medical evidence to support it. It was a clear and pathetic attack by Margaret Cunneen to discredit witnesses and justify not reinstating charges against Scott Volkers.

I think the Volkers matter is important because it really pulls back the curtain and we can see what Cunneen is like behind closed doors. She clearly does favours for friends and gives them the dodgy advice they want to justify their decisions if need be. Cunneen would have never dreamt her dodgy advice would be before a Royal Commission.

The Cunneen/Volkers scandal was uncovered at the Royal Commission into Child Sexual Abuse last year and Cunneen should have been sacked then. Cunneen tries to make out she is some sought of hero for victims of sexual abuse. What a lie that is, which the Volkers matter shows. How many other criminals has Cunneen helped walk free?

Interviews with Ray Hadley on 2GB and Channel 7

Over the last couple of days, Cunneen has done soft interviews with Ray "Jelly Back" Hadley and Channel 7 News. She did not get asked any tough questions nor did "Jelly Back" raise Stephen

Fletcher, Roger Rogerson or her disgraceful conduct in the Scott Volkers matter.

Margaret Cunneen complained that *"murderers and terrorists"* would not be treated the way she was. Well, she should know, look at the above photo of her and Roger Rogerson and how well she treated him. She looks like a love-struck groupie with her big smile, not a Senior Crown Prosecutor who should have nothing to do with criminals.

Multi-agency Taskforce phone tap referral to ICAC

Who leaked the story about the phone taps is unknown, although the journalist who broke the story, Kate McClymont, now says it was a law enforcement officer. Leaking the phone tap referral to the media was the right thing to do because Cunneen was busy lying and deceiving the public and telling us it was some frivolous and vexatious complaint from her sister. This was deliberately designed by Cunneen to give her an excuse and to make ICAC look stupid, and it was not true.

Cunneen said she took on the legal challenge for her family. What a lie. They have not been cleared and they also have a huge shadow over their integrity. If she really cared about her family, she would not hang around criminals.

ICAC

The Independent Commission Against Corruption (ICAC) has been criticised by some for wasting time in the Cunneen matter because it was not a serious matter and ICAC is meant to focus on serious and systemic corruption. Margaret Cunneen's relationship with Roger Rogerson alone raises suspicions of serious and systemic corruption that needs investigating and that would justify ICAC investigating Margaret Cunneen.

If the laws are not strengthened to sideline the High Court and made retrospective so Cunneen can be investigated by ICAC then there will have to be a government inquiry. Otherwise, it is the government who will be seen to be corrupt and that is what will worry them and hopefully make them do the right thing. The Greens are already pushing for the relevant law changes *"to shore up ICAC'S powers"* in May.

This story has a long way to go and goes to the heart of government and judicial corruption so I will be keeping a close eye on it.

End of article

It's blatantly obvious that the Special Commission of Inquiry headed up by Margaret Cunneen needs to be investigated in a public inquiry as all the evidence points to it being a stitch-up to protect corrupt paedophile protecting police.

Peter Fox wrote a book about his experience titled "Walking Towards Thunder" "The true story of a whistleblowing cop who took on corruption and the Church" which was published in 2019.

They describe it on the Booktopia website as:

'All that is necessary for the triumph of evil is that good men do nothing.'

Former Detective Chief Inspector Peter Fox is a hero in many people's eyes. A police officer with 36 years' service in the Hunter region, he rose to national prominence in 2012 for his major role in speaking out for the victims of abuse within the church. He had been at the coalface fighting these heinous crimes for decades. He had worked with the victims and supported their families. He knew an enquiry was long overdue. His decision to become a whistleblower helped trigger Prime Minister Julia Gillard's historic decision to establish a far-reaching Royal Commission into the sexual abuse of children in institutions.

He had no idea what speaking up would unleash. Peter's dedication and focus cost him his career, his health, and also affected his wife's health. He and his family were threatened. Former friends shunned him. But the victims and the families that he supported consider him their champion. To them, he is a hero.

Walking Towards Thunder details the cumulative horrors our police face every day, it reveals the cover-ups and the way sexual predators were moved around. It shows the backlash he faced and the lengths those in power will go to avoid facing the truth. Confronting and inspiring, this is an unforgettable story.

About the Author

Former Detective Chief Inspector Peter Fox is a 36-year veteran of the NSW Police Force, during which time he investigated countless child sexual abuse cases in the Hunter Region of New South Wales. In November 2012, Peter Fox put his job on the line and went public with claims of systemic cover-up of institutional child abuse. His voice helped prompt the Royal Commission into Institutional Child Sexual Abuse.

As a whistle-blower, Peter has made many enemies and many have tried to discredit him. However, the victims and their families are strong in their support of the man who was always there for them, and who helped give them a voice. Peter continues to fight for victims and speak out against those who took advantage of their power to target and silence victims of abuse.

End

I focused on Peter Fox in this chapter because it shows that at the highest levels of government, they deliberately handed such a serious complaint against the police and church to be covered-up by a well-known crook like Margaret Cunneen.

To update the above article:

Margaret Cunneen's friend Roger Rogerson, and another former police officer, Glen McNamara, were sentenced to life in prison for the murder of 20-year-old drug dealer Jamie Gao in 2016.

They charged Scott Volkers again in 2017 after Margaret Cunneen's perjured evidence at the Royal Commission. But a judge permanently stayed the charges against Volkers because of the time delay which is very disturbing and once again shows how alleged paedophiles and paedophiles get special treatment by the judiciary.

In December 2018, the federal government announced that they had appointed Margaret Cunneen to a panel to review legislation for setting up the Commonwealth Integrity Commission. The CIC will investigate government corruption so it is scandalous that they would appoint someone like Cunneen to review the legislation.

Chapter 15

Prime Minister Scott Morrison confirms judicial paedophile protection racket

In September 2019, Scott Morrison and the federal Attorney-General Christian Porter announced plans for mandatory sentencing of paedophiles because 28% of paedophiles convicted of federal child sexual abuse crimes do not receive jail sentences.

On the 24th of September 2019, I published an article titled "Prime Minister Scott Morrison confirms judicial paedophile protection racket with 28% not going to jail" as per below.

Prime Minister Scott Morrison confirms judicial paedophile protection racket with 28% not going to jail

Prime Minister Scott Morrison announced on the 3rd of September 2019 that 28% of paedophiles convicted of federal laws do not go to jail, so the government is introducing mandatory sentencing laws. The minimum inference that can be drawn is that Australian judges and magistrates are running a paedophile protection racket.

If 28% of paedophiles convicted of federal laws aren't going to jail what is the real number of paedophiles that are knowingly being let off in Australia when state laws are added? 40%? 50%?

The judges that let paedophiles off are deliberately and knowingly breaking the law as they know they should be sending the paedophiles to jail. So why aren't the judges sending the paedophiles to jail? Without a doubt, some judges are paedophiles themselves and some would be taking bribes. Whatever the case, it needs investigating by authorities in a major way and this website has been shining a light on the issue for a long time.

The government press release is in full below:

Mandatory jail sentences for child sex offenders

Media release

The Hon. Christian Porter MP
Attorney-General
Minister for Industrial Relations
Leader of the House

The Hon. Peter Dutton MP
Minister for Home Affairs

Paedophiles would face mandatory jail sentences and the most serious offenders could be jailed for life under sweeping changes to Federal sentencing laws to be introduced to Parliament next week.

The Crimes Legislation Amendment (Sexual Crimes Against Children and Community Protection Measures) Bill 2019 will also make it harder for serious offenders to get bail, while repeat offenders will have to stay in prison for longer.

The Bill reflects the Morrison Government's commitment to keeping Australians safe and creates new offences to capture evolving forms of child exploitation such as being the administrator of a website that functions for the purpose of distributing child abuse material.

Attorney-General Christian Porter said 28 percent of child sex offenders convicted of federal offences in 2018-19 did not spend one day in jail – a statistic totally out of step with community expectations.

"It simply beggars belief that nearly a third of all child sex offenders who were sentenced last year were not required to spend a single day behind bars, despite the devastating and life-long impacts that their crimes have on their young victims and their families," the Attorney-General said.

"And when jail terms were handed out, the average length of time that offenders spent in custody was just 18 months.

"The changes being introduced by the Morrison Government will ensure that a jail term becomes the starting point for all child sex offenders, while maximum penalties will also be increased to better reflect the gravity of these types of crimes, including a new life term for the worst offenders." Minister for Home Affairs Peter Dutton said the Australian Federal Police received almost 18,000 reports of child exploitation involving Australian children or Australian child sex offenders last year, which was almost double the number from the previous year.

"Sentences need to reflect community expectations and act as a significant deterrent to others, which is why these sorts of despicable crimes must result in significant penalties, not simply a slap on the wrist which is often the case," Mr Dutton said.

"Our Government is at war with these predators and all those who would seek to do harm to children.

"The message we are sending to paedophiles is that it won't matter how good their lawyer is, a prison cell will be waiting for them when they are convicted. This is what the community expects and this what the Morrison Government intends to deliver.

"I would urge the Labor Party, who failed to support these reforms in the last Parliament, to listen to the Australian People and put community safety first when it comes time to vote on this Bill." The Bill complements a broad package of reforms already introduced by the Coalition during the last Parliament, which strengthened laws relating to child sexual abuse and created new protections for the community.

This included tough new measures to stop child sex offenders from travelling overseas to abuse children and the introduction of Carly's law, which targets online predators who use the internet to prepare or plan to sexually abuse children.

The new Bill will vastly improve justice outcomes and community safety through:

- Mandatory minimum sentences for serious child sex offences and for recidivist offenders

- A presumption against bail for serious and repeat offenders to keep them off the streets

- Increased maximum penalties across the spectrum of child sex offences, including up to life imprisonment for the most serious offences

- Presumptions in favour of cumulative sentences and actual imprisonment

- Ensuring that all sex offenders, upon release from custody, are adequately supervised and subject to appropriate rehabilitative conditions

- Preventing courts from discounting sentences on the basis of good character where this is used to facilitate the crime.

The Bill will be introduced to Parliament next Wednesday. (Click to see on the Attorney-Generals website)

On the 3rd of September 2019, Prime Minister Scott Morrison tweeted: "28% of child sex offenders sentenced in Australia last year did not serve one day in jail. That's just not OK, not even close. These offenders are the lowest of the low & we're going to ensure they go to jail with new mandatory sentencing laws." and in the same Tweet Scott Morrison posted the below video:

Hypocrisy by Prime Minister Scott Morrison

Scott Morrison is talking tough on jailing paedophiles, yet he is good friends with Hillsong Church Pastor Brian Houston who, as I reported in July, is currently under investigation by the NSW Police for concealing his father raping children.

I wrote on the 13th of July 2019:

Prime Minister Scott Morrison and his wife were on stage leading prayers in front of 21,000 people on Tuesday night (9/7/19) with the Hillsong Church's Brian Houston who is still under investigation by the NSW police for concealing the sexual abuse of children by his father Frank Houston.

In 2014 while giving evidence at The Royal Commission into Institutional Responses to Child Sexual Abuse Brian Houston admitted he knew his father had abused children and he had failed to report it to the police so it is not a fact that is in dispute or a fact that Scott Morrison wouldn't know.

There are many reasons, which I outline below, why Scott Morrison should have never been on stage with paedophile protector Brian Houston who is under investigation by the NSW police. (Click here to read more)

In recent days Scott Morrison has embarrassed himself and Australia when it was revealed that Morrison tried to take Brian Houston to the US and Washington to rub shoulders with President Donald Trump but the Whitehouse refused Brian Houston clearance which was almost certain to be because of the current NSW police investigation.

One of the people who was abused as a child by Brian Houston's father, Frank Houston, is Brett Sengstock who was abused from the age of seven. Brian Houston and the Hillsong Church are refusing to pay compensation to victims even though they are meant to and Brett Sengstock, who is also battling cancer, is being forced by Brian Houston to fight every step of the way for compensation. Scott Morrison would have to know this, yet he still is good friends with Brian Houston and helps him promote the Hillsong Church which many regard as nothing more than a money-making scam.

"I have written about Brett Sengstock before and I spoke to him on Sunday and he said in relation to the Scott Morrison / Brian Houston White House scandal:

"This is an absolute slap in the face to sexual abuse survivors, the survivors who attended the Royal Commission and to the Australian laws. It makes Scott Morrison's apology to sexual abuse survivors look like it means absolutely nothing. It's invalid. And Scomo parading around with Brian Houston isn't a good look. What are Scott Morrison's people thinking or is there a deeper problem or reason behind all of this? Scott Morrison would be fully aware of the police investigation, I'm positive."

Brett Sengstock is currently raising funds to help with his ongoing legal battles for justice and also to help with his recovery from cancer treatment. He has a crowdfunding page on GoFundMe if you would like to help. (Click here for Brett's GoFundMe page)

I agree that there should be mandatory sentencing laws for paedophiles but that alone will not solve the problem of paedophiles being let back on the streets by the corrupt judges, prosecutors, and police who are currently letting the paedophiles off without any real punishment. This is a problem that has been known for years.

I wrote an article titled "Child Abuse Royal Commissioner Justice Peter McClellan outlines failures of judges and prosecutors" in April 2017 and said:

In a speech on the 13th of April 2017 the Chairman of the Royal Commission into Institutional Responses to Child Sexual Abuse, The Hon Justice Peter McClellan AM, raised issues regarding the failure of judges and prosecutors to do their jobs properly and therefore fail victims of child sex abuse.

Justice Peter McClellan is also an NSW Supreme Court judge and it is almost unheard of for judges to criticise their fellow judges, so it is a big call. And as I have reported in the last few posts it is not just members of the public that are raising issues of judicial failings and corruption. Many members of the legal fraternity are also raising issues themselves as the problem is now out of control. (Click here to read more)

Former police officer Peter Fox, who is a whistleblower on child sex abuse cover-ups in the church and NSW police force, has recently published a book on the subject titled Walking Towards Thunder and he said recently:

"In my book Walking Towards Thunder I explain how NSW Police collaborated with the Catholic Church to implement blind reporting, a controversial clergy abuse protocol, despite legal advice that blind reporting conflicted with the law." (Click here to see reviews and a description of his book)

The ABC reported: "Blind reporting occurs when an organisation passes on an allegation of child sex abuse, but strips the report of the name of the victim, meaning police are unable to investigate the report." In NSW it "has potentially allowed hundreds of perpetrators to continue to abuse children." (Click here to read more)

You don't have to go any further than what Justice Peter McClellan and Peter Fox have said to know that the problem covers the judges who fail to jail the paedophiles, the prosecutors who fail the victims and the police who fail to investigate and charge paedophiles. It is not a minor problem; it is a protection racket concealing a national epidemic.

Last year I was convicted and sentenced to 18 months jail for calling Justice Clifton Hoeben a paedophile and registrar Christopher Bradford a suspected paedophile and known bribe-taker in court on the 3rd of February 2017. Which I deny. It was reduced to 4 months on appeal. I was already in the line of fire of the judges for an email I sent to the Supreme Court outing 15 judges, 2 registrars and 1 magistrate as paedophiles, suspected paedophiles and raising issues of judicial bribery. I published the email and the names of the judges in an article titled "Paedophile priest gets 3 months jail for raping 3 boys by NSW Supreme Court's Justice Hoeben" (Click here to read the article)

The judges who stitched me up for some jail time because I outed them as paedophiles or suspected paedophiles are some of the same judges who are protecting the paedophiles by not jailing them or giving them very light sentences. I was, in fact, stitched-up for some jail time for exposing them.

Scott Morrison is talking tough on the issue, but he is at best only putting a band-aid on the problem if that. The mandatory sentencing laws were meant to have been put before parliament 2 weeks ago but have not been heard of since Scott Morrison's big announcement on the 3rd of September.

I'll keep following up on this issue.

End of article

On the 16th of July 2020, Federal Parliament passed laws introducing mandatory minimum sentences for child sex offenders. But when looked at closely it quickly becomes obvious the new mandatory sentencing laws will achieve little and reinforces Scott Morrison's nickname "Scotty from Marketing" as he has used the new laws to sound like he is doing something about the problem when in reality he is not doing much as all. The new laws only address federal laws and crimes and have no effect on state laws which many, if not most, paedophiles are charged with.

From September 2019 until the new laws were introduced July 2020 the rate had gone up from 28% to 39% of paedophiles convicted of federal child sexual abuse crimes did not receive jail sentences. The problem was never the laws, it has always been the corrupt judges. And what is the percentage of paedophiles charged with state laws who do not go to jail and why didn't Scott Morrison mention it?

Chapter 16

Paedophile judge Francois Kunc is also a senior member of the world's biggest paedophile ring

On the 23rd of November 2019, I published an article titled "Podcast of Supreme Court of NSW – Seven v Dowling – Allegation Chief Justice Tom Bathurst is a paedophile – Has Justice Kunc had a sexual relationship with Dr Nicky McWilliam – Judicial bribery etc." as per below.

Podcast of Supreme Court of NSW – Seven v Dowling – Allegation Chief Justice Tom Bathurst is a paedophile – Has Justice Kunc had a sexual relationship with Dr Nicky McWilliam – Judicial bribery etc.

In the below recording (KCoA Podcast) of myself, Justice Kunc and Seven's barrister Kieran Smark some of the issues that are discussed are 1. Allegations Chief Justice Tom Bathurst and other judges are paedophiles and suspected paedophiles 2. Justice Kunc's personal relationship with Nicky McWilliam and Bruce McWilliam and has Justice Kunc and Ms McWilliam previously had a sexual relationship 3. Judicial bribery 4. Perceived and actual bias.

It doesn't matter whether you are a lawyer or have no understanding of the law the below podcast will be a real eyeopener to what is really happening in Australian courts and how corrupt they are. The first couple of minutes starts off slow but then it gets right into the corruption that has been ongoing for years in this matter and against me.

A brief background to the proceeding in the podcast.

Kerry Stokes and his associated companies have been running numerous SLAPP lawsuits against me since 2014 to try to silence me from writing about their criminal conduct and corruption. The matter in the podcast is Seven West Media & Seven Network v Shane Dowling matter: 2017/116771. They instituted it in early 2017 against the publisher of the website SevenVersusAmber and later it was changed to be against me.

In July 2017 Seven also instituted contempt proceedings against me, for the third time if you include two of the other matters, but at about the same time Kerry Stokes and Seven took control of the SevenVersusAmber website. The proceedings have been dragging on for a long time and no final hearing date has been set, as Justice Kunc refused to set one, and it should have been thrown out long ago for want of prosecution. Seven's contempt hearing is set down to be heard on the 2nd of December 2019.

In July this year, I instituted contempt proceeding against Seven Network (Operations) Limited, Seven West Media Limited, Kerry Stokes, Bruce McWilliam, Tim Worner, barrister Kieran Smark and their lawyers Richard Keegan, Martin O'Connor and Alexander Latu. It is set down for the 3rd of December 2019.

On Friday the 15th of November 2019 Seven's lawyer Richard Keegan emailed Justice Kunc's associate, without my consent, saying they wanted the matter set down as they had a Notice of

Motion they wanted to be heard for better particulars in my contempt proceedings against them. Even though I objected on numerous grounds Justice Kunc set it down for Friday the 22nd of November. I then asked for two applications by me to be set down on the same day. One for Justice Kunc to stand down for perceived and actual bias and an application for the matter to be transferred to Brisbane, but I found out on Friday (22/11/19) at the hearing that my applications weren't set down.

That shows actual bias by Justice Kunc as he heard Seven's application on the 22/11/19 but refused to hear my applications even though they were requested on the same day (15/11/19) and one was for perceived and actual bias which should have taken precedent.

Barrister Kieran Smark was in court, but he was one of the respondents for my contempt proceedings against Seven etc and in a situation like that he can't represent the others which he was in effect doing. As the podcast shows, I raised it numerous times and Justice Kunc allowed it, which once again shows actual bias and corruption.

Click below to listen to the podcast. Justice Kunc and Kieran Smark SC were at the Supreme Court of NSW in Sydney and I was in Queensland on the phone as I moved permanently from Sydney a couple of weeks ago.

Both Justice Kunc and Seven's barrister Kieran Smark are ducking and weaving throughout the podcast as I try to hold them to account.

Justice Francois Kunc   Shane Dowling   Kieran Smark SC

0:00 / 57.08   HD ◠ ⤬

You can also watch it on YouTube: Click here

Click below to listen to the audio version:

Audio Player

Use Up/Down Arrow keys to increase or decrease volume.

(There is one mistake in the podcast. I said that Justice John Sackar said they all need their own representation for contempt matters against them. It was actually Justice Clifton Hoeben who said it in a related matter)

I have recorded court twice before when I was in court in Sydney and published it (Click here to see the recordings) and no one complained and numerous judges were aware of it. It is legal to record phone calls in Queensland and my motivation for recording the above call was to expose the corruption.

Justice Kunc should have stood down from this matter when previously requested especially given his personal relationship with Dr Nicky McWilliam and her husband Seven's Bruce McWilliam. (Click here to read the judgment where he refused to stand down)

In 2016 Justice Kunc received papal honours for his lifetime contribution to the Church in Sydney and he was named a Knight Commander of the Order of St Gregory the Great.

Bishop Terry Brady at Cathedral House with papal honour recipients (from left) Justice Francois Kunc, Gemile Mellick and Neville Moses

Justice Kunc is a senior member of the Catholic Church which has been running the world's largest paedophile ring for decades and this matter also deals with unchallenged allegations, by me, that Chief Justice Tom Bathurst and other judges are paedophiles or suspected paedophiles. On that basis alone Justice Kunc should be nowhere near the case and should have recused himself from hearing it.

To make the bias and/or perceived bias worse Chief Justice Tom Bathurst ordered senior court staff to have me jailed by making a false complaint to the police in September 2016 because I made the allegations about him and others being paedophiles or suspected paedophiles. The evidence is before the court in this matter because the applicants subpoenaed the evidence from the NSW police.

I asked Justice Kunc in the podcast if he would like to apologise to all the survivors of the paedophile priests in the Catholic Church, but he refused to.

That's just the start of the evidence that says Justice Kunc and the Supreme Court of NSW should have nothing to do with this matter or any matter involving me. I'll have plenty more to say on this matter in the future.

End of article

As I said at the end of chapter 5, the contempt proceedings against me that were listed for hearing on the 2nd of December 2019, as per above, have still not been heard. The hearing of the Notice of Motion for contempt is now scheduled for hearing on the 1st and 2nd of February 2021 to be heard by Justice Kate Williams.

Chapter 17

Paedophile protection by the Court of Appeal and the High Court of Australia

On the 11th of May 2019, I published an article titled "High Court of Australia's Justice Keane and Justice Edelman caught protecting their bribe-taking and paedophile judicial mates" as per below.

High Court of Australia's Justice Keane and Justice Edelman caught protecting their bribe-taking and paedophile judicial mates

The High Court of Australia has refused my special leave to appeal application for them to hear my appeal for contempt of court for calling Justice Clifton Hoeben a paedophile and Registrar Christopher Bradford a suspected paedophile and known bribe-taker. While it is disappointing, it is not a total loss as it takes us inside the High Court of Australia, and we can start writing first-hand about corruption by the High Court judges with the first two being Justice Patrick Anthony Keane and Justice James Joshua Edelman.

The full judgment by Justice Keane and Justice Edelman is below with the bottom line being "this application for special leave to appeal would not enjoy sufficient prospects of success to warrant the grant of special leave to appeal". What stands out about the full judgment is that it is not any longer than the line I just quoted, which does nothing more than scandalise the High Court of Australia.

Written judgments are meant to keep the judges accountable. For example, a long-detailed judgment addressing all the issues shows that a judge has at least tried to do their job. A judgment that has no reasons and is only one line and that addresses no issues shows that the judges have not justified anything at all, let alone their decision to refuse my special leave to appeal application. Keane and Edelman should be sacked immediately. If ever there was a need to give fully detailed reasons it is when there are serious allegations of judicial corruption and blatant perceived bias in the lower court's judgment.

What makes it worse is that at the time I was charged and convicted of contempt of court in 2017 Chief Justice Tom Bathurst had ordered senior court staff to stitch me up for jail time in September 2016 for an email I had sent to all the Supreme Court judges in accusing 15 judges, 2 registrars and 1 magistrate of being known paedophiles, suspected paedophiles and raising issues of judicial bribery. I was ultimately charged by the police in June 2017 but the charge was withdrawn because it was a malicious charge. Under those circumstances, it was even more reason why the High Court of Australia should have allowed special leave to appeal for the full court to hear the appeal.

The judge who convicted me of contempt for what I said in court on the 3rd of February 2017, Justice Helen Wilson, said in court that it was not what I said, but where I said it and how I said it, that resulted in me being found guilty of contempt. She then gave an example and said that if I called her a bribe-taker outside of court, she would not care less. I then asked her what if I called her a paedophile outside of court and she said it is not up to her to give me legal advice even though she had just given me legal advice about calling her a bribe-taker.

I had an almost identical conversation with Justice Clifton Hoeben on the 4th of May 2019 where he told me not to call him or any other judges of the court a paedophile. I asked him about calling him a bribe-taker and he said I couldn't call him that either. I then told Justice Hoeben about Justice Helen Wilson saying that I could call her a bribe-taker outside of court and I asked Justice Hoeben if I could call him a paedophile outside court and he said it was not for him to give me legal advice.

The reason I raise the issue of Justice Wilson and Justice Hoeben in effect saying I can say what I want, outside court in relation to judicial corruption, is that they had no choice to say that given the police charge was dropped for the email I sent to the Supreme Court judges in September 2016. That email is still on my website as part of an article I wrote in September 2016 titled "Paedophile priest gets 3 months jail for raping 3 boys by NSW Supreme Court's Justice Hoeben" and is also on the banner in the video below which I filmed at the High Court of Australia in Canberra on Friday (10-5-19). The reason the police charge was dropped is because the email I sent was clearly me raising issues of government corruption which is protected by the constitution as political communication and that is outlined in the 1997 High Court precedent Lange v ABC.

What Justice Wilson did was rewrite the law when she found me guilty of contempt because a Victorian Court of Appeal judgment, Herald & Weekly Times Ltd & Bolt v Popovic [2003] VSCA 161, in effect says if you raise allegations of criminal conduct against judges "whether in or out of court" that would be covered by 1997 High Court precedent Lange v ABC. This is another reason why the High Court needed to hear the matter because now we have 2 state Supreme Court judgments which contradict each other in regards to the Australian public's rights to political communication.

This leaves the allegations I have made in the email unchallenged and it also scandalises the High Court of Australia as they are the ones who have ultimate responsibility to protect the reputation of the courts.

The below video is me, Shane Dowling, outside the High Court of Australia (10-5-19). The video is an unfinished project as it was raining the day of filming and I thought I would just leave it as is but it was worth the trip and I will go again soon as we are going to start focusing heavily on the High Court. (A thank you to Ian in Canberra who helped with filming on the day)

Below is the full High Court judgment. To call it the "full judgment" is really a bad joke given the judgment is only one line with no reasons given.

Dowling v Prothonotary of the Supreme Court of New South Wales [2019] HCASL 96 (17 April 2019)

Last Updated: 17 April 2019

DOWLING

v

PROTHONOTARY OF THE SUPREME COURT OF NEW SOUTH WALES

[2019] HCASL 96

S22/2019

1. The appeal foreshadowed by this application for special leave to appeal would not enjoy sufficient prospects of success to warrant the grant of special leave to appeal. The application should be dismissed.

2. Pursuant to r 41.08.01 of the *High Court Rules 2004* (Cth), we direct the Registrar to draw up, sign and seal an order dismissing the application.

P.A. Keane   J.J. Edelman

17 April 2019

.

The High Court's scandalous decision also allows me to make allegations of corrupt and criminal conduct against the High Court as well as Justice Keane and Justice Edelman because their lack of reasons to support their judgment is powerful circumstantial evidence of corruption.

The High Court judges were always going to protect their corrupt mates but before we start making allegations, we needed documented evidence and now we have that.

The question I would like to know is how often the High Court judges sweep judicial corruption matters under the carpet. A lot of the judges in the lower courts wouldn't hand down the corrupt judgments they do if they didn't know they were protected by the High Court judges.

New federal laws need to be introduced sacking judges who refuse to give detailed written reasons for their judgments.

I'll be making other applications in the High Court of Australia with the first being in a matter of days so we will be going back inside the High Court and possibly expose more corruption.

End of article

I made several other applications to the High Court of Australia in relation to the other matters and they were given the same treatment of being dismissed but with no detailed reasons given.

The above obviously deals with my matters where the High Court refused to deal with them even though there was blatant perceived bias and real bias by the Supreme Court judges as well as unchallenged allegations of criminal conduct against the Supreme Court judges. It must be remembered that the High Court judges come from the lower courts and they will always protect their mates.

The High Court released Cardinal George Pell, in a unanimous judgment, from jail on the 7th of April 2020 after he had been convicted by a jury of sexually abusing two boys.

The High Court of Australia in effect found that the jury should have taken into account evidence from witnesses, who supported Pell, when the jury had obviously found the evidence from those witnesses was not credible. The net effect is that the High Court of Australia legalised perjury.

Justice Stephen John Gageler was one of the judges and he attends the Catholic church every week with his family, as reported on Wikipedia and other media articles, which leaves it open to an apprehension of bias given Cardinal George Pell is the most senior Catholic in Australia.

I find it hard to believe that Justice Gageler's family did not put pressure on him to uphold Pell's appeal. It was a unanimous decision of 7 judges but at least Gageler should have stood down and it was a scandalous judgment that undermines people's confidence in the judiciary as it also sidelines juries.

Chapter Eighteen

Becoming a fugitive on the run

After I was released from jail in December 2018 all of Kerry Stokes' SLAPP lawsuits will still afoot and when Justice Clifton Hoeben was appointed as the defamation list judge he made it clear that I would not be getting a fair go in the Supreme Court of NSW. I published an article on the 4th of May 2019 about the day in court before Justice Hoeben titled "Five Sheriff's Officers used to intimidate journalist Shane Dowling by the Supreme Court's Justice Clifton Hoeben" which is below:

Five Sheriff's Officers used to intimidate journalist Shane Dowling by the Supreme Court's Justice Clifton Hoeben

Five Court Sheriffs were used to try to intimidate me on Friday (3/5/19) in the NSW Supreme Court by Justice Clifton Hoeben while he aided and abetted Kerry Stokes and Capilano Honey in their SLAPP lawsuits against me.

I was in court for directions for the 2 criminal contempt applications I had made in the Capilano Honey matter and also in the Kerry Stokes, Ryan Stokes and Justine Munsie matter. I was also in court for the hearing of Capilano Honey's application to strike out my defence.

Justice Hoeben had pre-planned his intimidation game as he was looking after the defamation list and there were other lawyers and barristers in court for other defamation matters and he did not want them to see what he was up to. My 2 matters were listed near the top, but he said he would hold both over until the end knowing all the other lawyers and barrister would be gone.

I noticed one Court Sheriff at the beginning but the full 5 did not show up until just before Justice Hoeben started to deal with my matters and they sat in the back of the courtroom for my full hearing. I asked Justice Hoeben about the 5 Court Sheriffs and how it was disgraceful and a waste of taxpayer's money, but he wouldn't answer. At the start of the hearing, Justice Hoeben started lecturing me on the court's code of conduct about when I could talk, when I had to sit down and not to interrupt anyone etc.

Then suddenly Justice Hoeben said that I was also not to call him a paedophile or any other judges of the court a paedophile and that I knew what would happen if I did. He was implying that I would be jailed, and the 5 court Sheriffs were obviously to reinforce the threat.

I thought that's a first for any judge to say that but not surprising given I spent 4 months in jail last year for calling Hoeben a paedophile and registrar Christopher Bradford a suspected paedophile and known bribe taker in court in February 2017.

I said to Justice Hoeben what if I called him a "bribe-taker". He said I couldn't call him that either.

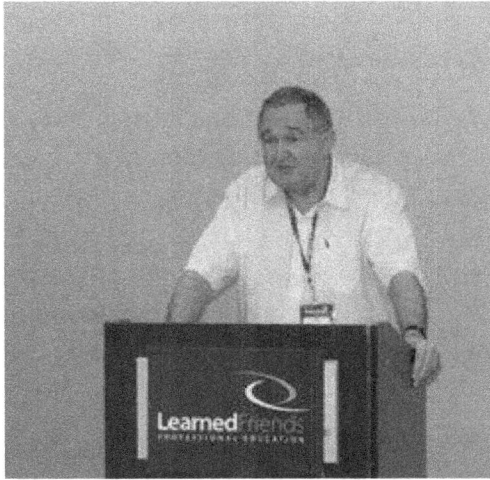

Justice Clifton Hoeben

Now I am sure everyone reading this article would think "what the hell is Justice Hoeben doing hearing any matter involving Shane Dowling and why didn't Mr Dowling ask Justice Hoeben to stand down for perceived bias if not real bias".

Well, I did ask Justice Hoeben to stand down from hearing any matter involving me when I was in court for directions on the 22nd March 2019, but he refused. I also asked Justice Hoeben to stand down again on Friday (3/5/19) and this time I referred to documented evidence in an affidavit as to why he should stand down and once again he refused. There is enough evidence in the affidavit to show that Chief Justice Tom Bathurst wanted me stitched up for jail as far back as September 2016 and given that any of my matters should be dealt with by interstate judges.

As part of the affidavit, there is also an article that is still on my website that says Justice Hoeben is a known paedophile and he did not regard that as a reason why he should stop hearing the matter. (Click here to see the article)

At this point, Hoeben has not published any written reason for his refusal to stand down on the 22nd of March 2019 so I wonder if he will publish reasons for his refusal to stand down on Friday (3/5/19) as he gave no reasons when we were in court.

Not only did Justice Clifton Hoeben refuse to stand down from hearing the matter he summarily dismissed my 2 criminal contempt charges in the Capilano Honey matter and also in the Kerry Stokes, Ryan Stokes and Justine Munsie matter. This was scandalous as a barrister had shown up to deal with the directions for the 2 criminal contempt matters and Justice Hoeben's action to dismiss them seemed to even surprise the barrister.

I can only assume that Kerry Stokes right-hand man Bruce McWilliam has called in another one of those judicial favours he likes to brag about to journalists. (Click here to read more)

Blatant bias by the court

Justice Hoeben said I needed leave of the court (permission by the court) to file the Notice of Motion for criminal contempt and he was refusing for both matters. He said I would have to file a separate summons which has the effect of starting a new case and would be a lot more expensive for me and waste more time.

Hoeben claimed it was because I also charged the lawyers with contempt and they were not parties to the proceedings, but their barrister did not complain. Also, I said that the notice of motions for contempt could go ahead against the people who were parties in the matters and Hoeben still said no. Hoeben then said the proceedings had been going too long and the contempts were irrelevant to the matters.

Hoeben also said that the Stokes/ Munsie matter was finalised except for costs. I said that is not correct as it is set down for final orders to be argued at the end of the month and that could be confirmed by asking their barrister Sandy Dawson or lawyer Richard Keegan who were there. I said it also could be confirmed by me checking my email on my mobile and reading out the email from the judge's chambers or for Hoeben to contact the judge's chambers.

Hoeben refused all options to verify that the Munsie / Stokes matter had further argument to go and said he was correct and that only costs in the Munsie matter was left to be decided and he did not want to reopen it with my contempt motion.

This shows blatant bias by the court because Kerry Stokes and Seven have filed 3 Notice of Motions for contempt against me where I was found guilty twice and fined $2000 the first time (which I never had to pay) and jailed for 4 months the second time for breaching suppression orders. The third contempt proceedings by Seven is still afoot and they are trying to jail me again.

So why didn't the court make them file summonses? That is not perceived bias, that is real bias. And why didn't Justice Hoeben say anything on the 22nd of March when the Capilano Honey contempt matter was first in court for directions?

Threatened with contempt at least 10 times during the course of the hearing

On Friday Justice Hoeben threatened me with jail over 10 times. I said their lawyer Richard Keegan had perjured himself and I received a warning. I said that their barrister Sandy Dawson had lied, and I received a warning, I said that Justice Hoeben was biased and I received a warning and on it went.

Hoeben became aggressive when he warned me. Hoeben never used the word jail. He would just say "you know what will happen". He's an absolute grub who's unfit to be a judge.

Numerous SLAPP lawsuits

Kerry Stokes and his companies have 4 SLAPP lawsuits against me and have been playing delaying tactics with 3 which are the Capilano Honey matter, the Munsie / Stokes matter and the Jane Doe matter. I had to file a notice of motion to have the Capilano

Honey matter listed again as Justice Hoeben and Capilano refused to. Justice Rothman threatened to close the Munsie/Stokes matter a few weeks ago because the applicants had done nothing to finalize it.

And in the Jane Doe matter, which is a well-known on-air host at Channel 7, a well-known actress at Channel Seven and 2 former staff members which have been suing me since December 2016, I had to email them directly this week because Justice Hoeben and their lawyers ignored my emails. When I emailed them their lawyer Richard Keegan emailed me and said in effect, they had been waiting for a final hearing date. Well, that means they have been waiting since August 2018 which is a lie as you can get a date in a matter of days if not hours.

The Jane Doe matter still hasn't gone anywhere or been set down for directions or final hearing as Justice Hoeben refused my request again in court on Friday. After arguing with Hoeben he said to send his associate another email which he'll probably ignore again.

The only matter they are pushing is the Seven Network and Seven West Media v Shane Dowling matter where they are trying to jail me in relation to a website that I never owned and which Kerry Stokes / Seven now own.

Towards the very end of the hearing, and after another threat by Justice Hoeben of being jailed, I grabbed my stuff and said I've had enough of the threats and went to walk out and I said that I would apply to have the matter removed to the High Court which is what I will do soon.

Justice Hoeben's and the court's conduct is clear and blatant vindictive revenge against me for the judicial corruption articles I have published on my website as well as the court continuing to help facilitate Kerry Stokes' and Capilano Honey's SLAPP lawsuits.

Having 5 Court Sheriffs for my hearing was not the first time they have had court sheriffs to try and intimidate me. I wonder how many $100,000's of taxpayers' money have been spent by the court trying to silence me, intimidate me and deny me natural justice? Every taxpayer should be horrified at the lengths that government employees and courts will go to hide corruption and persecute journalists and whistleblowers.

I spoke to the Court Sheriffs at the end of the hearing and they were fine. They didn't say so, but they knew they had been used and sent to the court in numbers to try and intimidate me.

I will not say too much but there are some positives to come out of Friday's hearings with the obvious one being clear evidence of judicial corruption and I'll write more about that in the near future.

End of article

A couple of weeks later on the 15th May 2019, the NSW police paid another visit to my residence after another frivolous and vexatious complaint by the Supreme Court of NSW. I published the below article titled "NSW Police harass journalist Shane Dowling after another malicious complaint from Australian judges" on the 22nd May 2019.

NSW Police harass journalist Shane Dowling after another malicious complaint from Australian judges

I received a harassing visit from the NSW police last Wednesday (15/5/19) and the complaint seems to have been made by staff at the NSW Supreme Court. Although the complaint could have come from the High Court of Australia given I had visited there a few days before to film a video and then I published an article titled "High Court of Australia's Justice Keane and Justice Edelman caught protecting their bribe-taking and paedophile judicial mates." (Click here to read the article)

The court staff would have told lies to the police and the court staff know it. They knew what they were doing when they made the complaint as they had done it before which led to a malicious police charge which was withdrawn by the CDPP.

I sent the below email complaining to the CDPP and NSW police senior management on Monday 20/5/19 at 3.30pm and asked for a response from both the CDPP and NSW police by 5pm today, Wednesday 22/5/19. At the bottom is the response I received from the CDPP but I have not had a response from the NSW police at the time of publishing this article. If I receive one, I will update this post.

From: SHANE DOWLING
Sent: 20 May 2019 15:30
To: Sarah.McNaughton@cdpp.gov.au;
full1mic@police.nsw.gov.au
Cc: andrew.colvin@afp.gov.au
Subject: Harassment by the CDPP and NSW Police- Contempt of the High Court of Australia by the CDPP and NSW Police – Formal complaint

Dear Ms Sarah McNaughton – Commonwealth Director of Public Prosecutions and Mick Fuller – NSW Police Commissioner

Just after 12pm on Wednesday the 15th of May 4 NSW police officers visited my residence and tried to harass, bully and intimidate me into stop reporting on my website and social media why I was in jail last year for contempt of court and also to stop complaining about Justice Clifton Hoeben. (See attached business card from Detective James Gatward)

From the conversation, I had that day I take it that Detective James Gatward had been in contact with the CDPP before the police visited me and he was there representing the CDPP to some degree as well.

I was jailed last year for 4 months as I was found guilty of calling Justice Clifton Hoeben a paedophile and Registrar Christopher

Bradford a suspected paedophile and known bribe-taker when I was in court on the 3rd of February 2017. I was also jailed for breaching suppression orders twice by writing articles reporting on why I had been charged with contempt of court.

Some of the things that were said to me by Detective James Gatward on the 15/5/19 were:

1. I needed to stop writing emails to the court calling Justice Clifton Hoeben a paedophile and bribe-taker and if I don't stop I could be charged with using a carriage service to menace, harass or cause offence (s 474.17 – Criminal Code Act 1995). Detective Gatward referred to an email I sent to the court in April 2019. That email, in fact, was in March and went to the Premier, Attorney-General, Chief Justice Bathurst and Justice Hoeben complaining that Justice Hoeben would not stand down from hearing numerous defamation matters involving me even though I did 4 months jail for calling Justice Hoeben a paedophile. (See attached email to Premier Gladys Berejiklian, Attorney-General Mark Speakman, Chief Justice Tom Bathurst and Justice Clifton Hoeben)

2. Detective Gatward made it clear he had spoken to people at the NSW Supreme Court recently who had complained about me. I assume it was the same people (Chief Justice Tom Bathurst, Chris D'Aeth and Rebel Kenna) who were behind the malicious complaint that led to the police charge in 2017 that was withdrawn by the CDPP. From the conversation, it also sounds like Detective Gatward might have spoken to Justice Hoeben.

3. Detective Gatward said a complaint had been made by the court at a higher level and it had filtered down to them.

4. I needed to stop calling people paedophiles and bribe-takers on my website and that I could be charged with

criminal defamation. Is Detective Gatward also a defamation lawyer?

5. I could be charged again for the email that I sent to the court in September 2016 even though I was previously charged by the NSW police and the CDPP withdrew the charge in March 2018. (See attached letter from the CDPP) I assume Detective Gatward had recently spoken to the CDPP about me possibly being charged again even though no crime had been committed.

6. Detective Gatward said words to the effect that he didn't want to have to come back and take my computer etc. It was a blatant attempt to intimidate me.

7. I said the police charge in 2017 was a malicious charge as it was political communication protected by the 1997 High Court judgment Lange v ABC and Detective Gatward said it wasn't. How would he know?

8. Detective Gatward confirmed he knew I still had matters before the court that Justice Hoeben was dealing with. On that basis alone Detective Gatward should not have been telling me what I can and can't say about Justice Hoeben as it could and would be construed as an attempt to interfere in the administration of justice by attempting to intimidate me as a party to the matters that are still in court and as a witness in the matters.

9. Defective Gatward confirmed he knew I had been to Canberra to film a video and I have written an article about 2 High Court of Australia judges only a few days before. On that basis, Detective Gatward had to of known that on Tuesday the 14th of May 2019, the day before his visit, I had filed an application in the High Court asking for the Seven v Dowling matter be removed to the High Court. That matter also deals with the allegations of Justice Hoeben being a paedophile and the police charge

and evidence from 2017. Once again the police visit could be construed as an attempt to interfere in the administration of justice in the High Court of Australia as I published links to the application and supporting affidavit on Twitter the night before the police visit.

10. I believe the complaint and police visit is likely linked to my visit to Canberra on the 10th of May 2019, the video I filmed outside the High Court and the article I published on the 11th of May titled *"High Court of Australia's Justice Keane and Justice Edelman caught protecting their bribe-taking and paedophile judicial mates"*. (Click here to read the article)

What is very disturbing is that accusing government employees of crimes such as bribe-taking is expressly dealt with by the High Court of Australia in the 1997 judgment Lange v ABC and the 2004 judgment Coleman v Power where the High Court ruled it is protected under the Australian constitution as political communication even if it is untrue as long as the person saying it believes it is true. Justice Helen Wilson wrote in her judgment when she sentenced me to jail for contempt words to the effect that she has no doubt that I believe what I say.

Detective Gatward was factually wrong on many points. I said I had not written to the court accusing Justice Clifton Hoeben of being a paedophile since I was released from jail and Detective Gatward said I had.

I later rang Detective Gatward at 3.33pm the same day and spoke to him for 38 minutes. I phoned him to ask for another meeting to correct his false allegations and he could only refer to an email I sent to the court where I wrote about why I was in jail to back up his claims against me. He then said that I had written that Justice Hoeben had not denied the allegation that he is a paedophile and that was evidence of me harassing just Hoeben. So what? That is a fact and part of the story that I was writing about so it's not harassment.

During the phone call Detective Gatward also said:

1. I should see a doctor and get therapy even though he knew I had 4 mental health exams and all cleared me of any mental health issues. Why would Detective Gatward say that?

2. I should stop the numerous court cases and litigation. I pointed out that I had not instituted the matters and he said words to the effect that if I close my website the matters would go away. Once again this could be construed as an attempt to interfere in the administration of justice.

3. I said I was going to file a malicious charge claim against the NSW Police for the 2017 police charge and he said words to the effect that I shouldn't. What right does he have to give that advice?

What makes the above worse is there was no legal basis for the police to even come and see me. It was a blatant attempt to interfere in the administration of justice. On the 3rd of May 2019 at a hearing, Justice Hoeben had 5 Court Sheriffs in court to try and intimidate me and Justice Hoeben threatened me with jail over 10 times for what I said in court as I tried to represent myself. I wrote an article about it titled *"Five Sheriff's Officers used to intimidate journalist Shane Dowling by the Supreme Court's Justice Clifton Hoeben"* and wrote:

Five Court Sheriffs were used to try to intimidate me on Friday (3/5/19) in the NSW Supreme Court by Justice Clifton Hoeben while he aided and abetted Kerry Stokes and Capilano Honey in their SLAPP lawsuits against me.

I was in court for directions for the 2 criminal contempt applications I had made in the Capilano Honey matter and also in the Kerry Stokes, Ryan Stokes and Justine Munsie matter. I was also in court for the hearing of Capilano Honey's application to strike out my defence.

Justice Hoeben had obviously pre-planned his intimidation game as he was looking after the defamation list and there were other lawyers and barristers in court for other defamation matters and he didn't want them to see what he was up to. My 2 matters were listed near the top, but he said he would hold both over until the end knowing all the other lawyers and barrister would be gone.

I noticed one Court Sheriff at the beginning but the full 5 didn't show up until just before Justice Hoeben started to deal with my matters and they sat in the back of the courtroom for my full hearing. I asked Justice Hoeben about the 5 Court Sheriffs and how it was disgraceful and a waste of taxpayers money but he wouldn't answer. At the start of the hearing, Justice Hoeben started lecturing me on the court's code of conduct about when I could talk, when I had to sit down and not to interrupt anyone etc.

Then all of a sudden Justice Hoeben said that I was also not to call him a paedophile or any other judges of the court a paedophile and that I knew what would happen if I did. He was implying that I would be jailed, and the 5 court Sheriffs were obviously to reinforce the threat.

I thought that's a first for any judge to say that but not surprising given I spent 4 months in jail last year for calling Hoeben a paedophile and registrar Christopher Bradford a suspected paedophile and known bribe taker in court in February 2017.

I said to Justice Hoeben what if I called him a "bribe-taker". He said I couldn't call him that either. (Click here to read the full article)

What happened in court on the 3rd of May 2019 is almost identical to what happened when Detective Gatward and 3 other police officers visited me on the 15th of May. I was in court again on Friday the 17th of May for directions in the frivolous and vexatious Jane Doe v Dowling matter and once again Justice Hoeben refused to stand down from hearing the matter, warned me not to call any judges of the court or him a paedophile or call them corrupt. There were also 4 court sheriffs in the court to try and intimidate me again. My matter was the first to be heard in the defamation list and all 4 court sheriffs left the court as I did which proves they were only there to intimidate me.

Once again, we have powerful evidence that the NSW Police and the CDPP are working with the courts to interfere with court cases and to intimidate litigants including up to the High Court of Australia.

As you both know I am a journalist and I will be publishing a story on this matter so could you please respond by 5pm on Wednesday the 22nd of May 2019. I would like a separate response from both of you. I will also be filing this email and any response with the High Court of Australia as evidence why all matters involving me need to be removed to the High Court of Australia as it is obvious I will be denied natural justice from the NSW Supreme Court.

Regards

Shane Dowling
Kangaroo Court of Australia

Below is the reply from the CDPP that I was emailed at 4.16pm today (22-5-19)

CDPP

Australia's Federal Prosecution Service

Telephone
Facsimile
www.cdpp.gov.au

Your Reference:

Our Reference:

22 May 2019

Shane Dowling
Unit 7 / 4 Park Parade
BONDI NSW 2026

Dear Mr Dowling

Your email correspondence dated 20 May 2019

I refer to you email sent at 3.30pm on Monday 20 May 2019, addressed to the Commonwealth Director of Public Prosecutions, and others.

The function of the Commonwealth DPP is to prosecute crimes against the Commonwealth and to provide advice to referring agencies. It has no investigative power or function and relies on investigative agencies to refer briefs of evidence to support a prosecution, which the CDPP then assesses in accordance with the Prosecution Policy of the Commonwealth.

This Office is unable to assist you in relation to the matters that you have raised in your email of Monday 20 May 2019.

Yours faithfully

For Director

The issue of judicial corruption is legally protected because it is political communication and for the police to harass me at any time in an attempt to silence me is scandalous, but they did it a few days before a federal election which needs a public investigation.

End of article

Detective James Gatward and the 3 other police officers he was with who visited me as mentioned above were from the Fixated

Persons Investigation Unit who investigate people with mental health issues who are fixated on an issue and who might become violent.

Because I wrote to politicians and the court complaining about Justice Hoeben hearing my matters somehow, I was a fixated person. I have no doubt the reason Detective Gatward wanted me to go see a doctor and get therapy was so he could say that I have admitted that I have mental health issues and then he could take action against me. He was trying to stitch me up.

Another problem for the police is that I have no history of violence simply because I am not a violent person.

The Fixated Persons Investigation Unit were used by a corrupt judiciary and corrupt police force to harass a journalist at the taxpayer's expense.

By September 2019 I had finally decided it was time to move back to Queensland which is where I am originally from and I moved on the 7th of November 2019. The main motive to move was the fact that I was never going to get justice in NSW courts with the judges and court staff making that clear and also because I had the threat of further police harassment hanging over my head. I figured that there was no point hanging around to just be stitched up again at any time that suited them and by moving it would also improve my chances of defending myself.

I published an article on the 17th of December 2019 titled "On the run with fugitive Australian journalist Shane Dowling" and said:

"I'm arguably a fugitive journalist given I moved interstate to avoid the police and courts in NSW but the main person chasing me and trying to jail me again is actually the media companies Seven West Media, the Channel Seven Network and SWM's nutter chairman Kerry Stokes."

"The definition of a fugitive is: "A fugitive from justice, also known as a wanted person, can be a person who is either convicted or accused of a crime and hiding from law enforcement in the state or taking refuge in a different country in order to avoid arrest"

After I moved I still had the Capilano Honey & Ben McKee v Shane Dowling matter and the Seven Network v Shane Dowling matter to deal with which I was hoping to have transferred to the Supreme Court of Queensland and I made an application in both matters.

But Justice Kunc refused to make a decision in transferring the Seven Network matter and said the Supreme Court of NSW would hear Seven's Notice of Motion to have me charged with Contempt of Court which they made clear they wanted me jailed again.

By this time, I was forced to appear via the phone as I was in Queensland and I started recording the hearing. I told Justice Kunc I was recording, and he spat the dummy. I published an article on the 23rd of November 2019 titled "Podcast of Supreme Court of NSW – Seven v Dowling – Allegation Chief Justice Tom Bathurst is a paedophile – Has Justice Kunc had a sexual relationship with Dr Nicky McWilliam – Judicial bribery etc." which has an audio copy of the hearing and I published the article in full in chapter 16.

If you have never heard a corrupt judge in full flight it is worth going to my website and having a listen.

On the 7th of February 2020 the Capilano Honey v Shane Dowling matter was set down for a quick directions hearing which I recorded, and it is probably one of the most powerful articles because the corruption is so blatant. I published an article on the 15th of February 2020 titled "Justice John Sackar recorded corruptly acting as counsel for Kerry Stokes' Capilano Honey" as per below:

Barrister Monique Cowden   Justice John Sackar

Justice John Sackar recorded corruptly acting as counsel for Kerry Stokes' Capilano Honey

Justice John Sackar was caught corruptly acting as the barrister/counsel for the Kerry Stokes' controlled Capilano Honey in a 5-minute recording as per below on the 7th of February 2020. The recording should end the careers of Justice Sackar and Capilano Honey's barrister Monique Cowden. I certainly don't miss Sackar in the recording and I call him a grub, a common criminal and did use a bit of colourful language but he deserved it and I was within my legal rights. (See Coleman v Power – High Court of Australia 2004)

There is no more powerful evidence of corruption then what comes out of someone's own mouth and that is why at about the 4:30 minute mark Capilano's barrister Monique Cowden warned Justice Sackar that I might be recording the hearing and when I said I was Justice Sackar quickly finished the phone call. I was in Queensland on the phone and they were in court in Sydney at the NSW Supreme Court.

Justice Sackar and the court have been ducking and weaving trying to work out what to do since Friday (7/2/20) when they found out I was recording the hearing. If you listen to one video on this website this is the one you should listen to.

There are five key issues that you should focus on, although trained lawyers will notice many more abuses of the law when listening to the below recording.

Issues: 1. Justice Sackar says at the beginning that he has already spoken to Capilano's barrister Monique Cowden before I was phoned for the hearing and she had said there are 2 matters to be dealt with. One a hearing date and two an application by me to transfer the matter (to Queensland). That constitutes private communication between Capilano and Justice Sackar. What else did they talk about?

2. Capilano's barrister makes no argument against having the matter transferred to Queensland. Justice Sackar argues for Capilano why it shouldn't be transferred. That shows Justice Sackar acting as Capilano's barrister/counsel which is blatant corruption. How did Justice Sackar know that Capilano didn't want the matter transferred and who told him?

3. In the recording, I say a number of times that the last time I was in court before Justice Sackar, for the Jane Doe v Dowling matter, there were 5 court sheriffs in court to bully, harass and intimidate me to deny me natural justice. Justice Sackar refuses to deny it because it is true. He also refuses to say why the court sheriffs were in court which confirms it was to bully, harass and intimidate me to deny me natural justice. (It was actually 4 court sheriffs, not 5, that day as I reported last year in an article)

4. Justice Sackar refuses to say why he has never published his reasons for denying me interrogatories and discovery in the Jane Doe matter and why he failed to recuse himself at the hearing on the 14 June 2019 even though he knows Bruce McWilliam who is Kerry Stokes top lawyer at Seven and his wife Nicky. Justice Sackar has since emailed me the transcript for that day but still refuses to publish the reasons which is a breach of common law because he doesn't want people to see his lies and abuse of the law.

5. The matter for the directions hearing in the recording is Capilano Honey Limited and Ben McKee v Shane Dowling 2016/299522 which was heard on Friday the 7th of February 2020. Both Capilano Honey and Ben McKee are based in Brisbane and since last year I am in Queensland and about 2 hours travel to Brisbane. There is no basis for the matter to be heard in NSW except that Kerry Stokes and Bruce McWilliam have the judges in their hip pockets.

That is why you will hear Justice Sackar say a couple of times that I am arguing the matter should be transferred to Queensland because there are a couple "witnesses" in Queensland which is crap. He knows that but he is deliberately trying to downplay the reason why it should be transferred and that is because all parties are bases in Queensland. Once again Justice Sackar is acting as Capilano's barrister/counsel which is blatant corruption.

Justice Sackar grants Capilano leave to apply for hearing dates before he has decided if the matter will be transferred which is the cart before the horse because he knew that he would deny transferring the matter. Sackar also fails to order a jury to hear the matter.

capilano-honey-v-shane-dowling-justice-sackar-7-2-20-mp4

(You might need to turn the volume up on the above recording as it is hard to hear the judge and the barrister because they were also using a mobile phone. The judge claims the court had technical issues with their phone system which they also claimed they had on another occasion.)

Just so there is no doubt, the phone call was recorded for my own legal protection and it is being published as political communication exposing government corruption which is protected as per the 1997 High Court judgement Lange v ABC which invalidates any laws that restrict political communication so there is nothing they can do.

This is a SLAPP lawsuit that has been going on since October 2016 and only now has a hearing date been set in Sydney when all parties are in Queensland. It is part of several SLAPP Lawsuits by Kerry Stokes and his associated companies.

Barrister Monique Cowden

After the hearing, Justice Sackar knew he was in trouble because his crimes had been recorded by me, so he shifted responsibility to Chief Justice Tom Bathurst

In December 2019 the listing manager, Milio Cesta-Incani, for the Supreme Court emailed us because there was no future court date which led to the matter being set down for a directions on Friday the 7th of February. (Click here to read the email chain)

On the recording Justice Sackar grants Capilano Honey leave to apply to have the matter listed for final hearing but he had second thoughts afterwards and is clearly worried by my recording his corrupt conduct and his associate sent an email late Friday afternoon (7/2/20) saying:

Dear parties

This morning application was made to approach the Registry to obtain a hearing date in the above matter.

His honour indicated at the time that that course was appropriate. However would you please confirm in writing by return that the matter is ready for hearing and that three days is thought best estimate.

As indicated this morning, his Honour is not in control of the listings and the matter will have to go to the Chief Judge in Common Law or the Chief Justice for allocation.

I responded on Monday the 10/2/20 at 9.09am:

Dear Ms Young

The matter is clearly not ready for hearing on many grounds and besides that, it should have been transferred to the Queensland Supreme Court in Brisbane as both the applicants are based in Brisbane and I am based just outside of Brisbane and Justice Sackar is well aware of that. We all know this is a SLAPP lawsuit being aided and abetted by the court.

Can you please advise when Justice Sackar will publish his reasons for his decisions at Friday's (7/2/20) hearing?

Can you also advise why Justice Sackar has failed to publish his reasons for the hearing in the associated Jane Doe & Ors v Shane Dowling matter which was heard on the 14th of June 2019 where

Justice Sackar refused to recuse himself and dismissed my application for interrogatories and discovery?

Regards

Shane Dowling

Justice Sackar emailed me the transcript for the Jane Doe matter but has refused to publish his reasons and has failed to publish reasons for the hearing as per the above recording.

On Tuesday the 11/2/20 at 19.13 am Sydney time the listing manager tried a swifty and emailed me saying that Justice Sackar had ordered the matter be set down for hearing. I emailed him back putting him in his place. (Click here to read the email chain)

Then I hit the jackpot. The listing manager, Milio, emailed me on Friday the 14/2/20 saying: "*Chief Justice Bathurst confirms that this matter be set down for hearing to commence on 25th May 2020 at 10.00am with a hearing estimate of 3 days.*"

That email tied Chief Justice Bathurst directly into the corruption. So, I sent Chief Justice Bathurst, NSW Attorney-General Mark Speakman and others the below email:

From: SHANE DOWLING
Sent: 14 February 2020 10:32
To: chambers.chiefjustice@courts.nsw.gov.au; office@speakman.minister.nsw.gov.au; icac@icac.nsw.gov.au; judcom@judcom.nsw.gov.au
Cc: Alexander Latu <alexander.latu@addisons.com>; Martin O'Connor <Martin.OConnor@addisons.com>; Richard Keegan <richard.keegan@addisons.com>; SCO – Listings (Shared Mailbox) <sc.listings@justice.nsw.gov.au>; sandy.dawson@banco.net.au; Monique Cowden <mcowden@level22.com.au>
Subject: Criminal conduct by Chief Justice Tom Bathurst. RE: Supreme Court proceedings: 2016/00299522 Capilano Honey

Limited v Shane Dowling – Notice of Listing of Hearing on 25 May 2020

Dear Chief Justice Tom Bathurst and Attorney-General Mark Speakman

Can you please explain the following:

1. Why has the matter 2016/00299522 Capilano Honey Limited v Shane Dowling not been transferred to the Supreme Court of Queensland given both applicants, Capilano Honey and Ben McKee, and myself live in Queensland? (Both applicants are based in Brisbane and I am in Queensland within 2 hours travel of Brisbane)

2. Are you directing that I represent myself by phone in the matter as I will not be travelling to NSW?

3. Why has the court not set a jury?

4. Given Chief Justice Bathurst instructed court staff (Chris D'Aeth and Rebel Kenna) in September 2016 to make a frivolous complaint to the NSW police and CDPP after I sent an email to judges of the court outing Chief Justice Bathurst as a known paedophile as well as 17 others why is Chief Justice Bathurst having anything to do with my matter?

5. Can you advise why Chief Justice Tom Bathurst refused to make a statement to the police or deny the allegation that he is a paedophile?

6. Have you listened to the recording from last Friday's (7/2/20) direction hearing in the matter where Justice Sackar made if very obvious he was acting on instructions to aid and abet Capilano Honey and Ben McKee?

Please respond by 5pm today.

Regards

Shane Dowling

I also emailed barrister Monique Cowden and asked her why she warned Justice Sackar that I might be taping the phone call. The answer is obvious. I had already recorded and published calls of court in November 2019 so that was no surprise to the lawyers. But they obviously didn't realize how blatantly and openly corrupt Justice Sackar would act in their favour and then they became worried.

Neither Chief Justice Tom Bathurst or Monique Cowden have responded to the questions in my emails at this point and I doubt they will.

I will follow-up with formal complaints to the relevant authorities which will include the NSW Attorney-General Mark Speakman and NSW Premier Gladys Berejiklian. Yes, they might do nothing although the recording is powerful evidence which will make it very difficult to ignore. But if they do nothing then we can go to town on social media for them covering up judicial corruption which they won't like.

End of article

Chapter 19

The Damian Speers hoax phone calls

With me recording the telephone court hearings after I moved to Queensland it became a big concern for the Supreme Court of NSW and the judges as their corrupt conduct was being exposed and broadcast on my website. Lawyers for Seven and Capilano also complained about me recording and publishing the hearings but it didn't stop me.

So, they changed tack and had someone phone me on Thursday the 27/2/2 claiming to be a court staff member and threatening me with contempt charges if I kept on recording the hearings. I published an article on the 29th of February 2020 titled "NSW Supreme Court call police to investigate threatening hoax phone call to journalist Shane Dowling" as per below:

NSW Supreme Court call police to investigate threatening hoax phone call to journalist Shane Dowling

The NSW Supreme Court CEO Chris D'Aeth has made a formal complaint to the police in relation to a threatening phone call, as per below, I received from a person who said they were "Damian Speers" and that he was calling from the NSW Supreme Court at the direction of Justice Kunc. I spoke to the police briefly on Friday and they have started an initial investigation.

It turns out that it was a hoax call and no Damian Speers has ever worked for the court but what is probably more disturbing is that Justice Kunc tried to cover it up and has refused to answer questions on the matter. I also recorded Justice Kunc's disturbing conduct and his attempted cover-up which is also below.

The key elements below are the recording of the hoax call from "Damian Speers", the recording of Justice Kunc trying to cover it up and the letter from the Supreme Court CEO Chris D'Aeth.

If "Damian Speers" is found he is looking down the barrel of at least 2 criminal charges. Firstly, section 474.17 the Criminal Code Act 1995 which is "using a carriage service to menace, harass or cause offence" and secondly, impersonating a government official as well as possible other charges.

Background

I moved to Queensland in November 2019 because I was getting harassed by the NSW Supreme Court on the instructions of Chief Justice Tom Bathurst. This had gotten worse over the last few years during the course of the numerous SLAPP lawsuits that Kerry Stokes and his associated companies had taken out against me.

I was jailed twice for contempt and breaching suppression orders that had no legal basis. When in court they would have up to 5 court sheriffs there to intimidate me and while at home I was the subject of 2 false and malicious complaints to the police by the court. It resulted in my unit being raided once by the police in 2017, computer taken and a malicious charge that was later dropped in relation to an email I sent to the court and also another intimidatory visit from the coppers in 2019.

There are two SLAPP lawsuits left to be dealt with. Seven v Dowling and Capilano Honey and Ben McKee v Dowling. I applied to have both matters transferred to Queensland, but they are refusing to do so or give reasons why.

Since I have been in Queensland, I have continued with the court proceedings in NSW over the phone and I have recorded the proceedings for my own physical and legal protection because of the widespread judicial corruption and harassment.

I recorded the interlocutory hearing in the Seven v Dowling matter on 22/11/19 and published it on this website in an article on the 23/11/19. (Click here for the recording and article) Seven West Media weren't happy when I published the recording and their lawyers Richard Keegan sent me the below email:

From: Richard Keegan
<richard.keegan@addisonslawyers.com.au>
Sent: 25 November 2019 18:52
To: 'SHANE DOWLING'
Cc: Alexander Latu <alexander.latu@addisonslawyers.com.au>

Subject: Seven Network (Operations) Limited & Anor v Dowling: recent publications

Dear Mr Dowling

We refer to your most recent publication on the Kangaroo Court of Australia website and associated Facebook and Twitter accounts in which you publish a recording of the hearing before his Honour Justice Kunc on 22 November 2019, referred to as a "podcast" in your various publications. We note the "podcast" has also been published on YouTube under your name.

We are writing to advise you that the recording and publication of Friday's hearing appear to breach Section 9 and/or 9A of the *Court Security Act* 2005 (NSW) (the Act) and we intend to bring your conduct to Justice Kunc's attention. You will be aware that the breach of the Act brings with it criminal liability.

In the meantime, we suggest you remove all publications of the "podcast".

Regards

Richard Keegan | Special Counsel

ADDISONS

D +61 2 8915 1075 | M +61 410 554 357 | F +61 2 8916 2075

E richard.keegan@addisonslawyers.com.au

Level 12, 60 Carrington Street, Sydney NSW 2000

End of email

When the matter was back for further hearings on the 2nd and 3rd of December 2019 Justice Kunc would tell me at the start of each session that I was not to record the hearing and he asked if I understood. I said no each time. At this point, I have not published those recordings and because of that maybe Seven and the court thought I wouldn't publish any more court proceedings.

On the 7th of February 2020, I recorded the Capilano Honey and Ben McKee v Shane Dowling hearing where I requested the matter be transferred to Queensland. Justice Sackar refused to transfer the matter and refused to give reasons why. The recording shows clear bias by Justice Sackar and I published an article with the recording on the 15th of February 2020 titled "Justice John Sackar recorded corruptly acting as counsel for Kerry Stokes' Capilano Honey".

The recording was very damming of Justice Sackar and at that point, the court and Kerry Stokes's Seven and Capilano, who both use Kerry's same lawyers, would have known that I was not scared of the judges and I was going to keep on recording and publishing the hearings which would expose the corruption during those hearings.

I have no doubt that my lack of fear of judges and their instructions not to record the hearings was the reason that the judges, the court and/or people associated with Kerry Stokes and his companies tried the below phone call to try and intimidate me not to record the court hearings.

2 Phone calls

On Wednesday the 26/2/20, I received a phone call at 5.23pm that lasted 21 seconds from a person who asked if I was Shane Dowling and they said they were from the Crown Solicitors Office. I recognized the voice as someone who had previously made threatening calls to me and I told them to send me an email and I hung up. Their phone number did not show up.

On Thursday the 27/2/20 I received a phone call at 5.15pm that lasted over 3 minutes and is below in full. Some of the key issues that I have noted after listening to the recording are:

1. The person identified themselves as Damian Speers and said they were calling from the NSW Supreme Court.

2. At 21 seconds, he said "The judge wants us to remind you that it is an offence to record court proceedings"

3. At 42 seconds: he said he is with the Prothonotary's office. While I knew there was a Prothonotary which is Rebel Kenna to my knowledge there was no "Prothonotary's office" which was confirmed to me the next day in a phone call to the court.

4. At 1:05: in relation to call the day before he said that someone called Patrick or Amanda would have called me from the Crown Solicitors office.

5. At 1:10: he says "We have directions from the judge for you not to record the proceedings".

6. At 1:25: he says "We just want to remind you that the judge does not want you to record the proceedings and put them up on the internet otherwise you will be dealt with for contempt of court. We have instructions that you will be dealt with for contempt"

7. At 1.41: he says " We would also like you to take down the recording if you could of the last time you were in court before the justice in the Seven West matter"

8. At 1:58: he says he reports to the Chief Justice Tom Bathurst.

9. At 3:23 he says "I have the authority of the Chief Justice to do this"

I published the above phone call from Damian Speers on YouTube, Facebook and Tweeted it on Thursday night (27/2/20) a few hours after it happened. I then emailed the court as per below:

From: SHANE DOWLING
Sent: 27 February 2020 21:30
To: Mary Boneham <mary.boneham@courts.nsw.gov.au>
Cc: Richard Keegan <richard.keegan@addisons.com>; Alexander Latu <alexander.latu@addisons.com>; kstokes@seven.com.au; rstokes@seven.com.au; Kieran Smark <smark@smark.com.au>; sandy.dawson@banco.net.au; mcowden@level22.com.au; Justine Munsie <justine.munsie@addisonslawyers.com.au>; Martin O'Connor <Martin.OConnor@addisons.com>; Rebecca Lennard <Rebecca.Lennard@courts.nsw.gov.au>
Subject: Threatening phone call from Supreme Court staffer Damian Speers RE: Seven Network (Operations) Limited & Anor v Dowling – 2017/116771

Dear Justice Kunc

I received a threatening phone call today from someone called Damian Speers saying they were from the NSW Supreme Court.

They made it clear they were calling in regards to the Seven West Media matter and told me I needed to delete a previous article on the matter.

I recorded the call and it can be heard here:
https://youtu.be/AS21pjmz4bo

Damian Speers mentions a couple of times in the phone call that he is calling on your behalf Justice Kunc and he also says he is calling with Chief Justice Tom Bathurst's authority.

The phone call also clearly implicates Seven West Media and I have no doubt that Kerry Stokes or someone associated with him is involved in some way with the phone call and it is consistent with the corrupt conduct of Seven's lawyers to date.

Regards

Shane Dowling

Kangaroo Court of Australia

End of email

I also emailed Kerry Stokes and his lawyers who did not respond.

The directions hearing took place at 9.30am (NSW time) Friday the 28th of February 2020 and Justice Kunc was ducking and weaving as the below recording shows. He refused to answer any questions. Some of the key points from the recording are:

1. I asked Justice Kunc if he instructed Damian Speers to call me. He refused to say or deny it. Why?

2. Just Kunc had to have known I had received a hoax threatening phone call claiming to be calling on behalf of Justice Kunc because Kunc would know if he had given his consent for someone to call on his behalf or not. Justice Kunc would have to have known the crime of using a carriage service to intimidate and harass had been committed but he tried to cover it up. Why?

3. Justice Kunc highly likely knew if Damian Speers existed and if that is the case Justice Kunc also tried to cover-up the crime of someone impersonating a government employee. Why?

If you listen to the recording below of Justice Kunc and the one above of Damian Speers they are both identical and singing from the same song sheet in the context of they both want me to stop recording the hearings which suggests that the fake Damian Speers was calling on behalf of Justice Kunc which would explain why Justice Kunc refused to answer the questions I asked him.

(Click on the triangle on the left below to listen to the recording of the hearing)

Bishop Terry Brady at Cathedral House with papal honour recipient Justice Francois Kunc

I called the NSW Supreme Court executive office an hour after the hearing at 10.45am (NSW time) and spoke to a lady called

Naomi. I asked her if there was a Damian Speers who worked at the Supreme Court and she said she had not heard of him. I said he told me he worked in the Prothonotary section. She said there is a Prothonotary and but there is no Prothonotary section. She said she would check the computer and then she said she would ask the CEO.

A couple of seconds later the CEO Chris D'Aeth was on the phone and said he was about to email me a letter. I asked him if there was a Damian Speers who worked there, and he said no and that he would be making a complaint to the police. I received the below letter via email at 10.48am (NSW time)

Supreme Court
of New South Wales

Executive Office

Law Courts Building, Queens Square
Level 5, 184 Phillip St, Sydney 2000
GPO Box 3, Sydney 2001
website: www.supremecourt.justice.nsw.gov.au
Email: sc.enquiries@justice.nsw.gov.au

ABN: 77 057 165 500

Mr Shane Dowling

By email only: shanedowling@hotmail.com

28 February 2020

Dear Mr Dowling,

Telephone call – 27 February 2020

I refer to your email correspondence to the chambers of Justice Kunc regarding a telephone call purportedly from the Supreme Court by a person describing themselves as Damian Speers.

There is no current or former employee of the Court registry, or judicial staff, called Damian Speers (or with a similar spelling).

Following enquiries with the Crown Solicitor's Office they have also confirmed they do not have an employee called Damian Speers.

Such is the serious nature of this hoax call I have referred this matter to the NSW Police for investigation.

Yours sincerely,

Chris D'Aeth
Executive Director and Principal Registrar

Cc: Chambers of Justice Kunc
Crown Solicitor's Office

(It's the same Chris D'Aeth that made a malicious complaint to the police about me a couple of years ago on the instruction of Chief Justice Tom Bathurst)

The letter raises a number of questions and points to the decision by the court to make the compliant only being taken after they knew I had recorded Justice Kunc trying to cover-up the hoax call and its associated crimes. If Justice Kunc had passed on or had plans to pass on, my email and his knowledge of the hoax call to Chris D'Aeth then why didn't he tell me at the hearing at 9.30am?

Chris D'Aeth went and made a formal complaint to the police at about 12pm and I received a call from the police at about 12.15pm and another call an hour or so later. I have no doubt that the complaint to police was only made to cover themselves because my recordings exposed them and that the court and its staff don't really want the police to investigate because it will uncover judicial corruption.

I will be making my own complaint to police by Monday and we see where we go from there.

But make no mistake, there are a lot of worried people hoping like hell that "Damian Speers" is never found.

Previous threatening phone calls

In 2017 after I published an article titled "Chief Justice Bathurst has journalist charged with contempt for accusing him of corruption" I received the first threatening phone call from a person I have no doubt was the same person as the "Damian Speers". I made a complaint to the then Crown Solicitor which I published the email in an article in April 2017 which is below.

Dear Ms Lea Armstrong – NSW Crown Solicitor

I am currently being pursued by the NSW Supreme Court for contempt of court which is being handled by Jillian Caldwell (Special Counsel for Crown Solicitor) in your office which you may or may not be aware of. The matter has been afoot since February and further background information can be found in the attached email.

I wish to make a formal complaint in relation to a threatening phone call that I received from a male who identified himself as being from the Crown Solicitors office or the Solicitor General's office. When I took the call I had no doubt the person was calling from your office. What happened is below:

"At 8.11pm on Tuesday the 14/2/17 I received a call on my mobile phone (0411 238 704) from an unknown number from a male who identified himself as calling from the Crown Solicitors office or the Solicitor General's office. He gave me a name but I forget what it was. I told him he should not be calling me that time of night and that he could have called me today or tomorrow. He said he would call back tomorrow and asked me if the mobile was the best number. I asked what it was about, and he said that if I did not take down the 2 videos on my website that Registrar Bradford would have me incarcerated as he was very upset. He also said I should apologise to Registrar Bradford."

"I went off at him and said he should not be calling me that time of night about it. He again said that Registrar Bradford was very upset. I said to call me tomorrow and hung up."

"At 4.25pm on Wednesday the 15/2/17 I received a missed call from an unknown number."

I have a few questions:

1. *Can you confirm if anyone in your office called me at 8.11pm on Tuesday the 14/2/17? Can you confirm if Jillian Caldwell is aware of anyone calling me?*

2. *If it was someone in your office can you please tell me their name and position?*

3. *Given that it is possible that several federal laws and state laws have been breached (E.g. 474.17 Using a carriage service to menace, harass or cause offence) can you advise of what action you will take?*

4. *What next step do you suggest I should take?*

Can you please respond ASAP?

Regards

Shane Dowling

Lea Armstrong swept the complaint under the carpet and did nothing. What it shows is "Damian Speers has been around a while and seems to be the go-to-guy when the court and people such as Kerry Stokes want to intimidate litigants.

Summary

This whole scandal is about me recording and publishing the corruption by judges in the NSW Supreme Court and there are plenty of people who are worried about it and they got desperate and tried to stop it but it has backfired badly.

When investigating a matter like this the first question to ask is who would benefit from the "Damian Speers" phone call. The first person would be Justice Francois Kunc who I now have on numerous recordings of lying, deceiving and acting corruptly while sitting on the bench working as a judge. The second person is Kerry Stokes and his associated companies as the caller even mentioned Seven West Media. The third likely person would be Chief Justice Tom Bathurst given his vendetta against me using taxpayers' funds.

There is already enough evidence above to charge Justice Kunc with attempting to conceal a serious indictable offence.

One thing is for certain is that "Damian Speers" has links to the court and likely Kerry Stokes as well via his lawyers or employee Bruce McWilliam. I have had about 5 or 6 calls from "Damian Speers" since the first call in 2017 and I wonder how many other people he has threatened on behalf of others while impersonating government officials. When he made the first call in 2017, I actually did believe he was from the Crown Solicitors Office, so I am sure he has fooled others as well.

Damian Speers would be well advised to hand himself in once he has read this article, and he will read it, because it is just a matter of time before he is caught. His voice is all over the internet and he'll be on the run for the rest of his life if he doesn't hand himself in. Also, he will get a discounted sentence if he confesses his crimes and maybe walk scot-free if he gives the others up who paid him to make the call.

The police are investigating the matter after the complaint by Chris D'Aeth and I will be making my own complaint. But if the police sweep it under the carpet we won't worry because this website is now in full investigation mode and the number one priority is to find "Damian Speers".

I believe "Damian Speers" is a lawyer or works in the legal system somewhere because he knows the lingo from the calls I have had from him and likely works in Sydney. If you recognise his voice please contact me which you can do anonymously via email or snail mail etc with the details on the about page.

End of article

I had a call from NSW police officer Lauren Drake the same day that Chris D'Aeth emailed me the above letter saying her had referred it to the police. She was working on the front counter at the Day St Station in Sydney's CBD. I told her the 3 main suspects for the hoax call would be Justice Francois Kunc, Chief Justice Tom Bathurst and Kerry Stokes' Seven West Media. She made it very obvious she was not keen to do anything with the complaint which was no surprise to me as I had no doubt the court had only made the complaint to cover themselves as they knew I would be publishing the tapes in the above article.

I knew the NSW police would do nothing, so I sent an email on the 1st March 2020 to the NSW Police Commissioner Mick Fuller as per below:

From: SHANE DOWLING <shanedowling@hotmail.com>
Sent: 01 March 2020 22:24

To: 'full1mic@police.nsw.gov.au'
<full1mic@police.nsw.gov.au>
Cc: 'hamm1jor@police.nsw.gov.au'
<hamm1jor@police.nsw.gov.au>; 'juri1kri@police.nsw.gov.au'
<juri1kri@police.nsw.gov.au>;
'SECRETARIAT@police.nsw.gov.au'
<SECRETARIAT@police.nsw.gov.au>;
'with1sel@police.nsw.gov.au' <with1sel@police.nsw.gov.au>;
drak1lor@police.nsw.gov.au
Subject: Supreme Court complaint regarding using a carriage service to harass and intimidate and impersonating a government official

Dear Mick Fuller - Commissioner of the NSW Police Force

I received a threatening and harassing phone call from a "Damian Speers" on Thursday (27/2/20) who said he worked for the NSW Supreme Court and was calling on behalf of Justice Kunc and he had Chief Justice Tom Bathurst's authority to make the call and he wanted me to stop recording the court hearings which I have been doing since I moved to Queensland as they have refused to transfer the matters to Queensland. I recorded the Damian Speers call and published it that night. I also raised the matter with Justice Kunc's staff that night via email.

The next morning at a directions hearing at 9.30am Justice Kunc tried to sweep "Damian Speers" threatening phone call under the carpet and I called him out on it numerous times but he kept ducking and weaving. I also recorded the hearing call which I have also now published.

After the hearing Chris D'Aeth – CEO and Principal Registrar of the NSW Supreme Court made a complaint to the Day St police regarding the harassing and threatening phone call I received because they said there was no "Damian Speers" working at the Supreme Court.

The complaint was made by the court which they are entitled to do as someone impersonated one of their staff but I have no doubt that they only made the complaint to cover themselves because they knew that I had recorded Justice Kunc trying to cover it up and they knew I would publish it. I also have no doubt Chris D'Aeth and the court want the police complaint swept under the carpet.

The recordings of the threatening phone call from Damian Speers, the hearing with Justice Kunc and other details are in an article I published Saturday night 29/2/20 which is here: https://kangaroocourtofaustralia.com/2020/02/29/nsw-supreme-court-call-police-to-investigate-threatening-hoax-phone-call-to-journalist-shane-dowling/

I spoke to a Constable Lauren Drake a couple of times on Friday (28/2/20) after Chris D'Aeth had apparently visited the Day St police station to make a formal complaint and from what I could make out she wasn't planning on doing much.

The matter before Justice Kunc is the Seven West Media and Seven Network v Dowling matter which also involves the Day St police as they illegally took my computer in 2017 after a malicious complaint by Chris D'Aeth and the Supreme Court and then gave the computer to Seven as per the below email chain.

The prime suspects behind the call would be Justice Kunc, Kerry Stokes's Seven and their lawyers who have made it clear they want me to stop recording the court hearings because they are trying to stitch me up. Chief Justice Tom Bathurst would also be a suspect.

Damian Speers has made a number of calls to me before and I suspect has made many other similar calls to other people and he is likely a lawyer who works in the justice area.

In those circumstances at the very least the Day St police station should not be investigating the complaint and given the gravity of the crime which undermines justice it really should be given to senior police. In fact, the matter should really go to the federal police. I haven't made a formal complaint to anyone yet, but I will.

Please respond ASAP.

If you plan on covering it up now or in the future, then you will own it.

Regards

Shane Dowling

Kangaroo Court of Australia

I called the Day St police station on the 6th of March 2020 and made the following notes:

Called Day St Police - 10.55am 6/3/20 - They said that Lauren Drake went on leave on Saturday the 29/2/20 which is the day after Chris D'Aeth made a complaint about Damian Speers. Not back until the 20/3/20 doing the night shift. Starts day shift on the 28th of March.

No other officer allocated the complaint. Event number 73308625

I had spoken to constable Lauran Drake on Friday the 28th of February which was the day that Chris D'Aeth made the police complaint, I phoned her late on Friday 28th and left a message for her to call me which she didn't then on Saturday the 29th she went on holidays for 3 weeks and no other officer was allocated the complaint. A very obvious cover-up.

I decided to make my own complaint to the QLD police, but they refused to take my complaint once they realised it involved government corruption in NSW. I made a complaint about the QLD police refusing to take my complaint and I recorded a couple of phone calls with an Inspector Bruce Kuhn which make interesting listening, to say the least. I published an article on the 12 April 2020 titled "Queensland copper Inspector Bruce Kuhn recorded trying to sweep NSW government corruption under the carpet" as per below:

Queensland copper Inspector Bruce Kuhn recorded trying to sweep NSW government corruption under the carpet

Below are 2 telephone recordings of Queensland police officer Inspector Bruce Kuhn lying, deceiving, ducking and weaving in relation to a complaint I made about officers at the Coolangatta police station refusing to take a complaint from me.

Inspector Kuhn was meant to investigate my complaint against the Coolangatta police officers and his lies are that blatant and obvious it is embarrassing and reminds me of the saying that it would be comical if it wasn't so criminal.

The phone calls I had with Inspector Kuhn are only short but are a must-listen for everyone as you can hear for yourself a senior police officer refusing to do their job and then lying and deceiving to try to cover it up.

There are 2 main lies that Inspector Kuhn repeats a number of times. Firstly, that the reason the police officers at the Coolangatta station refused to take my complaint, which was about a harassing and threatening hoax phone call I received a few weeks ago, is because of my conduct after they refused to take my complaint. Think about it, it's ridiculous. How can my conduct after they refused to take my complaint then be the reason they refused to take my complaint?

Secondly, Inspector Kuhn said no crime had been committed in relation to the harassing and threatening hoax phone call, but he admitted he hadn't listened to the phone call so how would he know.

After the first phone call, Inspector Kuhn realised he was in trouble with his lies and he phoned again the next day to try and fix the issue, but he only dug a bigger hole for himself.

Inspector Kuhn also tried to say that it was an NSW police matter even though the NSW police and Federal police said it was a Queensland police matter given I was in Queensland when I received the hoax phone call. Although the NSW police could still investigate the person impersonating a court staff member which they are meant to be doing now. (Click here to read more)

The police and other law enforcement agencies avoid investigating government corruption like the plague and that is why the Queensland police don't want to know anything about it because the hoax phone call leads back to judges of the NSW Supreme Court.

I recorded the hoax phone call and published it in an article on the 29th of February titled "NSW Supreme Court call police to investigate threatening hoax phone call to journalist Shane Dowling". In the article, you can also listen to Justice Francois Kunc refusing to answer questions about the hoax phone call which is disturbing given the call involved someone impersonating a court staff member and making threats to me on behalf of Justice Kunc. That points to Justice Kunc having knowledge of and/or involvement in the hoax call. (Click here to read more)

In the phone calls below, you will also hear that the police officers at the Coolangatta police station were considering charging me with disorderly conduct when I went back to the station to get their names so I could make a complaint about them refusing to take my complaint.

The first phone call below from Inspector Bruce Kuhn was on the 19th of March 2020.

The second phone call below from Inspector Bruce Kuhn was on the 20th of March 2020. He knew his lies from the day before didn't add up and he tried to fix the problem but only made it worse.

I will follow the above matter up with a further complaint higher up the ladder. This is a stock standard example of where the cover-up is worse than the original crime.

End of article

I made a complaint against Inspector Bruce Kuhn and I received an email response on the 9th June 2020 with a letter attached dated the 5th June 2020 from a G K Sheldon – Superintendent – Assistant District Officer - Gold Coast District sweeping my complaint under the carpet. I'll continue to drive the matter through the proper channels.

Chapter 20

Chapter summaries

I will summarise the key points from the chapters here which is what you would do in a court of law when making out your case. In the final chapter which will be called "Closing arguments" I will put all the pieces together.

I had already been on the receiving end of Kerry Stokes SLAPP lawsuit, Munsie v Dowling, from April 2014 when in September 2016 I sent the email to all of the judges of NSW Supreme Court putting them on notice that I would be naming 15 judges, 2 registrars and 1 magistrate as known paedophiles and suspected paedophiles and raising judicial bribery allegations by the ABC and Fairfax Media in an article I was about to publish.

That was the spark that lit the fire for Chief Justice Tom Bathurst to throw everything he had at me to have me jailed and destroyed but in doing so he exposed the underbelly of the court like it has never been seen before because I was in a position to document it and report it. And fortunately for me, the Australian Federal Police, the Commonwealth Director of Public Prosecutions and a magistrate in the local court would not play his game otherwise I would have likely done more jail time.

The fact that I did jail time is not that important except for the fact that it shows how corrupt and how far the likes of Chief

Justice Tom Bathurst and the 2 judges who jailed me, Justice Ian Harrison and Justice Helen Wilson, will go to silence journalists from revealing the truth. They do not want anyone to know about what is happening in the courts and the crimes of the judges which in this case is the judges protecting and looking after paedophiles.

I had been making allegations of judicial bribery for many years and writing to the judges making the allegations, but it was not until I started making allegations of judges being paedophiles that they started trying to jail me.

Former High Court of Australia judge Dyson Heydon

I am close to finishing this book and only a couple of months ago a scandal breaks in the media (22/6/20) that former High Court of Australia judge Dyson Heydon allegedly sexually harassed and sexually assaulted many females in the legal fraternity over many years.

A report was given to the media that said Dyson Heydon sexually harassed at least six young female Associates when he was a judge of the High Court from 2003 to 2013. Chief Justice of the High Court, Susan Kiefel, issued a statement saying, "We are ashamed that this could have happened at the High Court of Australia."

Other media reports named lawyers who said they had been sexually assaulted and/or harassed by Dyson Heydon. This has led to Dyson Heydon's conduct being referred to the Australian Federal Police for a possible criminal investigation and some barristers referring Heydon to the Office of the Legal Services Commissioner for disciplinary action and possibly being struck off as a lawyer/barrister.

It has become obvious that hundreds of people in the legal fraternity have known for many years Dyson Heydon allegedly sexually harassed / sexually assaulted young females working for him and other females, yet nothing was ever done or said.

What the Dyson Heydon scandal shows is that the whole legal fraternity will act as one when covering up sex crimes at the highest levels in the legal system.

The scandal is the identical situation you get when judges act corruptly or look after paedophiles by giving them lenient sentences. No one says anything, except on rare occasions and then it is quickly swept under the carpet.

I will quickly summarise the key points from the chapters and then move on to the broader issues.

Chapters one to five dealt with Kerry Stokes and his associated companies and their SLAPP lawsuits against me. The history of all four matters are remarkably similar as per the brief outline below and it is the same sort of corruption that happened against me in the defamation matters that judges use when protecting their paedophile mates.

Munsie v Dowling (Kerry Stokes, Ryan Stokes and their lawyer Justine Munsie sued me for defamation)

Instituted in April 2014 at an ex parte hearing (secret hearing without my knowledge or consent). A super-injunction was issued (where I could not even tell anyone there was a court case afoot) with wide-ranging suppression orders and non-publication orders were also issued.

The applicants instituted contempt charges against me because I published an article telling people they were suing me for defamation.

The super-injunction, suppression orders and non-publication orders were lifted a few days later because there was no legal basis for them. A couple of weeks later Justice Peter Hall heard a notice of motion which was a back-door appeal and re-instated the non-publication orders. Peter Hall is now the Commissioner of the NSW ICAC.

I was fined $2000 for breaching the super-injunction, suppression orders and non-publication orders. Although I never had to pay it.

I had my defences kicked out and I was not allowed interrogatories (where they have to answer written questions), discovery (where I can subpoena documents), I could not subpoena people to give evidence and there was no jury for the final hearing even though I requested one.

All three applicants, Kerry Stokes, Ryan Stokes and Justine Munsie refused to give evidence and would not sign affidavits.

Justice Stephen Rothman heard the final hearing in April 2017 and handed down his judgment 14 months later in May 2018 in the applicant's favour and awarded them costs. They acted that corruptly during the matter they cannot enforce the costs.

Capilano Honey v Shane Dowling (Capilano Honey and CEO Ben McKee sued me for defamation)

Instituted in October 2016 at an ex parte hearing (secret hearing without my knowledge or consent). A super-injunction was issued (where I could not even tell anyone there was a court case afoot) with wide-ranging suppression orders and non-publication orders were also issued.

This was identical to the way the Munsie v Dowling matter was started with the same barrister, Sandy Dawson SC, and the same lawyers Richard Keegan and Martin O'Connor from Addisons Lawyers. It was also before Justice Peter Hall who heard the back-door appeal in the Munsie v Dowling matter.

It was before Justice Hall late on Friday the 7th of October 2016 and on Monday the 10th of October 2016 it was before Justice David Davies who continued orders and at the request of barrister Sandy Dawson SC referred the matter to the registrar to have me charged with contempt because I published an article telling people they were suing me for defamation.

There was no legal basis for the super-injunction, suppression orders and non-publication orders and they were lifted in 2018. Capilano appealed and lost in a unanimous decision in my favour.

The NSW Crown Solicitor's office wrote to me in February 2019 and told me that the court would not be charging me with contempt.

The final hearing was on the 25th, 26th and 27th of May 2020 but ran over time to include the 28th of May and the afternoon of the 3rd of June.

I had most of my defences thrown out by Justice Clifton Hoeben who continued to deal with the matter even after I did 4 months jail in part because I was found guilty of calling him a paedophile.

I was not allowed interrogatories (where they have to answer written questions), discovery (where I can subpoena documents), I could not subpoena people to give evidence and there was no jury for the final hearing even though I requested one.

Justice Richard Button heard the matter, reserved his judgment and then went on holidays and at the time of writing this book (September 2020) we are awaiting a decision.

Jane Doe and Ors v Shane Dowling (Four females suing for defamation paid for by Seven)

Instituted in December 2016 at an ex parte hearing (secret hearing without my knowledge or consent). Suppression orders and non-publication orders were issued to protect a well-known on-air host at Channel Seven and a well-known Channel 7 actress who was alleged by Amber Harrison to have had sexual relationships with the then Seven West Media CEO Tim Worner.

The proceedings were paid for by Seven West Media and it became clear they couldn't care less about the women and they were there to protect Seven, the Directors and Tim Worner.

The same legal team from the Munsie v Dowling and Capilano v Dowling matters were used which were barrister, Sandy Dawson SC, and lawyers Richard Keegan and Martin O'Connor from Addisons Lawyers.

In February 2017 two former female Channel 7 employees were added as applicants.

The first two applicants instituted contempt proceedings against me because I refused to take their names down from my website as I knew there was no legal basis for the court orders and because I was taking a stand against corrupt judges issuing corrupt suppression orders. I had decided to take that stand a few months earlier in the Capilano Honey matter. I was sentenced to four months in jail in August 2017.

All four women refused to give evidence at the hearing or sign affidavits. I was not allowed interrogatories (where they have to answer written questions), discovery (where I can subpoena documents), I could not subpoena people to give evidence and there was no jury for the final hearing even though I requested one.

All four women were named in a legal document that Amber Harrison filed with the Australian Human Rights Commission which meant they could not sue for defamation because it is protected by the defence of "Absolute Privilege."

Justice Desmond Fagan heard the final hearing in August 2019, and he pointed that out to barrister Sandy Dawson that it was protected by "Absolute Privilege" and there was a long debate about the issue. In September 2019 when Justice Fagan handed down a judgment in the applicant's favour and Fagan said no legal document naming the four women was tendered as evidence which was a lie.

The four women were awarded $150,000 each and indemnity costs were awarded against me. I have written to them asking for an itemised bill, but they have refused to send me one. I have no doubt the reason is that Kerry Stokes is worried that I will publish the bill which will show how much Seven West Media paid for the case. It will also raise many questions such as why was Seven West Media paying for 2 former female staff to sue me for defamation concerning allegations that they had sexual relationships with former Seven CEO Tim Worner?

Seven Network & Seven West Media v Dowling

As I previously said: In April 2017 Seven West Media and its subsidiary the Seven Network instituted proceedings against the unknown owner of the website sevenversusamber.com claiming the owner breached suppression and/or non-publication orders issued in Seven's proceedings against Amber Harrison. The matter was known as Seven versus Publisher X.

A few months later Seven changed the name of the respondent from Publisher X to me claiming I was the owner of the website. The matter is now known as Seven Network (Operations) Limited & Ors v Shane Dowling.

At about the same time Seven started suing me the ownership of the website sevenversusamber.com was transferred to Kerry Stokes and/or Seven West Media as they claimed they owned the copyright to the word "seven". The international body who oversees domain name disputes ordered the transfer of the name to Stokes and/or Seven.

The case is going nowhere, and a Notice of Motion filed in 2017 to have me charged with contempt has now been set down for hearing on the 1st and 2nd of February 2021 to be heard by Justice Kate Williams.

The same lawyers from the Munsie, Capilano and Jane Doe matters, Richard Keegan and Martin O'Connor, are running the case although they are using a different barrister, Kieran Smark SC, this time. Mr Smark has been used in the Jane Doe matter a few times and was the one who had me jailed for contempt as I assume barrister Sandy Dawson refused to do it. Mr Smark also acted pro bono for Beekeeper Simon Mulvany against Capilano Honey until Mr Mulvany sacked him after Mr Smark was caught colluding against Simon Mulvany with Capilano's lawyers Richard Keegan and Sandy Dawson SC. I published an article on the 3rd of June 2017 with all the evidence and details titled "Capilano Honey tried to have recorded evidence of their misogynistic CEO destroyed before court case" which is a fascinating read for the straight-out stupidity of the lawyers to document their corrupt conduct in a Deed of Release they wanted Simon Mulvany to sign.

The real scandal about the SLAPP Lawsuits

After what happened in 2017, with the contempt charge and police charge, all my matters before the NSW Supreme Court should have had an interstate judge appointed and I made numerous applications before different judges but they all refused my applications. All the judges refused to write detailed judgments with the reasons why I sought an interstate judge to hear my matters.

The key grounds for my applications to have interstate judges to hear the matters was that in February 2017 I had been charged for calling Justice Clifton Hoeben a paedophile and Registrar Christopher Bradford a suspected paedophile and known bribe-taker. In June 2017 I was also charged by the police for sending the September 2016 email to all the judges of the Supreme Court of NSW naming 15 judges, 2 registrars and 1 magistrate as known paedophiles or suspected paedophiles and also raising allegations of the Mafia $2.2 million judicial bribe. The complainants in the police charge were CEO and Principal Registrar of the NSW Supreme Court Chris D'Aeth and Registrar Rebel Kenna. This paragraph has key details and evidence why I should have had an interstate judge hearing my matters, but you will not see this evidence in any written judgments because the judges wanted it covered up.

It was obvious I was never going to get a fair go in NSW courts. But the only thing that a court must decide is whether there is perceived bias. That is, would the average person think there is a chance that I would not get a fair go. Given the evidence in the previous paragraph, I think the whole country would agree that at the very least there was a good chance that I would not get a fair go.

The reasons the judges wouldn't put key evidence in their written judgements is because they know the average person and the whole legal fraternity would be horrified that they were hearing the matters and that they had not stood down and requested an interstate judge hear the matters. It would have also shone a light on the fact that there are serious allegations against judges going unchallenged.

An example is that I moved to Queensland in November 2019 and I made an application on the 7th of February 2020 at a directions hearing to have the Capilano Honey matter transferred to the Supreme Court of Queensland as the applicants, Capilano Honey and Ben McKee, are also based here. Justice John Sackar, who is good friends with Seven West Media's Commercial Director Bruce McWilliam and his wife Nicky, refused to transfer the matter. Bruce McWilliam is the one running the SLAPP Lawsuits against me on behalf of Kerry Stokes

I recorded the hearing which lasted just over 5 minutes and published an article on the 15th of February 2020 titled "Justice John Sackar recorded corruptly acting as counsel for Kerry Stokes' Capilano Honey". It only goes for 5 minutes but it was enough time for Justice Sackar to expose his blatant corruption as he admits he had communication with Capilano's barrister Monique Cowden before they called me which constitutes private communication and Justice Sackar was running Capilano's arguments for them with no input from Capilano's barrister. Once again Justice Sackar breached common law and refused to publish written reasons for his decisions.

Barrister Sandy Dawson SC was Capilano's barrister since October 2016 and the final hearing dates in May 2020 were set down when he was in court but for some reason, he had jumped ship before the final hearing. I can only assume it got too hot for Dawson, even for a corrupt barrister like him.

Another example is Justice Richard Button who also refused to have the Capilano Honey matter transferred to Queensland. He at least he did publish reasons, Capilano Honey Ltd v Dowling (No 2) [2020] NSWSC 661, but he failed to give detailed reasons.

Justice Button in his judgment makes no mention of the fact that I did jail time after I was found guilty of calling his boss the Chief Judge at Common Law Justice Clifton Hoeben a paedophile and Registrar Christopher Bradford a suspected paedophile and known bribe-taker which I argued showed perceived bias and the matter should be transferred on that evidence alone.

Justice Button also made no mention in his judgement of the fact that Chief Justice Tom Bathurst ordered staff to make a complaint to police in regards to the September 2016 email which I named Chief Justice Tom Bathurst and Justice Hoeben as known paedophiles. In total, I named 15 judges, 2 registrars and 1 magistrate as known paedophiles or suspected paedophiles and raised allegations of the Mafia's $2.2 million judicial bribe of NSW judges.

The jail time I did and the judicial paedophile allegations I made against Supreme Court judges were raised by me as other powerful reasons why the matter should be transferred to Queensland and if it was in the judgment the average person would agree that it should be transferred. So, Justice Button watered it down in his judgment and wrote:

"He has also submitted that he just cannot get a fair trial in New South Wales, because of all the negative interactions that he has had with other Supreme Court judges."

Justice Button says that I claimed that I "cannot get a fair trial in New South Wales, because of all the negative interactions". That is a blatant distortion of the truth and conceals the powerful reasons why it should have been transferred.

Other judges were just as dodgy when writing their judgements as to why they would not stand down from hearing the matters or have an interstate judge appointed etc. At one-point Justice Clifton Hoeben, as defamation list judge, was hearing directions for the Capilano and Jane Doe matters in 2019 even after I had done jail time for calling him a paedophile in court. Hoeben refused to appoint another judge to hear the matters even when there was blatant bias. The first time I asked him to recuse himself he refused to publish a judgment why he wouldn't stand down but after the second application a week later he did publish a judgement but he refused to publish the key facts just like Justice Button as I outlined above.

Justice Hoeben did eventually publish a judgement on the 13th of May 2019, Capilano Honey Ltd v Dowling (No 3) [2019] NSWSC 539, and said at paragraph 17 concerning my application for him to stand down from hearing the matter:

"When this matter was reached on Friday 3 May 2019, the defendant objected to me hearing it. He did so on the basis of an email sent by him to the Court on 7 September 2016 in which he had referred to me and other Judges of the Court as "paedophiles". This email was attached to an affidavit of the defendant, dated 2 March 2018. This was the first occasion that I was made aware of this email and of the fact that a report to similar effect had been placed on the "Kangaroo Court" website."

It is not believable that he had just heard of the email and the article on my website where I call him a paedophile.

But what is even a bigger lie by Justice Hoeben is the fact that he made no mention in his judgment that I had done 4 months in jail in 2018 after I was found guilty of calling him a paedophile in court which I raised as the main reason why he shouldn't be hearing the case. Not only did I raise it as an issue but he had to have known and that is why he had 5 Court Sheriff's in court to intimidate me and that is why he said: "not to call him a paedophile or any other judges of the court a paedophile and that I knew what would happen if I did."

Paedophile priest gets 3 months jail for raping 3 boys by NSW Supreme Court's Justice Hoeben

By the time I posted the article titled "Paedophile priest gets 3 months jail for raping 3 boys by NSW Supreme Court's Justice Hoeben" on the 8th of September 2016 I had been publishing the Kangaroo Court of Australia website for almost 6 years focusing on judicial corruption and the associated government corruption.

Over that time it became clear the biggest elephant in the room in the legal fraternity that no one wanted to talk about or address was the protection that paedophiles were receiving from judges, magistrates and others who were meant to enforce the law.

I came to this conclusion from my observations reporting on judges and the courts and also from watching the scandalous stories of survivors at the Royal Commission into Institutional Responses to Child Sexual Abuse who outed the judges, police and prosecutors who failed them and protected the paedophiles. Anyone who watched the Royal Commission, which ran from 2013 to 2017 would have come to the same conclusion. The public hearings went from 2013 to 2016 and the Royal Commission's website says they heard from survivors in 8,013 private sessions, held between May 2013 and November 2017" and that was only the tip of the iceberg.

Even though the Royal Commission was in progress from 2013 until 2017 it did not stop judges protecting paedophiles during that time. For example, the article I published in September 2016 focused on the fact that Father Robert Flaherty was sentenced in August 2016 to a non-parole period of 3 months jail for abusing and raping 3 boys yet the Royal Commission didn't send it final Report to the government until December 2017.

Judge Garry Neilson, who still sits on the NSW District Court and who I named as a paedophile in the September 2016 email and article, used his position to support paedophiles and incest. I published an article on the 11th of July 2014 titled "Has Judge Garry Neilson outed himself for being a paedophile given he implied incest and paedophilia are OK?" which is below. Remember when you are reading the below article that the Royal Commission into Institutional Responses to Child Sexual Abuse had been in progress for 18 months when Judge Neilson made the comments he did and handed down the judgment he did.

Has Judge Garry Neilson outed himself for being a paedophile given he implied incest and paedophilia are OK?

District Court Judge Garry Neilson has used a court of law to try to justify incest and paedophilia as being OK and acceptable to the public. What Judge Neilson has done is make it clear to everyone that he is a sick and perverted person who should be in jail. Judge Neilson said that *"the community may no longer see sexual contact between siblings and between adults and children as "unnatural" or "taboo"* and:

"District Court Judge Garry Neilson said just as gay sex was socially unacceptable and criminal in the 1950s and 1960s but is now widely accepted, "a jury might find nothing untoward in the advance of a brother towards his sister once she had sexually matured, had sexual relationships with other men and was now 'available', not having [a] sexual partner"."

"He also said the "only reason" that incest is still a crime is because of the high risk of genetic abnormalities in children born from consanguineous relationships "but even that falls away to an extent [because] there is such ease of contraception and readily access to abortion"." (Click here to read more)

This came to light during the course of an appeal in the Court of Criminal Appeal in the last few days and Judge Neilson has at least one similar previous judgement which needs investigation as well.

Judge Garry Neilson *"who compared incest to homosexuality this week — and suggested it was no longer taboo — once gave an incestuous rapist a lighter sentence because he did not ejaculate inside his young niece or "treat her roughly".* (Click here to read more)

Background

Judge Neilson is currently hearing a case that involves a man raping his sister. Judge Neilson made his scandalous comments during the course of the proceedings and disallowed certain evidence. The prosecution has appealed. From what I can tell they have appealed both the disallowing of evidence and also asked for another judge given Judge Neilson's comments which clearly show he is a sick person and not fit to be a judge.

Circumstantial case that Judge Neilson is a paedophile

When Judge Garry Neilson started making the scandalous statements in court, he knew what would happen. All judicial officers know what they say in court is recorded and dissected by many parties including the media and they are fully aware of the consequences. They also know what they say in court can be used as grounds for an appeal and then three judges will have a good look at what they said. Judge Neilson would have been fully aware that an appeal was guaranteed once he said what he did. So, what was Judge Neilson's reason for knowingly ending his own career?

1. It is one thing to defend a person accused of being a paedophile as they might not be guilty but that is defending the person, not the act. The only people that I have heard of that defend paedophilia as an act or as a crime are paedophiles

themselves. I have never heard of anyone else defending it as an act or as a crime.

2. Judge Neilson knew exactly what he was doing, and he knew it would get media attention. It seems like a deliberate rallying call to other paedophiles to support the issue as they are under attack from the Royal Commission into Institutional Responses to Child Sexual Abuse which is currently in progress. (Click here to read more on their website)

3. Judge Neilson must be close to the mandatory retirement age of 70 so he would know there is little damage that can be done to him from a financial or career viewpoint. He will still get the full pension and I suspect this is part of his thinking in deciding to say what he has and when.

4. Judge Neilson should have been investigated previously given his scandalous judgement in the matter where he *"gave an incestuous rapist a lighter sentence"* as quoted above.

5. Judge Neilson could and should be charged with the criminal offence of Scandalising the Court as he would have been fully aware that he was undermining the public's confidence in the courts before he said what he did. So why did he do it? In my view, only a paedophile would say and do what he did knowing he was damaging the judiciary's reputation.

Peter Hollingworth when he was Governor-General of Australia defended a paedophile priest and Hollingworth was forced to resign. Neilson should not be given the luxury of resigning and should be sacked as soon as possible.

I spoke to the Attorney-General's office on Thursday regarding Judge Neilson and they asked for my feedback (I am told they asked for everyone's feedback who called that day as the matter had only been reported in the media a few hours).

I said words to the effect that *"there is a good chance that Judge Garry Neilson is a paedophile as they get off on pushing the boundaries and he would have been fully aware that there would be media attention regarding his comments. He has to go as he damages the reputation of all judges and the courts while he is still a judge.*" My viewpoint would not have been greatly different from most people I suspect.

I should give credit where it is due as the relatively new Attorney-General Brad Hazzard has moved fast and Judge Nielson has now been suspended from hearing criminal matters.

The SMH is reporting:

Mr Hazard had initially refused to be drawn on Judge Neilson's comments while MRM's trial was pending but in an about-face he issued a statement on Friday saying he had to refer the Judge to the commission because "confidence in the judiciary is a critical part of ensuring broader community support for the legal system".

Mr Hazard said he was acting on behalf of the community and that he had also written to the Chief Judge of the district Court, Reg Blanch, requesting that Judge Neilson not sit on any criminal trials until the commission had examined his complaint.

It is understood that on Thursday a senior NSW official referred the NSW judiciary to the royal commission after it was determined it could be defined as an "institution". (Click here to read more)

The commission referred to above that will investigate Judge Neilson is the Judicial Commission on News South Wales which is mostly a toothless tiger as they have no powers themselves and only make recommendations to the government. But at least that is a start and it must be noted that the Judicial Commission did recommend that the state government consider sacking Magistrate Jennifer Betts and Magistrate Brian Maloney in 2011. Both were directed to address parliament and show cause why they shouldn't be sacked. (Click here to read more)

It is also noteworthy that Judge Neilson has also been referred to the Royal Commission into Child Abuse that is currently afoot. That is what should happen, and it would be explosive to see Judge Neilson in the witness-box justifying his statements. There has been a very strong rumour for a long time that a paedophile ring operates in the Australian judiciary and I think it is something that has to be looked at closely especially given Judge Neilson's comments.

There really needs to be an independent Royal Commission into the judiciary by itself but let's start with Judge Neilson at the Child Abuse Royal Commission. If the Royal Commission does not call Judge Neilson as a witness, then the Royal Commission is saying that judges are above being accountable.

End of Article

For Judge Garry Neilson to say what he did and to protect paedophiles like he did while the Royal Commission was in progress shows what contempt he had for the Royal Commission. I was given a tip-off that Garry Neilson had abused boys when they were Scouts in the 1980s and I investigated as much as I could, but Scouts Australia who had already had an adverse finding made against them at the Royal Commission for protecting paedophiles refused to respond to questions. I published an article on the 26th of July 2014 titled "Scouts Australia refuse to answer questions re Judge Garry Neilson who supported paedophilia and incest" but the investigation never went any further.

Garry Neilson's support of paedophiles and incest attracted widespread media attention which forced the government and judiciary to act. Judge Neilson was taken off criminal trials and the Judicial Commission of NSW set up an inquiry after a complaint from the NSW Attorney-General which meant he could have been referred to the NSW Parliament for possible dismissal as a judge. What happened? Nothing. Because judges always protect judges and the Judicial Commission of NSW is overseen by the Chief Judges in NSW, Chief Magistrate in NSW, and a few other token appointments.

The Chief Executive of the Judicial Commission of NSW is Mr Ernest Schmatt and it says on their website "Mr Schmatt held senior legal and management positions in the public sector before his appointment, in October 1987, as the first Deputy Chief Executive of the Judicial Commission. In March 1989, he was appointed to the position of Chief Executive of the Judicial Commission." He has been there for 33 years and been in the Chief Executive position for 31 years. The Deputy Chief Executive, Mr Murali Sagi, "commenced employment with the Commission in 1992" which means he has been there 28 years. I find their length of time in roles that are meant to keep judges accountable very disturbing and they should be moved on.

I never felt a need to go through what evidence I used to name the 15 judges, 2 registrars and 1 magistrate as known paedophiles or suspected paedophiles in the September 2016 email. If they had responded to the email, which I allowed them to respond, then I would have detailed the evidence. But as I said above, I named Judge Garry Neilson as a paedophile and there is no doubt in my mind he is because the only people who would defend and protect paedophiles are other paedophiles which the same can be said for the others on the list and none of them complained either and that's why the email and article are still on my website.

The magistrate I named on the list as a known paedophile, Doug Dick, gave the former head of Bega Cheese Maurice Van Ryn bail in December 2014 after he had pleaded guilty to sexually abusing six boys aged eight to 16 and even though Maurice Van Ryn had abused another victim while previously on bail. There were calls for magistrate Doug Dick to be sacked, and he should have been, but he is still a magistrate. The decision was appealed, and Maurice Van Ryn was jailed a few weeks later after his bail was revoked.

In September 2015 Maurice Van Ryn was sentenced to 13 years jail with a non-parole period of 7 years for abusing 9 boys and girls between the ages of 8 and 15. It looks like more victims came forward after the original guilty plea and the sentencing. Maurice Van Ryn was sentenced to a further 9 years jail in 2019 after being charged with abusing another boy. His earliest release in now 2029.

Why would Doug Dick give bail to a confessed paedophile again who was waiting to be sentenced to lengthy jail term when the paedophile had recent history of abusing a child while previously on bail? The only answer I could come to was that Doug Dick is himself a paedophile and as he had to of known that he had no legal right to give Maurice Van Ryn bail.

In Chapter 7 I collated parts of the police statements by Supreme Court employees Chris D'Aeth, Rebel Kenna and Detective Kristijan Juric from the NSW police which showed Chief Justice Tom Bathurst directing court staff to stitch me up for jail time even though there was no legal basis to do so. While the NSW police did eventually charge me for sending the September 2016 email it was only after I raised in court during my contempt charge before Justice Wilson that no action or complaint had been made concerning the email. Once it got to court and the NSW police were forced to pass the prosecution of the charge over to the Commonwealth Director of Public Prosecutions the charge was withdrawn by the CDPP.

Chapter 8 is titled "Three Australian Prime Minister protecting paedophiles and their protectors: John Howard, Tony Abbott and Scott Morrison". When you have people at the highest level of politics defending the actions of paedophiles it becomes easy to understand why paedophiles can infiltrate every level of society.

Having 2 former Prime Ministers and the current Prime Minister defending paedophiles and/or their protectors is very disturbing and something that should be investigated irrespective of anything else. It is worth noting that John Howard appointed

Dyson Heydon to the High Court of Australia in 2003 and Tony Abbott appointed Dyson Heydon to head up the Royal Commission into Trade Union Governance and Corruption in 2014. John Howard has recently stood by Dyson Heydon, as he did with George Pell, since Heydon has been exposed in the media for sexually harassing young female staff and others in the legal fraternity.

Doing jail for breaching the suppression orders in the Jane Doe matter speaks for itself which I covered in Chapter 9. There was never any legal basis for the suppression orders and there still is not to this day. At the time I was stitched up for the jail-time in 2017 behind the scenes Chief Justice Tom Bathurst and court staff were working overtime to have me jailed and they took advantage of the Jane Doe contempt matter and had Justice Ian Harrison jail me. Justice Harrison was one of the judges I named as a suspected paedophile in the September 2016 email and he shouldn't have been hearing the contempt matter but he refused to step down from hearing it and in the sentencing judgment he lies and deceives about the email and his knowledge of it. See the judgment: Doe v Dowling [2017] NSWSC 1037 published on the 10th of August 2017.

In June 2017 after the NSW police had charged me in relation to me to sending the email, after a complaint by Rebel Kenna and Chris D'Aeth, the police told me that they would be contacting the other people named in the email and that I could face possible further charges. If that is the case that means the police would have contacted Justice Ian Harrison before he sentenced me which is further reason Harrison should not have heard the matter.

In Chapter 10 I deal with being charged by the NSW Supreme Court for Contempt of Court for what I said in court on the 3rd of February 2017. But as the evidence shows that was just an opportunistic stitch-up as Chief Justice Tom Bathurst and the court had been trying to have criminal charges laid against me since I sent the paedophile judge list in the email on the 6th of September 2016.

It shows to what lengths the judges and the court will go persecuting someone who calls them out regarding their protection and support of paedophiles. None of them ever denied my allegations I made against them. Even Rebel Kenna who I named in the email as a suspected paedophile and who made a complaint to the police never denied the allegation in her police statement. Although given she made a complaint to the police it might be regarded as a denial.

Chapter 11: When Justice Helen Wilson issued orders for me to file and serve a Notice of a Constitutional matter on all the Attorney-Generals because I argued even if I had of said why they claimed I said in court it was protected as political communication, not one responded. I found it odd because what I was convicted of saying in court, naming one judge and one registrar, was a small quote of what I said in the email and what is published on my website where I name numerous judges as paedophiles and suspected paedophiles.

What I said in the email and on my website published in the 8th of September article titled "Paedophile priest gets 3 months jail for raping 3 boys by NSW Supreme Court's Justice Hoeben" is protected as political communication and not even the police who charged me asked me to take down the article or email and that's why they are still on my website to this day.

It is a further reason why the Attorney-Generals should have intervened in my Contempt of Court charge, but all the Attorney-Generals have a long history of protecting corrupt judges. It's also a further reason why the High Court of Australia should have heard my appeal.

The key evidence to take away from Chapter 12 which deals with the police charge is the timeline of the statements which shows the NSW police, Commonwealth Director of Public Prosecutions and Australian Federal Police all refused to charge me. We know this because the complaint was initially sent to the NSW Police on the 6th of September 2016 who did nothing. The complaint was then sent to the CDPP on the 21st of September 2016 after a meeting Chief Justice Tom Bathurst had with Chris D'Aeth. The CDPP did nothing except refer the matter to the AFP which the court was advised on the 26th of September 2016.

Only after I raised the email in court on the 4th of May 2017 as part of my defence during the contempt hearing before Justice Helen Wilson did the NSW police ultimately charge me which was 10 months after the initial police complaint.

The fact that paedophiles have been protected by the judiciary and law enforcement agencies is not something new and it was exposed badly during the Royal Commission into Institutional Responses to Child Sexual Abuse. As I said in Chapter 13 the starting point for jail sentences for paedophiles in South Australia is between 10 to 12 years as stated by the Royal Commission Chairman Justice Peter McClellan in a speech in April 2017. Compare that to 3-month non-parole period sentence for the paedophile priest Father Flaherty in NSW which I wrote about in the September 2016 email and article and for which the judiciary came after me for in a big way.

Chapter 14: Police protecting paedophiles is what led to the Special Commission of Inquiry in Newcastle in 2012 but the hit was put on the outcome from the start when they appointed known paedophile protector Margaret Cunneen to head up the Inquiry. Cunneen used her position to attack whistleblower Peter Fox and defend the police. Cunneen also has a long history of being friends with corrupt police including the infamous Roger Rogerson who is currently in jail for murder which makes Cunneen's appointment even more scandalous.

Cunneen released a report in May 2014 attacking Peter Fox and in July 2014 she was in the witness stand at the Royal Commission into Institutional Responses to Child Sexual Abuse perjuring herself like no tomorrow trying to justify scandalous advice she gave which led to alleged paedophile Scott Volkers walking free.

The new mandatory sentencing laws for paedophiles are a smoke screen for doing nothing regarding Australia's paedophile protection racket as I outlined in chapter 15.

In September 2019 Scott Morrison and the federal Attorney-General Christian Porter announced they would be introducing new federal laws for the mandatory sentencing of paedophiles. In April 2020, the High Court of Australia set a new precedent in the George Pell matter that allows paedophiles to walk free if they can get a witness to contradict the evidence of an accuser even if a jury finds the witness is not credible.

Just to recap "From September 2019 until the new laws were introduced July 2020 the rate had gone up from 28% to 39% of paedophiles convicted of federal child sexual abuse crimes did not receive jail sentences. The problem was never the laws, it has always been the corrupt judges."

Why do judges break the law, by failing to enforce the law, protecting so many paedophiles? That is the question that Prime Minister Scott Morrison and the federal Attorney-General Christian Porter should be asking but to date, they have refused to do so. And then they need to address the problem.

Chapter 16: Justice Kunc should have thrown the Seven Network & Seven West Media v Shane Dowling matter out of court a long time ago back in 2017 when he first started dealing with the case. All he has done is help expose his corruption and the underbelly of corruption in the Supreme Court of NSW and that is why his conduct is covered in detail in both chapter 5 and chapter 16.

The where numerous reasons why Justice Kunc should have recused himself from hearing the matter long before he did in June this year and he only did it then on the basis he was going on sabbatical and would not be able to hear the contempt charge until next year.

Justice Kunc has a personal interest in the case as he knows Seven's head lawyer Bruce McWilliam and his wife Nicky. Kunc also is a senior member the Catholic Church, which has a history of running the world's largest paedophile ring, as Kunc received a papal honour in 2016 and was named a Knight Commander of the Order of St Gregory the Great.

The Seven matter also deals with unchallenged allegations, by me, that Chief Justice Tom Bathurst and other judges are paedophiles or suspected paedophiles. That's because Seven subpoenaed the police paperwork for my charge, that was later dropped, as well as my computer from the police.

There are three good reasons why Kunc should have never been anywhere near the case and why he should be investigated for his corrupt conduct, blatant bias, and that's a major reason why I have named him in this book as a paedophile. I asked Kunc if he wanted to apologise to all the victims given his Pope appointed position as a Knight Commander of the Order of St Gregory the Great, but he refused. I suspect that Justice Kunc is friends with George Pell as Pell was based in Sydney for many years and maybe even Pell had a say in Justice Kunc's papal honour, but I never asked Kunc that, although I should have.

In Chapter 17 I dealt with 2 judges of the High Court and their refusal to grant me Special Leave to Appeal which is required before the full court of the High Court hears the appeal. There is nothing special with judges of higher courts protecting the corrupt and criminal conduct by judicial officers in lower courts who are their mates. Remember that Scott Morrison announced that 38% of paedophiles convicted of federal child sex crimes never went to jail and that wouldn't happen if judges of the High Court were handing down judgements that made sure that lower court judicial officers enforced the law correctly and honestly.

Becoming a fugitive and being forced out of NSW is self-explanatory which I covered in Chapter 18. Some of the key points are:

1. Chief Justice Tom Bathurst and the NSW Supreme Court were doing everything they could to deny me natural justice and jail me when they could.
2. The court would have up to 5 court sheriffs in court for the Capilano Honey / Kerry Stokes defamation matters to try to intimidate me and undermine me defending myself in court.
3. I was never allowed juries for the defamation matters, never allowed to issue interrogatories or discovery to subpoena documents from the other parties.
4. The Supreme Court of NSW would refuse me fee waiver for the appeals/applications I would make even though I was entitled to the fee waivers and to prove the point the High Court of Australia approved my fee waiver applications and my financial position hadn't changed.
5. The NSW police raided my home in 2017 and took my computers after a frivolous and vexation complaint by the Supreme Court of NSW staff Chris D'Aeth and Rebel Kenna.
6. The NSW police charged me with the frivolous and vexation complaint by the Supreme Court of NSW about an email I sent to the court as a journalist. The charge was later dropped as it would have failed and been very embarrassing for the court and prosecution who by the time it was dropped were the CDPP.
7. The NSW police visited me in May 2019 to intimidate me after another frivolous and vexatious complaint by the Supreme Court of NSW.
8. On several occasions someone associated with the NSW Supreme Court phoned me impersonating an employee of the NSW Crown Solicitors Office making threats that I

would be jailed if I did not take down certain articles from my website.

9. After I moved to Queensland someone associated with the NSW Supreme Court phoned me impersonating a Supreme Court of NSW employee and again making threats that I would be jailed if I did not take down certain articles form my website. I deal with the matter in Chapter 19.

The biggest scandal of Chapter 19 is that it shows how government corruption will be protected and covered-up across state borders with the Queensland Police lying and deceiving to in effect cover-up corruption in NSW Courts by refusing to investigate the Damian Speers hoax calls.

Chapter 21

Closing arguments

Whether you agree with me or not that numerous Australian judges are paedophiles, including the ones that I name in this book and on my website, one thing that can't be disputed and that is the fact that Australian judges are running a paedophile protection racket. We know that for sure because the statistics and judgments prove it.

Remember, none be of the judges I have named in the book and/or on the KCA website have denied the allegations I have made against them. And the judges named in the September 2016 email all refused to make complaints or give police statements when they had the opportunity as the police told me when I was charged in June 2017 that they would approach all the people named in the email. The judges who protect the paedophiles are just as bad as the paedophiles.

In 2019 28% of paedophiles convicted of federal child abuse crimes never went to jail and that same year the federal government said they would introduce mandatory sentencing because so many convicted paedophiles went free. Yet in the next 12 months, before the government legislated the new mandatory sentencing laws, the figure went up to 39% of convicted paedophiles never went to jail. Why? It is as if the judges thought to themselves "we better look after as many paedophiles as possible now before the new mandatory sentencing laws come into effect". If you have a better explanation let me know.

Just remember that there are already laws that say convicted paedophiles must go to jail. But the judges just ignore the law and knowingly break the law when they let paedophiles off with suspended sentences or community service etc. Justice Peter McClellan who was the Commissioner at the Royal Commission into Institutional Responses to Child Sexual Abuse went into detail how the Australian judiciary had failed survivors of child sex abuse.

The next area that proves that there is an Australian paedophile protection racket is the sentences and you only have to look at some of the recent ones over the last few years. Two examples already raised in this book are:

Father Flaherty who received 3 months for abusing 3 boys in 2016 which was a key element of the 2016 email and article where I named numerous paedophile and suspected paedophile judges.

Justice John North giving a confessed paedophile a suspended sentence in 2017 for abusing 2 girls. Justice North also issued a suppression order to protect the paedophile even though the victims objected. One reason Justice North gave for not sending the paedophile to jail is that he had not had sex education at school.

In May 2020 a paedophile was given a suspended sentence because of the Coronavirus and I published an article on the 16th of May 2020 titled "Supreme Court judges Justice Wilson, Hulme and Hamill give paedophiles a get out of jail free card during the Coronavirus crisis" as per below:

Supreme Court judges Justice Wilson, Hulme and Hamill give paedophiles a get out of jail free card during the Coronavirus crisis

Convicted paedophile, Robert Crick, who sexually abused his 5-year-old grandson has avoided jail after three Court of Appeal judges in the Supreme Court of NSW felt sorry for him because of his claimed health issues and they were worried he might catch the Coronavirus in jail.

This is a stock standard case where the courts deliberately rewrite the law in favour of paedophiles and come up with any and every excuse possible not to jail them. The problem of judges failing to enforce the law and jail paedophiles is so bad that Prime Minister Scott Morrison announced in September 2019 that the government was introducing new mandatory sentencing laws for paedophiles. (Click here to read more) Unfortunately, Scott Morrison has failed to follow through with the new laws at this point but if he had then Robert Crick would be in jail right now.

The Court of Appeal has set a precedent that now binds lower courts and single judges of the Supreme Court to follow. Will it also means is all paedophiles now get a "get out of jail free" card until after the Coronavirus crisis is over which could be years away?

Robert Crick's lawyers claimed his age and his health issues meant he was more at risk of catching the Coronavirus and because of that he should not be jailed.

In 2016 I wrote about paedophile catholic priest Father Robert Flaherty being sentenced in August 2016 to a non-parole period of 3 months jail for abusing and raping 3 boys in an article titled "Paedophile priest gets 3 months jail for raping 3 boys by NSW Supreme Court's Justice Hoeben."

In Father Flaherty case, the Court of Appeal should have increased his jail sentence but reduced it because Father Flaherty's lawyers did the big sob story that he suffered numerous health issues and only had 6 to 12 months to live.

Father Flaherty's lawyers told the court in February 2016 that he only had 6 to 12 months to live but almost 4 years later in

November 2019 Father Flaherty was charged was sexually abusing a 4th boy and is currently on bail awaiting trial. (Click here to read more) The Catholic Church kept paying Father Flaherty's rent, electricity and car lease etc after he was released from jail in 2016 until A Current Affair did a story on it. (Click here to read more)

How did Father Flaherty's lawyers get it so badly wrong in February 2016 when they told the court that he only had 6 to 12 months to live? How accurate are Robert Crick's claims of health issues and why in other cases, which are below, are health issues ignored by judges?

The SMH reported on the 28/4/20 in relation to Robert Crick:

A grandfather convicted of molesting his grandson the day before his sixth birthday will not be sent to prison because of the coronavirus pandemic.

The 76-year-old man, given the pseudonym of RC to protect the identity of his victim, was convicted in the District Court in July last year of twice digitally penetrating the five-year-old's bottom.

RC, a former public servant who also trained for five years as a priest, was then sentenced to an 18-month community order for sexual intercourse with a child under 10 years.

The Court of Criminal Appeal unanimously found this week that the sentence imposed by Justice Justin Smith SC was "manifestly inadequate".

"It is so far below the range of sentences that could be justly imposed for an offence of this nature that it could tend to undermine public confidence in the proper administration of criminal justice in the sentencing of offenders for the commission of serious sexual assaults upon very young children," Justice Helen Wilson said.

The maximum sentence for sexual intercourse with a child under 10 years is life imprisonment. (Click here to read more)

So, Justice Helen Wilson says the sentence *"could tend to undermine public confidence in the proper administration of criminal justice"* but she then lets the convicted paedophile free and the other two judges, Justice Robert Hulme and Peter Hamill, agreed. It is the 3 judges who have undermined the public's confidence in the courts, and they know it.

RC v R; R v RC [2020] NSWCCA 76 (Click here to read the judgment)

There was a suppression order on Robert Crick's name but for some reason, the suppression order was lifted because Channel 10 named him in the below video, interviewed his lawyer and tried to interview him which was broadcast on Tuesday (12/5/20).

Below is the story of another paedophile who has a long history of abusing more than 15 boys but on Friday (15/5/20) he was only sentenced to a minimum jail term of 7 months. But at least he did go to jail which is a bit better than Robert Crick being set free.

Catholic brother nicknamed 'The Rat' jailed for sex abuse of four Traralgon schoolboys

Marist Brother Gerard Joseph McNamara, 82, has begun his second stint in prison after pleading guilty to indecently assaulting Traralgon schoolboys in the 1970s.

McNamara was working at St Paul's Catholic College in Traralgon when he indecently assaulted more than 15 students between 1970 and 1975.

McNamara was sentenced in the Victorian County Court on Friday to 35 months in prison, with 28 months suspended, after pleading guilty to four charges of indecent assault and one count of common assault.

Since 2006, he has been sentenced three times for sexual offences against pupils but, until Friday, had only served nine months in jail.

On June 17, 2006 McNamara was sentenced to 36 months in prison, wholly suspended, for indecently assaulting seven boys aged between 11 and 13.

In December 2016 he escaped jail time again when he was given a wholly suspended prison sentence for abusing two young brothers at the school back in 1975.

It was not until September 2018, when McNamara came before the courts again, that he was ordered to serve nine months in prison for assaulting four boys aged between 11 and 15 years.

McNamara suffers glaucoma, skin diseases, prostate cancer, anxiety and depression.

He will be eligible to be released from prison before Christmas. (Click here to read more)

Marist Brother Gerard Joseph McNamara is 82 so he would also be a prime candidate to catch the Coronavirus. Will he now appeal given the Robert Crick precedent above?

Justice Robert Hulme

Serial paedophile Gerald Ridsdale given more jail time

The SMH reported on Thursday the 14/5/20:

Australia's most prolific paedophile priest, Gerald Ridsdale, is likely to die in prison after having his jail time increased again following another sentence for sexually abusing boys.

Ridsdale, due to turn 86 next week, was 25 years into a 33-year sentence and was eligible for parole in April 2022.

But his earliest release date is now April 8, 2025, after he was sentenced in the Melbourne County Court on Thursday for the abuse of another four boys in western Victoria in the 1970s.

Judge Gerard Mullaly set a maximum 10-year term with a non-parole period of four years for the 14 charges.

Taking into account Ridsdale's age and the likelihood of him dying in jail, three of those years are to be served cumulatively with the sentences he was already in jail for.

"At your age, my sentence may well mean that you are as a consequence more likely to die in custody," Judge Mullaly said. (Click here to read more)

Ridsdale is also very sick as the ABC reported:

The former priest appeared via videolink with a walker beside him, and also suffers from high blood pressure and arthritis.

He has also had a heart bypass and bowel surgery. (Click here to read more)

But the judge didn't give Ridsdale a "get out of jail free" card because of the Coronavirus and nor should he have. Ridsdale is now 86, also a prime candidate to catch the Coronavirus and also now in a position to appeal given the Robert Crick precedent above?

There are hundreds if not thousands more like Marist Brother Gerard Joseph McNamara and paedophile priest Gerald Ridsdale in jail or awaiting court and/or sentencing who will now be in a position to potentially benefit from the Robert Crick precedent which is dangerous for society.

Justice Helen Wilson is corrupt

Justice Helen Wilson wrote the judgment in the Robert Crick matter with Justice Robert Hulme and Justice Peter Hamill agreeing. All three need to be investigated as to why they handed down such a dodgy judgment. I will have more to say on them in the future.

The New South Wales Director of Public Prosecutions (DPP), Lloyd Babb SC, needs to appeal the Robert Crick matter to the High Court because if he doesn't hundreds of paedophiles will likely use the new precedent to try and get out of jail.

End of article

At a time when judges new mandatory sentencing for paedophiles was imminent three judges of the Supreme Court of NSW's Court of Appeal set a paedophile free with a suspended sentence. And remember we only had a Royal Commission into the cover-up of child sex abuse a few years ago but the judges still to this day protect paedophiles as the examples in the above article prove. Why? The only conclusion I can come to is because some of them are paedophiles but at the very least they are paedophile protectors which is also a crime.

No other type of criminals gets exemptions from jail because of the Coronavirus yet at least one paedophile has and maybe more will by using the precedent that has been set. Justice Wilson who was one of the judges who looked after the paedophile is the same judge who stitched me up for jail the second time.

The new mandatory sentencing laws only cover federal laws and not state laws which is a potential loophole that can and will be abused by judges to help paedophiles avoid jail and/or minimise the sentences they receive. How do I know? Because judges have been breaking the law to protect paedophile for years as per Marist Brother Gerard Joseph McNamara in the article above who has only been sent to jail twice for short sentences even though he has had multiple convictions for sexually abusing boys.

If judges have been able to give paedophiles non-custodial sentences in breach of current laws, previous laws and precedents then the same judges will work out ways to look after paedophiles circumventing the new mandatory sentencing laws.

One of the likely outcomes with the new mandatory sentencing laws is that judges might find more paedophiles not guilty by deliberately rejecting evidence etc as they did with me in the various defamation matters I spoke about at the beginning of the book. If you look at all the dirty tricks and lies by the judges in Kerry Stokes defamation matters against me they are the same dirty tricks sand lies the judges will use to protect paedophiles in the future to make sure they don't go to jail.

The solution

Obviously, not all paedophiles get protected by judges, but many do and the only solution is to have an open inquiry at a national level, set up a federal body to investigate judges and criminal investigations into suspect judgements by judges. The inquiry would need non-legal people on the committee overseeing it otherwise it would be a waste of time.

Food for thought

Final two points, we have a Prime Minister in Scott Morrison who has used his position to promote Brian Houston and Hillsong, while Mr Houston is under police investigation for protecting his paedophile father, by showing up to Hillsong's convention in May 2019 with his wife which gained widespread media coverage. Mr Morrison has also highly likely protected Brian Houston from criminal charges by phoning the NSW police the same as he phoned the NSW police when federal MP Angus Taylor was under investigation. I contacted the NSW Police and they refused to answer the questions I put to them except to say Brian Houston was still under investigation. Scott Morrison is the Prime Minister and the example he has set is that it is ok to protect paedophiles or at the very least protect paedophile protectors like Brian Houston. Houston admitted on national TV that he knew his father had committed a crime by abusing children and he also admitted that he failed to go to the police, so it is an open and shut case to charge Brian Houston but the NSW police refuse to do so.

And lastly, when the judges give paedophiles suspended sentences and/or manifestly inadequate sentences they know they are breaking the law and that's why they come up with ridiculous reasons such as Justice North saying in 2017 the paedophile hadn't had "sex education" as justification not to jail the paedophile.

The judges also know how much damage the suspended sentences and/or manifestly inadequate sentences do to the victims who want justice but feel betrayed by the court when justice is not done. The victims often say the court case is worse than the original abuse and for them at the end to not get justice when the paedophile has confessed or been found guilty by a jury or judge is scandalous. The judges know how much damage they do to the survivors, but the judges are so cold they don't care less.

The judges also know when they give so many paedophiles suspended sentences and/or manifestly inadequate sentences, as they do regularly, it means more children are being abused and the judges are complicit in that and should be jailed along with the paedophiles.

Shane Dowling rides again

I have not written this book hoping people feel sorry for me for being jailed in any way. If you do, don't. When I set up the Kangaroo Court of Australia website focusing heavily on judicial corruption that automatically made me a target for corrupt judges. I've been belted for two jail sentences and I've rolled with those punches and bounced back. If it happens again, I'll roll with it and bounce back again.

I publish a judicial corruption website so the judges coming after me has given me invaluable evidence of judicial corruption as they have bent every rule in the book trying to stitch me up. This has enabled me to be able to publish the evidence of corruption to the public to help expose the problem which undermines democracy on many, if not most, levels.

So, in that regards, I should probably thank Kerry Stokes for instituting his first SLAPP lawsuit against me in 2014 and his follow-up SLAPP lawsuits because without Stokes and the lawsuits I wouldn't have anywhere near the amount of firsthand experience and direct evidence of the judicial corruption that I do.

Thank you for buying and reading the book and I hope you got value from it.

If you would like to help, please visit the Kangaroo Court of Australia and join the free email subscription which is near the top right and top left of the main page and you will be sent an email when I publish a new article with is normally about twice a week. The email subscription is free, and you can unsubscribe at anytime.

The end

References

In the book, I have reprinted numerous articles from my website Kangaroo Court of Australia and below are the references used in the articles. Where the same articles have been referenced more than once in the book, I have only listed them once below. Numerous court judgments and transcripts which have links in the articles on my website are not listed, although some are, so please visit the website and search for the articles to use those links and watch the videos.

Chapter One to Chapter Five: No references

Chapter Six

KCA article: "Paedophile priest gets 3 months jail for raping 3 boys by NSW Supreme Court's Justice Hoeben" 8 September 2016

References

"Former SA magistrate sentenced to 25 years for child sex crimes" ABC http://www.abc.net.au/pm/stories/s361246.htm 7 September 2001

"Paedophile Catholic priest aged 72 sentenced to two years in prison" The Sydney Morning Herald https://www.smh.com.au/national/nsw/paedophile-catholic-priest-aged-72-sentenced-to-two-years-in-prison-20160225-gn3bq7.html 25 February 2016

"The Catholic priest, the Mollymook weekender and bedtime ghost stories for altar boys" The Sydney Morning Herald https://www.smh.com.au/national/nsw/the-catholic-priest-the-mollymook-weekender-and-bedtime-ghost-stories-for-altar-boys-20150911-gjkrdv.html 12 September 2015

"Abuse victims put Bega judge in dock" The Daily Telegraph (Behind paywall)

"Victims outraged over serial child rapist's lenient sentence" Nine News https://www.9news.com.au/national/victims-outraged-over-serial-child-rapists-lenient-sentence/080da3e8-337e-408b-ad1e-488653be4c28 13 October 2015

"NSW promises life in jail for child sex offenders" Business Insider Australia https://www.businessinsider.com.au/nsw-promises-life-in-jail-for-child-sex-offenders-2015-5 10 May 2015

"District Court Judge Kate Traill brings empathy and experience to child sexual assault trials" The Sydney Morning Herald https://www.smh.com.au/national/nsw/district-court-judge-kate-traill-brings-empathy-and-experience-to-child-sexual-assault-trials-20150929-gjxbqd.html 11 October 2015

Chapter Seven

KCA article: "Journalist charged by police for asking questions about judicial corruption" 24 June 2017

References

"Obeid awarded $162,000 for defamation" The Sydney Morning Herald https://www.smh.com.au/national/obeid-awarded-162-000-for-defamation-20061013-gdol7g.html 13 October 2006

Chapter Eight

KCA article: "Australian paedophile support ring, which includes 2 former PM's, out themselves in their support of George Pell" 2 March 2019

References

"Liberal senator Bill Heffernan says former prime minister a suspected paedophile" The Sydney Morning Herald https://www.smh.com.au/politics/federal/liberal-senator-bill-heffernan-says-former-prime-minister-a-suspected-paedophile-20151020-gke2o0.html 21 October 2015

"Malcolm Turnbull urged to investigation former prime minister paedophile claims by sex abuse survivors" News.com.au https://www.news.com.au/national/politics/malcolm-turnbull-urged-to-investigation-former-prime-minister-paedophile-claims-by-sex-abuse-survivors/news-story/b1c9dd8e7530803c45ae3029809778c0 21 October 2015

"Bill Heffernan 'paedophile list' allegation: former royal commissioner James Wood hits back" The Sydney Morning Herald https://www.smh.com.au/politics/federal/bill-heffernan-paedophile-list-allegation-former-royal-commissioner-james-wood-hits-back-20151021-gkeawj.html 21 October 2015

"Tony Abbott vouched for Catholic priest later struck off by Vatican" The Daily Telegraph https://www.dailytelegraph.com.au/news/national/tony-abbott-vouched-for-catholic-priest-later-struck-off-by-vatican/news-story/f7a36be19325f974025d75c971c427aa 6 February 2013

"Abbott insisted on Nestor reference" The Sydney Morning Herald https://www.smh.com.au/national/abbott-insisted-on-nestor-reference-20130217-2eksx.html 17 February 2013

"Tony Abbott linked to Catholic priest dumped after child abuse case" News.com.au https://www.news.com.au/national/tony-abbott-linked-to-priest-in-web-of-intrigue/news-story/330cac03e0185f90de63328b71100e2b 8 February 2013

"Abbott criticised for supporting priest" The Sydney Morning Herald https://www.smh.com.au/politics/federal/abbott-criticised-for-supporting-priest-20130324-2gnjm.html 24 March 2013

KCA article: "NSW Police confirm PM Scott Morrison's mate Hillsong's Brian Houston still under investigation for concealing paedophile father" 13 July 2019

References

"Jeffrey Epstein charged with sex trafficking, reports say" The Guardian https://www.theguardian.com/us-news/2019/jul/07/jeffrey-epstein-charged-with-sex-trafficking-reports-say 7 July 2019

"Bill Clinton and Jeffrey Epstein: How Are They Connected?" The New York Times https://www.nytimes.com/2019/07/09/nyregion/bill-clinton-jeffrey-epstein.html 9 July 2019

"Donald Trump's Labour Secretary Alex Acosta quits over role in Jeffrey Epstein sex scandal" ABC https://www.abc.net.au/news/2019-07-13/epstein-sexual-abuse-case-acosta-resigns-trump-cabinet/11305996 13 July 2019

"Trump labor secretary who cut Epstein deal plans to slash funds for sex trafficking victims" The Guardian https://www.theguardian.com/us-news/2019/jul/09/labor-secretary-alexander-acosta-sex-trafficking-budget-cut 10 July 2019

"Jeffrey Epstein: how US media – with one star exception – whitewashed the story" The Guardian https://www.theguardian.com/us-news/2019/jul/13/jeffrey-epstein-alex-acosta-miami-herald-media 13 July 2019

"Politics goes to church at Hillsong" The Sydney Morning Herald https://www.smh.com.au/national/politics-goes-to-church-at-hillsong-20050705-gdlmp8.html 5 July 2005

"Assemblies of God" Wikipedia https://en.wikipedia.org/wiki/Assemblies_of_God

"Royal Commission into Institutional Responses to Child Sexual Abuse" Wikipedia https://en.wikipedia.org/wiki/Royal_Commission_into_Institutional_Responses_to_Child_Sexual_Abuse

"Assemblies of God in New Zealand" Wikipedia https://en.wikipedia.org/wiki/Assemblies_of_God_in_New_Zealand

"Hillsong Church" Wikipedia
https://en.wikipedia.org/wiki/Hillsong_Church

"Scott Morrison calls for 'more love' as he prays for Australia at Hillsong conference" The Guardian
https://www.theguardian.com/australia-news/2019/jul/10/scott-morrison-calls-for-more-love-as-he-prays-for-australia-at-hillsong-conference 10 July 2019

"Hillsong's Brian Houston failed to report abuse and had conflict of interest – royal commission" The Guardian
https://www.theguardian.com/australia-news/2015/nov/23/hillsongs-brian-houston-failed-to-report-abuse-and-had-conflict-of-interest-royal-commission 23 November 2015

"Hillsong farewells a lost sheep pioneer" The Sydney Morning Herald https://www.smh.com.au/national/hillsong-farewells-a-lost-sheep-pioneer-20041113-gdk3uq.html 13 November 2004

"60 Minutes: Hillsong Church founder under police investigation over handling of father's sex crimes" Nine News
https://www.9news.com.au/national/60-minutes-brian-houston-hillsong-church-founder-under-police-investigation/a6ee85b6-39a9-4810-8530-9dd1f2f377bf 18 November 2018

"Andrew Scipione" Wikipedia
https://en.wikipedia.org/wiki/Andrew_Scipione

"The Royal Commission into Institutional Responses to Child Sexual Abuse" https://www.childabuseroyalcommission.gov.au/

"The National Redress Scheme"
https://www.nationalredress.gov.au/

"Five per cent of applicants processed through National Redress Scheme amid 'wave of reforms'" ABC
https://www.abc.net.au/news/2019-07-01/five-per-cent-of-victims-paid-out-through-redress-scheme/11265456 1 July 2019

KCA article: "Hillsong Church Pastor Brian Houston perjured himself at the Child Sex Abuse Royal Commission. The evidence." 5 October 2019

References

"Case Study 18: Australian Christian Churches" Royal Commission into Institutional Responses to Child Sexual Abuse https://www.childabuseroyalcommission.gov.au/case-studies/case-study-18-australian-christian-churches 2017

KCA article: "NSW Police refuse to deny PM Scott Morrison has interfered in the investigation into paedophile protector Brian Houston" 28 November 2019

References

"Morrison toasts 'unconventional' Trump – but Hillsong pastor reportedly rejected from guest list" The Guardian https://www.theguardian.com/australia-news/2019/sep/21/morrison-toasts-unconventional-trump-but-hillsong-pastor-reportedly-rejected-from-guest-list 21 September 2019

"PM stands by Angus Taylor despite NSW police investigation into doctored document" The Guardian https://www.theguardian.com/australia-news/2019/nov/26/nsw-police-investigating-doctored-document-angus-taylor-used-in-clover-moore-attack 26 November 2019

"Scott Morrison under fire for calling NSW Police Commissioner amid Angus Taylor forgery probe" ABC https://www.abc.net.au/news/2019-11-27/albanese-turnbull-criticise-morrison-over-fuller-taylor-call/11740174?section=politics 27 November 2019

"Scott Morrison refuses to release notes of call with NSW police chief over doctored document" The Guardian https://www.theguardian.com/australia-news/2019/nov/27/turnbull-says-morrison-should-not-have-called-nsw-police-chief-over-doctored-document 27 November 2019

Chapter Nine – No references

Chapter Ten

KCA article: "Chief Justice Bathurst has journalist charged with contempt for accusing him of corruption" 3 February 2017

References

"Judicial Commission of New South Wales Annual Report" Judicial Commission of New South Wales" https://www.judcom.nsw.gov.au/wp-content/uploads/2016/11/Judicial-Commission-Annual-Report-2015-16.pdf 2016

"Contempt of court" Judicial Commission of New South Wales https://www.judcom.nsw.gov.au/publications/benchbks/local/contempt_in_the_face_of_the_court.html

KCA article: "Free speech and political speech is being suppressed in Australia by the NSW Supreme Court" 8 April 2017

"Protections from statutory encroachments" Australian Law Reform Commission https://www.alrc.gov.au/publication/traditional-rights-and-freedoms-encroachments-by-commonwealth-laws-ip-46/2-freedom-of-speech/protections-from-statutory-encroachments/ 8 December 2014

"Coleman v Power [2004] HCA 39; 220 CLR 1; 209 ALR 182; 78 ALJR 1166 (1 September 2004)" AustLII http://www8.austlii.edu.au/cgibin/viewdoc/au/cases/cth/HCA/2004/39.html

"Coleman v Power" Wikipedia https://en.wikipedia.org/wiki/Coleman_v_Power

"This is why open justice is broken" Mondaq
http://www.mondaq.com/australia/disclosure-electronic-discovery-privilege/581148/this-is-why-open-justice-is-broken
30 March 2017

"Role of the NSW Crown Solicitor" NSW Crown Solicitor's Office
https://www.cso.nsw.gov.au/Pages/cso_aboutus/cso_crownsolicit or_role.aspx

"Lea Armstrong appointed NSW's first female crown solicitor" ABC https://www.abc.net.au/news/2015-06-10/nsw-appoints-states-first-female-crown-solicitor-lea-armstrong/6535522 10 June 2015

Chapter Eleven

KCA article: "Blogger charged with contempt ordered to serve Attorney-Generals with Notice of a Constitutional Matter" 11 June 2017

References

"Lange v Australian Broadcasting Corporation ("Political Free Speech case") [1997] HCA 25; (1997) 189 CLR 520; (1997) 145 ALR 96; (1997) 71 ALJR 818 (8 July 1997)" AustLII
http://www8.austlii.edu.au/cgi-bin/viewdoc/au/cases/cth/HCA/1997/25.html

"Lange v Australian Broadcasting Corporation" Wikipedia
https://en.wikipedia.org/wiki/Lange_v_Australian_Broadcasting_Corporation

"JUDICIARY ACT 1903 - SECT 78B Notice to Attorneys-General" AustLII http://www8.austlii.edu.au/cgi-bin/viewdoc/au/legis/cth/consol_act/ja1903112/s78b.html

"Constitutional litigation" Australian Government Solicitor
https://www.ags.gov.au/areasoflaw/case-studies/constitutional-litigation.html

Nationwide News Pty Ltd v Wills [1992] HCA 46; (1992) 177 CLR 1 (30 September 1992) AustLII http://www8.austlii.edu.au/cgi-bin/viewdoc/au/cases/cth/HCA/1992/46.html

"Theophanous v Herald & Weekly Times Ltd [1994] HCA 46; (1994) 182 CLR 104; (1994) 124 ALR 1 (1994) Aust Torts Reports 81-297 (12 October 1994)" AustLII http://www8.austlii.edu.au/cgi-bin/viewdoc/au/cases/cth/HCA/1994/46.html

"John Fairfax Publications Pty Limited v the Attorney General for New South Wales [2000] NSWCA 198 (2 August 2000)" AustLII http://www8.austlii.edu.au/cgi-bin/viewdoc/au/cases/nsw/NSWCA/2000/198.html

Chapter Twelve

KCA article "Chief Justice Tom Bathurst behind judicial paedophile and bribery cover-up evidence shows" 16 December 2016

References

"Sydney magistrate Graeme Curran appears in court charged with child sex offences" ABC https://www.abc.net.au/news/2017-11-22/sydney-magistrate-makes-first-appearance-on-child-sex-offences/9179310 22 November 2017

"Paedophile, 55, spared jail because he has high cholesterol and never had sex education lessons accused of abusing MORE children - and paid one victim $5,000 to silence her" Daily Mail https://www.dailymail.co.uk/news/article-5101707/Paedophile-spared-jail-accused-abusing-children.html 21 November 2017

"Prosecution Policy" Commonwealth Director of Public Prosecutions https://www.cdpp.gov.au/prosecution-process/prosecution-policy

"Conspiracy to have someone falsely charged" CRIMES ACT 1914 – SECT 41 Conspiracy to bring false accusation http://www5.austlii.edu.au/au/legis/cth/consol_act/ca191482/s41.html

Chapter Thirteen

KCA article: "Child Abuse Royal Commissioner Justice Peter McClellan outlines failures of judges and prosecutors" 22 April 2017

References

"Seeking 'justice for victims' (part I)" The Hon. Justice Peter McClellan AM, Chair, Royal Commission into Institutional Responses to Child Sexual Abuse addressed the Australian Lawyers Alliance NSW Annual State Conference. https://www.childabuseroyalcommission.gov.au/speeches/australian-lawyers-alliance-nsw-annual-state-conference 17 March 2017

"Seeking 'justice for victims' (Part II)" The Hon. Justice Peter McClellan AM Chair, Royal Commission into Institutional Responses to Child Sexual Abuse addressed the Modern Prosecutor Conference. https://www.childabuseroyalcommission.gov.au/speeches/modern-prosecutor-conference 13 April 2017

"'Survivors have waited too long': 4000 institutions named in sex abuse royal commission" The Sydney Morning Herald https://www.smh.com.au/national/survivors-have-waited-too-long-4000-institutions-named-in-sex-abuse-royal-commission-20170327-gv716h.html 27 March 2017

"Cardinal George Pell uninterested in Ridsdale sex claims, Royal Commission hears" The Sydney Morning Herald https://www.smh.com.au/national/cardinal-george-pell-uninterested-in-ridsdale-sex-claims-royal-commission-hears-20160301-gn6vyi.html 1 March 2016

"More child sexual assault cases in court but fewer convictions: Justice Peter McClellan" The Sydney Morning Herald https://www.smh.com.au/national/nsw/more-child-sexual-assault-cases-in-court-but-fewer-convictions-justice-peter-mcclellan-20170412-gvj9vb.html 12 April 2017

Chapter Fourteen

KCA article: "Prosecutor Margaret Cunneen lies to hide friendship with killer Roger Rogerson etc" 19 April 2015

References

"Phone taps the source of Cunneen investigation" The Sydney Morning Herald https://www.smh.com.au/national/nsw/phone-taps-the-source-of-cunneen-investigation-20150415-1mlvwi.html 16 April 2015

"An unusual meeting of minds" The Sydney Morning Herald https://www.smh.com.au/national/nsw/an-unusual-meeting-of-minds-20110506-1ec3q.html 7 May 2011

"Prosecutor Margaret Cunneen is fighting to save her career" The Australian https://www.theaustralian.com.au/weekend-australian-magazine/prosecutor-margaret-cunneen-is-fighting-to-save-her-career/news-story/d085c3ce39db6577dee75fa02cc96355 28 February 2015

"Margaret Cunneen and supporters jubilant after victory in ICAC battle" The Sydney Morning Herald https://www.smh.com.au/national/nsw/margaret-cunneen-and-supporters-jubilant-after-victory-in-icac-battle-20150417-1mn5e9.html 17 April 2015

"Has the Independent Commission Against Corruption gone too far?" ABC - 7.30 Report https://www.abc.net.au/7.30/has-the-independent-commission-against-corruption/5869932 5 November 2014

"Roger Rogerson" Wikipedia
https://en.wikipedia.org/wiki/Roger_Rogerson

"Margaret Cunneen queried whether swimmer's breasts big enough to be groped" The Sydney Morning Herald
https://www.smh.com.au/national/margaret-cunneen-queried-whether-swimmers-breasts-big-enough-to-be-groped-20140707-3bj0o.html 8 July 2014

"Julie Gilbert, allegedly abused by swimming coach Scott Volkers, reveals 'insult' over comments by prosecutor Margaret Cunneen" ABC https://www.abc.net.au/news/2014-07-08/swimmer-allegedly-abused-by-volkers-insulted-by-prosecutor/5582620 8 July 2014

"Cunneen's sister denies causing ICAC inquiry" The Sydney Morning Herald
https://www.smh.com.au/national/nsw/cunneens-sister-denies-causing-icac-inquiry-20150102-12h2gd.html 2 January 2015

"Greens to introduce bill to shore up ICAC's powers following Margaret Cunneen ruling" The Sydney Morning Herald
https://www.smh.com.au/national/nsw/greens-to-introduce-bill-to-shore-up-icacs-powers-following-margaret-cunneen-ruling-20150416-1mm98x.html 16 April 2015

Chapter Fifteen

KCA article: "Prime Minister Scott Morrison confirms judicial paedophile protection racket with 28% not going to jail" 24 September 2019

"Morrison toasts 'unconventional' Trump – but Hillsong pastor reportedly rejected from guest list" The Guardian
https://www.theguardian.com/australia-news/2019/sep/21/morrison-toasts-unconventional-trump-but-hillsong-pastor-reportedly-rejected-from-guest-list 21 September 2019

"Nearly seven years after an interview that changed history, Peter Fox launches a book" Newcastle Herald https://www.newcastleherald.com.au/story/6352071/former-hunter-top-cop-peter-fox-writes-the-wrongs-in-new-book-on-abuse-controversies/ 28 August 2019

"Walking Towards Thunder - The true story of a whistleblowing cop who took on corruption and the Church" Booktopia https://www.booktopia.com.au/walking-towards-thunder-peter-fox/book/9780733642845.html 27 August 2019

"Blind-reported child sex abuse cases may be reopened after hundreds not investigated" ABC https://www.abc.net.au/news/2016-04-20/blind-reporting-child-sex-abuse-leaves-hundreds-not-investigated/7340128 20 April 2016

Chapter Sixteen

"KCA article: "Podcast of Supreme Court of NSW – Seven v Dowling – Allegation Chief Justice Tom Bathurst is a paedophile – Has Justice Kunc had a sexual relationship with Dr Nicky McWilliam – Judicial bribery etc." 23rd November 2019

References

"Seven Network (Operations) Limited v Dowling [2019] NSWSC 1173 (4 September 2019)" AustLII http://www.austlii.edu.au/cgi-bin/viewdoc/au/cases/nsw/NSWSC/2019/1173.html

"Papal awards for Sydney trio" The Catholic Weekly https://www.catholicweekly.com.au/papal-awards-for-sydney-trio/ 8 March 2016

Chapter Seventeen

KCA article: "High Court of Australia's Justice Keane and Justice Edelman caught protecting their bribe-taking and paedophile judicial mates" 11 May 2019

References

"Herald & Weekly Times Ltd & Bolt v Popovic [2003] VSCA 161 (21 November 2003)" AustLII
https://www.austlii.edu.au/cgi-bin/viewdoc/au/cases/vic/VSCA/2003/161.html

Chapter Eighteen

No additional references

Chapter Nineteen

No additional references

Chapter Twenty

KCA article: "Has Judge Garry Neilson outed himself for being a paedophile given he implied incest and paedophilia are OK?" 11 July 2014

References

"Judge compares incest and paedophilia to past attitudes towards homosexuality, claiming they might not be taboo anymore" The Sydney Morning Herald
https://www.smh.com.au/national/nsw/judge-compares-incest-and-paedophilia-to-past-attitudes-towards-homosexuality-claiming-they-might-not-be-taboo-anymore-20140709-zt0v2.html 10 July 2014

"Calls for NSW judge Garry Neilson to step down as he says incest and paedophilia may no longer be considered 'taboo' in society" The Daily Telegraph
https://www.dailytelegraph.com.au/news/nsw/calls-for-nsw-judge-garry-neilson-to-step-down-as-he-says-incest-and-paedophilia-may-no-longer-be-considered-taboo-in-society/news-story/c7362e10a8878e4e23997fd5e4fa56e5 10 July 2014

"Peter Hollingworth" Wikipedia
https://en.wikipedia.org/wiki/Peter_Hollingworth

"Incest statements: Judge Garry Neilson referred to Judicial Commission" The Sydney Morning Herald https://www.smh.com.au/national/nsw/incest-statements-judge-garry-neilson-referred-to-judicial-commission-20140711-zt40v.html 11 July 2014

Chapter Twenty-One

KCA article: "Supreme Court judges Justice Wilson, Hulme and Hamill give paedophiles a get out of jail free card during the Coronavirus crisis" 16 May 2020

References

"A priest (previously jailed regarding three boys) is in court again re a fourth boy" Broken Rites Australia http://www.brokenrites.org.au/drupal/node/242 1 February 2020

"'They'd help me': Ex-priest accused of indecent assault confident of church support" Nine News https://9now.nine.com.au/a-current-affair/catholic-ex-priest-accused-assaulting-boy-claims-church-support/e1b42889-d3bc-465b-bf3e-4aaf824a20f5 January 2020

"Coronavirus pandemic saves convicted paedophile from prison" The Sydney Morning Herald https://www.smh.com.au/national/nsw/coronavirus-pandemic-saves-convicted-pedophile-from-prison-20200428-p54nzr.html 28 April 2020

"RC v R; R v RC [2020] NSWCCA 76" NSW Caselaw https://www.caselaw.nsw.gov.au/decision/5e8e56a5e4b0f66047e d89b9 22 April 2020

"Catholic brother Gerard McNamara jailed for nine months over 'repulsive' sexual abuse" ABC https://www.abc.net.au/news/2018-09-03/catholic-brother-gerard-mcnamara-jailed-for-nine-months/10195396 3 September 2018

"Catholic brother nicknamed 'The Rat' jailed for sex abuse of four Traralgon schoolboys" ABC
https://amp.abc.net.au/article/12252922 15 May 2020

"More jail time means Gerald Ridsdale is 'likely to die in custody'" The Age
https://www.theage.com.au/national/victoria/more-jail-time-means-gerald-ridsdale-is-likely-to-die-in-custody-20200514-p54sxy.html 14 May 2020

"Paedophile priest Gerald Ridsdale sentenced to 10 years' jail for sexual abuse of boys in 1970s" ABC
https://www.abc.net.au/news/2020-05-14/gerald-ridsdale-sentenced-for-1970s-sexual-abuse-of-boys/12248176 14 May 2020